THE NEW LAW
of
DEMAND
AND
SUPPLY

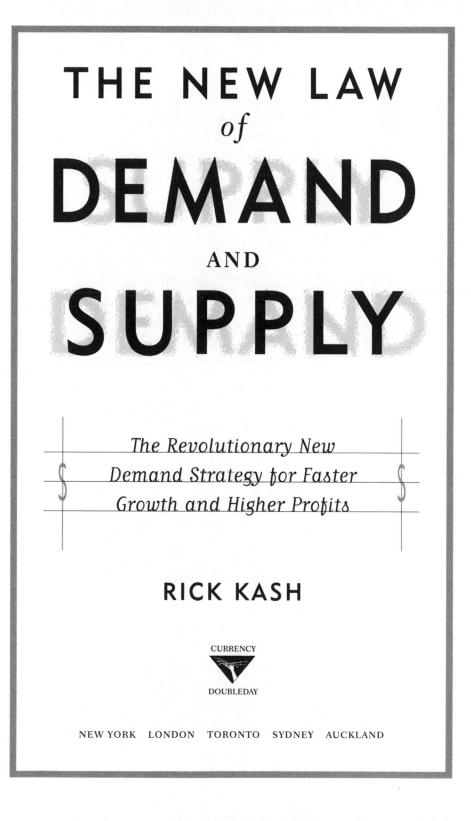

THE NEW LAW

of

DEMAND

AND

SUPPLY

The Revolutionary New
Demand Strategy for Faster
Growth and Higher Profits

RICK KASH

CURRENCY

DOUBLEDAY

NEW YORK   LONDON   TORONTO   SYDNEY   AUCKLAND

A CURRENCY BOOK
Published by Doubleday
A Division of Random House, Inc.
1540 Broadway, New York, New York 10036

Currency and Doubleday are trademarks
of Doubleday, a division of Random House, Inc.

Book Design by Lisa Sloane

Library of Congress Cataloging-in-Publication Data

Kash, Rick.
The new law of demand and supply : the revolutionary new demand strategy
for faster growth and higher profits / Rick Kash.—1st ed.
p.   cm.
I. Title.

HB801 .K355 2002
338.5'21—dc21
2001058288

ISBN 0-385-50432-2

PRINTED IN THE UNITED STATES OF AMERICA

First Edition: October 2002

Special Sales
Currency Books are available at special discounts for bulk purchases for sales promotions or
premiums. Special editions, including personalized covers, excerpts of existing books, and
corporate imprints, can be created in large quantities for special needs. For more information,
write to Special Market, Currency Books, 280 Park Avenue, 11th floor, New York, NY 10017,
or e-mail specialmarkets@randomhouse.com.

1   3   5   7   9   10   8   6   4   2

This book is dedicated to
Dr. Faith Price Kash,
the sunshine of my life,
who is in demand forever

ACKNOWLEDGMENTS

First and foremost, I would like to thank Adam Smith, whose insights and understanding of economics and business have proven to be timeless. In fact, given the contents and thesis of this book, it is likely that the influence of Mr. Smith has only begun to reach the full promise and potential of his brilliant insights written at the end of the eighteenth century.

As I built the original thinking for Demand Strategy, I had a felt need to create a bridge between Mr. Smith and the twenty-first century: by linking economists of the past two-hundred-plus years, I could understand how the original theory of supply and demand had evolved among leading economic thinkers. My enthusiasm for Demand Strategy continued to grow as it became clear that two centuries of independent economists have continued to build and expand the principles of supply and demand. In doing so they have provided the current business community with a clear understanding that we are entering an entirely new period of economic reality. The nineteenth and twentieth centuries were appropriately driven by supply, but as you will read in our first and second chapters, the American and worldwide economies have undergone massive changes so that we are now a demand-driven world economy versus one that is supply-driven. Recognizing and acting on this seminal change at the beginning of the twenty-first century will drive successful performance in companies both large and small.

This book and the reception it has enjoyed from the publishing community are due to the continuous energy and intellectual contribution from my partner, Jason Green, and our colleague, Dr. Venkatesh Bala. Their effort was unflagging. Their ideas were excellent. I could not have had two better partners in bringing our thoughts and experiences to realization as a manifesto for how to succeed in business in the twenty-first century.

Susan Beard used her role as The Cambridge Group's Director of Information Services to identify two people without whom this effort would never have started, let alone finished. I met Jim Levine because of his personal reputation and great business success as an agent for business authors. I retained him as an agent, and getting a friend and an adviser were just wonderful extra dimensions to our relationship. As a Harvard Ph.D., he had the capacity to retain and improve both important parts and subtleties of the text so that the expression of ideas within this book are both clearer and more accessible to its readers.

Donna Carpenter is perhaps the most successful ghostwriter of the last twenty years. This volume is just one example of what her unique style can bring to a book, making it more enjoyable to read and interesting to write. Donna, her partner, Maurice Coyle, and I had many seven A.M. meetings where we discovered our shared love of good coffee, great restaurants, and that the same movies touched our souls. Their instincts were superb at every step. They gently prodded and challenged me in ways that improved the book and made me respect the talent, insight, and experience that Donna and Mo provided. Thanks also to their colleagues at Wordworks: Deborah Horvitz, Larry Martz, and Helen Rees.

When I first met the Doubleday team, it was apparent that they were enthusiastic about *The New Law of Demand and Supply* as a book. During our lengthy first meeting, several people from Doubleday who attended made it clear that they fully understood what I was hoping to accomplish and that they shared my enthusiasm for the importance of understanding demand. I feel very fortunate to have had the wise counsel and personal commitment of editorial director Roger Scholl, whose guidance, gentle nudges, and then somewhat less-than-gentle nudges have contributed to every phase of this undertaking. I also want to thank Michael Palgon, deputy publisher and senior vice president of Doubleday Broadway, for his continuous enthusiasm and for bringing together the outstanding Doubleday organization so that this book and its ideas can be presented to its readers in the best possible way. I'd also like to thank two other key members of the Currency Doubleday team: David Drake, assistant director of publicity, and Meredith McGinnis, associate marketing director.

To the members of the Doubleday sales force, who spent so many hours and whose valued advice can be read in the chapters, seen in the graphics of the cover, and can be felt in the expanded title of the book, I want to offer my sincerest thanks.

Demand Strategy as a basis for running a company or a business enterprise of any size would not have been possible if not for my business partner of twenty years, Larry Burns. His early business successes formed the intellectual platform on which Demand Strategy has been built.

While every partner and associate of The Cambridge Group contributed constructive thoughts and gave of their valuable time, several people "volunteered" to play a more active role. To Bruce Onsager, Kevin Bowen, and Gloria Cox, I want to offer my gratitude for the suggestions you made, the constructive criticism you offered, and for being right almost all of the time.

The many case studies and corporate examples used in this book were the result of the great generosity of CEOs and senior managers who lead these companies. Their superior results have been achieved because of their great belief in the power of understanding the demand side of a business relationship before creating supply.

My thanks to Mike Ruettgers, the chairman of EMC, and to Peter Schwartz, director of executive communications, for helping me to fully understand how EMC experienced an 80,575 percent increase in its value on the New York Stock Exchange during the decade of the nineties. To someone whom I'm privileged to have as one of my closest friends, Phil Marineau, the CEO of Levi's, thanks for letting me know which parts of the early versions of the book were working and which needed further attention. Peggy Dyer, the senior vice president of Allstate Financial, as usual was able to pinpoint ways in which to make our points clearer and easier to understand.

Jim Kilts, the chairman and CEO of Gillette, as always was available whenever I needed him. His mastery of how underperforming companies can be turned around is one of the most interesting sections of this book. My former partner, Peter Klein, is currently the senior vice president of Gillette and it's not surprising that his incisive comments provided enhancements to our points of view.

When I first met Jane Thompson and tried to recruit her to The

Cambridge Group, it was clear that she was a very special talent. She helped shape the chapter on the remarkable success of the Sears Credit Card, and her contributions were significant given her role as executive vice president of the Sears Credit Division, where she managed to accomplish what most people thought was impossible. And, to John Delaney, who was the senior vice president of marketing working with Jane, thanks for the diligence in offering thoughts and comments for this text.

CDW, as you will read in this book, is an amazing company that created and successfully runs a unique business model. Michael Krasny, its founder, was my brother Gary's college roommate, and as always, Michael's comments on business in general were wonderful. Jim Shanks and Paul Kozak, two senior members of CDW's management, spent a great deal of time so that we fully understood the pivotal role of demand in the success of their company.

There is always something special about the founder of a company that becomes a nationwide success. The reasons for that success are always clear when you meet and talk with that founder. Angelo Mozilo, chairman of the board and chief executive officer, is one of the two founders of Countrywide Credit Industries. Angelo redefined the mortgage industry forty years ago and continues to do so today. Andrew Bielanski, managing director of marketing, and Susan Martin, senior vice president of public relations, were instrumental in making certain that we understood the breadth and commitment that Countrywide has to understanding demand before creating supply.

Vernon Hill, the chairman and CEO of Commerce Bank, has taken most of the assumptions of the banking industry and turned them inside out. In so doing, he showed how understanding demand enables meteoric growth and inelastic pricing no matter how strong the competition. Thanks to David Flaherty for making our familiarity with Commerce Bank so easy to achieve.

McDonald's redefined the restaurant business and continues to be a model for entrepreneurs. My thanks to David Green, senior vice president, International Marketing, Jack Daly, senior vice president, corporate relations, and Jack Greenberg, the chairman and CEO, for providing the access and the information so that we could share with the reader how demand was and continues to be at the forefront of McDonald's success.

Joe Lawler of R. R. Donnelley inspired me when the task ahead seemed daunting, and for that I will always be grateful. Bill Smithburg, former chairman of Quaker Oats, had an inspired vision for what Gatorade could be, and made that vision become a reality. He was also one of the earliest corporate supporters of Demand Strategy, within Quaker Oats and among other business leaders, and this support made it possible to apply and refine our earliest thinking. Without his confidence and support, this book might never have happened.

By anybody's standards, Medline has been extremely successful in the hospital supply business. Jon Mills, one of the two founders and inspirational leaders, was generous in sharing his time and in recounting the many innovations that have enabled Medline to achieve great success against competitors who used to be many times their size.

To Mitchell Posner, Marvin Zimmerman, and my daughter Amy, your candor was always constructive no matter how it felt at the time. Ed Lebar of Young and Rubicam was very helpful in making available the data from Brand Asset Valuator. And thanks to Karla Kapikian, who made everyone's use of that data much easier.

To the economists whose personal and academic critique were a constant source of inspiration, I want to thank our own Dr. Venkatesh Bala and his associates Saurabh Narain (Bank of America), Prof. Joseph Greenberg (McGill), Prof. Arun Agrawal (Yale), and Dr. Narayan Venkatasubramanyan (i2 Technologies).

To my father, the late Maurice S. Kash, I am forever grateful that he encouraged all of his sons to explore and to discover for themselves what goes on in this wonderful world of ours. It is this sense of life as a continuing adventure that enabled me to participate in the early thinking and ultimate formation of Demand Strategy and the New Law of Demand and Supply. To my mother, Frances Kash, whose achievements extended far beyond her training, she taught her three sons that if you understood demand, you could always create better supply.

And finally, to Lynise Anderson and Deborah Dean: No one could have been blessed with better friends and more talented business assistants. Thanks for trying to keep the many parts of my life organized while bringing together the best Demand Strategy book possible. And to our many clients whose personal confidence in The Cambridge Group and its partners enabled them to be the early practitioners of Demand Strategy, I'll always be grateful for their pursuit of relevance, innovation, and differentiation.

CONTENTS

CHAPTER 1

WHY DEMAND STRATEGY? WHY NOW?

or several years we were dazzled, confused, and ultimately numbed by talk of the new economy—a cybernetic wonderland, powered by microchips and liberated by the Internet, that would blow away the drab old rules and usher in a brave new era of business and finance. Of course, that vision has been seriously questioned with Wall Street's implosion and our first economic slump in a decade.

My colleagues and I at the consulting firm I lead, The Cambridge Group, have argued all along that it isn't the switch from the old economy to the new economy that has transformed business. Rather, it has been the shift from a supply-side economy to a demand-side economy that is changing forever the terms of commerce. While it was perfectly appropriate in the nineteenth and twentieth centuries to be supply-driven, the fundamental basis on which business economics function has now changed 180 degrees. Recognizing this change and the impact that it will have in determining the future success of companies cannot be overstated.

Historically, sellers have dominated nearly all markets. Today, buyers rule, and businesses that can't adapt to that sea change won't long survive.

From the Industrial Revolution to the end of the twentieth century, companies competed, for the most part, by supplying what they assumed their markets demanded. For two hundred years, this approach was successful because the world's economies on a broad scale were able to absorb virtually all of the supply that was being created. This is no longer the case, as many business leaders and economists now recognize.

Of course, businesses have always noted their customers' desires. As Lawrence A. Bossidy, the much-admired chairman of Honeywell International Inc., observed: "I doubt if there is a single company in [this] country that will not tell you that its first priority is satisfying customers. But do they behave that way? . . . Not many do."

Still, until recently the world's economies could absorb, on the whole, almost all of the supply that was created. As a result, it made little difference that ideas about demand were ignored and unsophisticated.

Today, as hordes of new competitors boldly and sometimes blindly enter nearly every marketplace and cause supply to outstrip demand, companies find themselves in a price squeeze. Their products have become or are in danger of becoming commodities that are entirely interchangeable. Therefore, they will have little choice but to compete on the basis of price alone. This results in a significant loss of profit. In the twenty-first century, they must realign their approaches to the market to reflect the realities of the demand economy or suffer the consequences as many companies have during the past year.

The distinction between the demand economy and the new economy is not a semantic one. My point is that it is not very useful—and may, in fact, be misleading—to talk about a new economy that is somehow supplanting the old one. It is both more accurate and more helpful to picture an economy that has been driven by supply but is now ruled by demand.

To alter the way a company acts, you must first address how its leaders think. I argue in this book that economic, technological, and societal forces have combined to create changes of such scope and magnitude that business leaders must rethink what they do in order to compete successfully—that is, to win.

To be successful requires a change in how you go to market and how you compete. Competitive advantage and continuous growth in sales and profits are available by making some rather simple changes that will have an enormous impact in the marketplace.

In this chapter I will explain the evolution of these changes. Drawing upon my nearly three decades of experience as an adviser and consultant to many Fortune 500 companies, such as Merrill Lynch, AT&T, Citibank, Levi Strauss & Co., R. R. Donnelley, McDonald's Corporation, PepsiCo, Inc., Du Pont, Pharmacia Upjohn, the Quaker Oats Company, and Sears, Roebuck and Co., I show how companies can prosper in the demand economy using what I call Demand Strategy.

Unlike the many supply-side approaches—such as reengineering, six sigma, and total quality management (TQM)—that so many organizations engaged in during the late 1980s and 1990s, Demand Strategy begins by thoroughly understanding existing and future demand, and only then creating the supply to satisfy it. In our experience, the process of creating supply cannot be optimized until the demand it is intended to satisfy is fully understood. This is a paradigm shift of major proportions, whether you are in the credit card business, the fast food business, or any other business. The way you involve target customers so that they can guide you in the creation of supply that meets their expressed demand will define the extent to which you will succeed and potentially dominate your markets.

Frequently I'm asked how Demand Strategy is different from customer focus, customer intimacy, or any of the many customer approaches (often spelled out in books) of the past few years. My response is that Demand Strategy is vastly different.

Customers are a critically important part of Demand Strategy, but demand goes far deeper and involves a greater array of forces and factors than customers alone can supply. In fact, companies that rely only on their customers can get themselves into trouble if they don't set a context within which they hear, understand, and evaluate what customers tell them. Listening to customers provides enormous value, but there must be a system of checks and balances through which you can validate all that you are being told by customers.

Before we even talk to a customer in Demand Strategy, we gather a fact base on past, current, and emerging demand, a process we call a *demand forces and industry factors analysis*. The purpose of this analysis is to understand what forces and factors cause significant changes in demand in any specific category. Some are obvious; others might surprise you. For example, what would you guess is the single most important attribute teenagers around the world want in their cars today? A sleek look? Extra power? A great sound system? All are good guesses, but all are wrong—they want a vehicle that offers them protection from physical harm and a car company that offers them emotional security. You'll read much more about this in Chapter 5.

Much of the trouble in the world's economy results from companies that listened only to their customers and built as much product as their customers thought they needed. In what will surely become a textbook account in business history, senior managers in the telecom industry were essentially told by their customer gurus to keep making more equipment and more bandwidth. As a result of listening to their customers and failing to put the information in context, the telecom companies now have an estimated twenty times more telecommunication capacity in the United States than we need. All too often, the business leaders failed to validate what customers said by putting it in the context of other information.

Unfortunately, there's a long list of highly visible companies that suffered the same fate: customers spoke convincingly about how much they wanted of a particular product, but once the manufacturer followed their advice, those same customers somehow disappeared and the products were failures. New Coke, for example, was highly preferred among some 201,000 people in market research, yet it failed miserably.

Why? Consumers gave Coke a very important answer to a critically important question: the new formulation of Coke tasted better than the existing formula. The Coca-Cola Company focused on this clear taste preference but failed to place that information into the broader context. Within this larger context the plan was to take away existing Coke and replace it with an entirely new product. The lesson is simple. Customer input must be understood in the larger context in which the business activity in question will take place.

The importance of context pertains to every issue and question in order to fully understand customer opinion, experience, and demand.

For example, when asked the isolated question "Would you buy more environmentally friendly products if they were conveniently available in your favorite stores?," consumers overwhelmingly say yes all the time. However, as the requirements of making products environmentally safe can be quite expensive, many product introductions have failed because those that are environmentally safe usually cost significantly more than the products consumers are used to purchasing. Had the price differential been a part of the earlier question, many companies would have saved lots of time and money.

More recently, financial services companies across the United States have looked at research telling them that consumers would like to "bundle" many of their financial services products with one provider. For example, checking accounts, credit cards, mortgages, and investments would be provided by one company that in turn would provide monthly statements and billing all in one envelope, often with financial incentives to the consumer for having multiple product relationships with one financial institution. However, after hundreds of efforts by companies large and small, the success stories of bundling financial services products are few and very far between. Among the most important reasons these efforts have failed has to do with the context. While at one level bundled products create simplicity and time savings, these pale in comparison to the concern about putting all of your financial eggs in one basket and giving up the opportunity to select individual service providers that excel in a single financial dimension like mortgages and investments.

You will have to look far and wide to find someone who believes more in customers than I do. However, while customer insight and needs are critically important, a business leader must know all the factors that might affect demand, some of which provide the needed context for understanding what customers say and what they really mean.

The forces and factors that cause changes in demand in a category are absolutely critical as a continuing source of information for companies that want to lead their categories or even be fast followers. If your company waits until customers are the source of news, it's already too late—because those customers are telling your competitors exactly what they're telling you.

Whenever companies tell me that they've learned something from their customers, I always ask: Which customers? Which segments are they in? Are they part of your targeted demand segments? Are they heavy users, or medium-to-light users? In other words, customers have different value to business managers, and so does the information they give you. Unfortunately, much marketing research is not as thorough as it should be and you end up with obvious or even misleading information.

Demand Strategy is holistic in that it considers legislation, economics, the economic environment, geography, demography, raw material costs, production costs, and psychographics, as well as the customer. None of these is as important as the customer; nonetheless, the customer cannot stand alone in providing the breadth and quality of information business leaders must have. In other words, customer information is absolutely necessary but wholly insufficient if it stands alone as the primary source of information and guidance.

Let's take a long look at the supply economy that has dominated the past two centuries.

THE SUPPLY ECONOMY

Two centuries ago Adam Smith's seminal treatise, *The Wealth of Nations,* set the terms for modern economic thinking. His best-known principle is the law of supply and demand. While the name of the law placed "supply" before "demand," Smith, in fact, didn't consider either element more important than the other.

Buyers drive demand. Total market demand, of course, refers to the number of customers who are able and willing to buy a product at a given price. When the price of a product increases, the demand for that product typically decreases.

It is producers who drive supply. A product's total supply depends upon the number of producers who are selling it at a specified price and the amount each producer is willing to supply at that price. In most instances, when the product's price increases, the number of producers supplying it also goes up, which in turn increases the supply available in the market. If the demand can't absorb the additional quantity, the price inevitably drops as producers try to unload inventory. If a shortage in supply occurs, competing buyers will bid prices up.

Adam Smith established another vital principle two hundred years ago, that of scarcity, or nonsubstitutability. Smith noted that products that are scarce relative to demand, and for which there are no close substitutes, command a higher price. And this price mechanism holds demand and supply in balance.

While Smith's ideas did not emphasize supply over demand, economists and companies in the centuries that followed did. I suggest that today we would more accurately represent the historic changes taking place in the markets if we reversed the sequence in order to describe how successful business managers must act as they go forward. We should embrace a new law of *demand and supply.*

In the old supply-driven model, there was no schism between theory and practice, between boardroom and classroom. Adopted by businesses the world over, it reflected the thinking and research of leading scholars in economics and business. In 1948, for example, when Nobel laureate Paul Samuelson of the Massachusetts Institute of Technology wrote his notable and widely used textbook, *Economics,* he asked three fundamental questions:

1. *What* commodities will be produced, and in what quantities? That is, of the numerous goods and services that can be offered, which ones will be selected?
2. *How* will they be produced? That is, who will make them, and what methods, resources, and technology will be used?
3. *For whom* will they be produced? Who will enjoy and benefit from the rendered goods and services? To put it another way: through what means will the nation's output be distributed among its population?

The 2001 edition of Professor Samuelson's book clearly indicates that the author continues to support his views of half a century ago: "Every society must have a way of determining *what* commodities are produced, *how* these goods are made, and *for whom* they are produced."

While his questions remain the right ones, we respectfully suggest that changes in every sphere of the economy over the past fifty years make it obvious that the sequence of Professor Samuelson's questions is no longer appropriate for businesses that seek to prosper.

In the demand economy of the twenty-first century, the first question that should be raised is *"For whom* are the goods intended, and which of their demands are we attempting to satisfy?" The question *"What* should be produced to meet this demand?" follows; and *"How* should they be produced?" is the last of the questions one should ask oneself. Today's demand economy is marked first and foremost by an oversupply in virtually every business category. As a result, each competitor must first select its target groups of customers, then create supply that more fully satisfies them than the supply offered by competitors. Unless you ask the "whom" question first, you will inevitably create supply that falls short of meeting demand and you will generate lower returns and less profit.

Needless to say, the changes in our world since *The Wealth of Nations* was first published are enormous. At that time, demand was omnipresent and supply dominated the equation. But the confluence of processes that would irrevocably change that balance was already beginning to take hold.

The twentieth century saw the advent of mass production, and as hundreds of thousands of people migrated from rural communities into cities, many family farms and cottage industries languished and eventually collapsed. In industrialized countries, the standards of living vastly improved, the middle class expanded, and a sophisticated consumer society began to take shape. Though people, of course, needed basic goods and services, they were, in addition, showing signs of the sociological phenomenon for which Thorstein Veblen coined the term "conspicuous consumption." The desire for material things, coupled with the capacity to buy them, created unprecedented demand, and industry could not keep pace. Mass markets emerged for new goods, services, and modern conveniences, including safety razors, washing machines, telephones, automobiles, motion pictures, airplanes, television, and computers, to name just a few.

In order to meet the challenges that new markets posed, techniques for mass production were continually developed and refined. One of the earliest shifts resulted in the division of labor, which divided complex activities into sets of simple tasks performed by individual workers.

A flood tide of discoveries, insights, techniques, and theories followed—including steam power, electricity, Henry Ford's assembly line, and Frederick Winslow Taylor's time-and-motion studies.

For the most part, these were profitable times for manufacturers because demand was growing as fast as, if not faster than, supply, and the balance of power in the economy was still weighted toward producers. With few exceptions, and with only a cursory glance in the direction of the customer, businesses could sell virtually all they produced. Most companies had pricing power as well, which gave them the freedom to increase prices without losing significant volume. Given their limited choices, consumers were frequently willing to pay whatever their desired goods cost. Henry Ford's now well-known quip—that customers could buy cars in any color they wanted, as long as it was black—exemplified precisely this balance of power.

Of course, there was competition within mass markets, resulting in lowered prices, but production efficiencies made it possible to drop prices and remain profitable. Moreover, lower prices attracted more customers. Typically, prices were set by adding a hefty percentage to production costs. Sellers thrived. As we know, the economic cycle sometimes brought hard times to manufacturers when demand temporarily waned as customers stopped buying what they wanted. However, such times acted as a spur to consolidation and offered opportunities for stronger enterprises to further increase supply efficiencies and broaden their distribution reach. When the economy revived once again, the suppliers could meet the flood of pent-up demand with even greater sales and profits. For the most part, supply-side economics ruled the day.

But in the early 1990s, the tectonic plates underpinning the world economy shifted. The supply economy was dead, killed by the producers themselves.

THE DEMAND ECONOMY

By the late 1990s, the United States had crossed the threshold to the demand economy. Supply was overflowing; it so saturated the markets that not even the robust economy that closed the twentieth century could absorb it. With a glut of goods and services, buyers could be excruciatingly selective, causing the pricing power producers had enjoyed to all but vanish. Furthermore, because all too often the products supplied resembled their competitors' products more than they differed from them, they became commodities, which forced price-based competition. In their drive for efficiency, companies lost sight of Adam Smith's tenet of nonsubstitutability: in order to keep a product's price high, it is vital that nothing can be closely or easily substituted for it.

Today the power that resides with the customer in our demand economy is beyond dispute. In fact, I would argue that the balance can only tip more in the same direction as the forces at work continue to assert themselves. Nearly a century ago, economist Joseph Schumpeter advised us to "always start from the satisfaction of wants, since they are the end of all production." It is time to take his advice seriously. Today and in the future, the company that satisfies the highest percentage of its most profitable customers' demand will take a major step toward regaining control of its pricing and profitability.

In a recent speech, Frederick W. Smith, chairman, CEO, and president of FedEx Corporation, and in my view one of the great business visionaries of our time, described the transformation this way:

> It is still the case that the vast majority of businesses continue to focus more on the supply side of the business equation than on the demand side. The traditional business question has always been: "How much product can we make and how fast can our workers make it?" But today, it is very clear that pushing product out the door certainly will not create competitive advantage.
>
> Today, most businessmen who are successful are asking a very different question. And that is simply: "What does my customer need, and when does that customer want it?" That, ladies and gentlemen, is a major shift of historic proportions. We are in the midst of a change of the entire flow of commerce. The

flow of all commercial information and all goods [must now] meet a new standard [for] demanding customer requirements.

Smith's own company has remade itself repeatedly in response to demand. FedEx recognized and then exploited the demand for worry-free package delivery on the part of anxious businesspeople and individuals who are willing to pay a premium for reliable, timely service. Over time, FedEx has earned its leading position by keeping its promise that every package will arrive "absolutely, positively overnight."

Many elements converge to create and perpetuate the demand economy and will be discussed in detail in the next section of this chapter. Some of the highlights include elements that have increased global oversupply and made demand more selective. Oversupply is increased through technology, productivity gains, availability of capital, and globalization. Meanwhile, instant information, the Internet, rapid changes in distribution channels, and shorter product life cycles make a demand-driven approach to markets mandatory.

■ Competition Has Grown on All Sides

No company can rely on being one of a few suppliers of its goods or services.

As recently as a dozen years ago, giant companies could easily block start-ups from entering many industries. But the barriers to entry have been greatly reduced. While the blockbuster initial public offerings (IPOs) of the late 1990s have vanished, upstart companies with new ideas and sound business plans can still tap into private-equity and venture-capital pools that are much larger and more international than has historically been the case.

Other factors have also reduced the barriers to entry. Previously a company that wished to sell, say, computer equipment had to assemble multiple core competencies, including design, engineering, manufacturing, distribution, and marketing, then make them work together effectively. Today an enterprise can focus on just one or two aspects, such as design and marketing, and hand off other competencies to outsourcing partners and "white-label" manufacturers who have the scale and expertise to manufacture the product quickly and cheaply. In electronics manufacturing alone, it is estimated that between 1999 and 2004 the outsourced volume will grow annually at nearly 30 percent a year, from $58 billion to $203 billion, increasing the proportion of outsourced production from 8 percent to 18 percent.

The trend toward outsourcing greatly reduces the effort and expense of creating supply and enables companies to move swiftly into new markets and join the competition there. For example, outsourcing production to companies such as Solectron Corporation helped new entrant Juniper Networks to successfully attack Cisco Systems' market dominance in its high-end Internet router markets. By the beginning of 2001, Juniper had racked up nearly 30 percentage points of market share, after starting virtually from scratch just two years earlier. The speed and size of this high-technology achievement underscore the fundamental change we must make in considering our competition.

▪ Commerce Is Global

Adam Smith would be pleased by international competition and global trade. Although Karl Marx is usually credited with the thought, it was Smith who first said that we are all better off doing precisely what we do best, whether we are households or entire nations. In Smith's words:

> It is the maxim of every prudent master of a family never to attempt to make at home what it will cost him more to make than to buy. . . . What is prudence in the conduct of every private family can scarce be folly in that of a great kingdom. If a foreign country can supply us with a commodity cheaper than we ourselves can make it, better buy it of them with some part of the produce of our own industry, employed in a way in which we have some advantage.

Smith's logic is as persuasive and relevant now as it was two centuries ago.

From the perspective of pricing power, globalization has a mixed track record. Lester Thurow, economist and former dean of the Sloan School of Management at MIT, warns that "globalization is forcing prices down. Production is being moved from high-cost to low-cost locations, and prices are falling as a result."

Globalization is driven by alliances and trade agreements (some, such as the European Economic Union—EEU—are designed to compete effectively with the United States), monetary policy, technology, the communications revolution, and supply-chain advancements. In these circumstances, companies can now open facilities around the world. Developing countries can move from supplying raw materials to producing products from clothing to computer chips as they become global commodities. What that means is that we are having to run faster and faster just to stay in the same place.

▪ The Increasing Pace and Complexity of Business Raise Risk

Improvements in communication technology, computing power, and manufacturing processes have all contributed to the accelerated pace of business. Dramatically shorter product life cycles are one consequence. Never again will we see a product like the conventional telephone, which took a century to move through the cycle of introduction, growth, maturity, and, with the advent of the wireless phone, decline. Today the wireless phone, introduced less than a decade ago, is already threatened by mobile Internet devices. Another example: Intel Corporation, from 1982 to 1993, introduced nine major new microprocessor products; from 1993 to 2000, however, it brought out more than a hundred new microprocessors—more than a tenfold increase.

Just-in-time inventory systems, facilitated by faster, cheaper, and better communication among manufacturers, suppliers, and logistics providers, also contribute to the increased speed of doing business.

Improvements in communication (especially the Internet) and greater standardization in technological platforms (for example, XML) have helped shape the trend toward "horizontal" businesses, in which companies rely upon partnerships and alliances for many parts of their business system rather than owning fully integrated operations. While overall efficiency has improved, the complexity of business has increased vastly, most notably in efforts to coordinate across corporate boundaries.

Shortened product life cycles narrow the window of time to pursue new market opportunities. The return from investments in research and development is riskier and must be recouped over a shorter period. Moreover, the need to coordinate closely with supply-chain members and other partners make mistakes costlier. Making the wrong product or introducing it at the wrong time can devastate profitability. In the demand economy, the need to understand demand and act on it quickly and effectively is at a premium.

■ Information Is Pervasive, and Communication Is Instantaneous

Companies find it exceedingly difficult, if not impossible, to keep information secret for very long. Big institutions used to have an advantage in the stock markets because they were the first to receive information, which they could act on before smaller players even heard the news. Now, as a result of changes in technology and the law, individual investors receive news at virtually the same time as institutional investors.

In everyday business, reverse engineering allows companies to copy the innovations of other companies seemingly overnight. When the Procter & Gamble Co. successfully introduced Febreze fabric deodorizer in 1998, the Clorox Company matched the product category the following year with FreshCare. Moreover, proliferating databases and e-mail marketing techniques enable competitors to find and pursue companies' best customers. As a result, innovative products quickly morph into commodities that compete at even lower prices.

▪ *Products Can Be Purchased Anytime, Anywhere*

Expanding consumers' choices even more, businesses have developed additional and alternative distribution channels, and in so doing have advanced the emergence of the demand economy. As we know, the opportunities for shopping, as well as the methods for delivering ordered goods, have vastly multiplied. For example, pizza, books, a full month of groceries, even mortgages and insurance can be purchased over the Internet and brought directly to your door, and you can comparison shop many different competitors with just a few keystrokes.

▪ *Purchasing Consortia Threaten to Squeeze Suppliers*

The shift from the supply economy to the demand economy is also visible in the business-to-business sector. Traditional competitors in a range of industries have formed partnerships to create electronic marketplaces, such as Covisint (for cars), Aero Exchange (for aircraft parts), and the WorldWide Retail Exchange. The initial gains accrue from improved efficiency in matching buyers and sellers. Over time, however, the greater transparency and information flow created by these marketplaces are likely to commoditize products and increase price competition. In turn, buyers are likely to obtain significant cost savings at the expense of sellers through the exchanges.

▪ *Traditional Buyer-Seller Relationships Must Be Broadened*

One client of ours, a large manufacturer of parts for home appliances, discovered recently that it was no longer enough to maintain close contacts with its major buyer, an appliance manufacturer. Instead, in order to compete effectively in a rapidly changing environment, it had to understand demand for appliances across each link in the chain starting with its parts factories and extending to consumers' homes. By understanding shifts in consumer demand and the changing retail landscape, our client was better able to anticipate and align with demand. In turn, these demand insights made the company a much more valuable partner for its appliance-maker customers.

More generally, the concept of demand has become broader and deeper than many business-to-business companies have realized. Responding to the demand chain, sometimes all the way to the final consumer, has become crucial to preserve profit margin and make the business grow.

That the basic nature of competition has changed is clear. Demand is strong and growing, but supply, which is easier to access than ever before, is overwhelming demand. As choices multiply, we see that Adam Smith's law still applies, but its terms have certainly been altered.

Unlike Smith's contemporaries, whose limited, predictable diet was provided by a small number of competing butchers, bakers, fishmongers, and greengrocers, today's consumers choose from hundreds of cuisines supplied by dozens of supermarkets, specialty stores, and even Internet food suppliers. Each seller must work extremely hard just to get a customer's attention, and then must whet her appetite and make her decide that this is the meal she wants.

As the consumer markets go, so goes the business-to-business trade. New technology can change products and processes overnight, and options multiply. A supplier's price may be less important to a purchasing company than its delivery time, its own supply chain's reliability, or the specialists on its payroll who assist the buyer. A customer company may be prestigious enough to demand, and receive, cut-rate prices or a loss-leader standard of service from the supplier. For example, we helped one client significantly increase its business with Wal-Mart Stores, Inc., by explaining how and why the retailer's customers shop for and buy our client's apparel products. While Wal-Mart was absolutely expert at what sold in its stores, it was far less confident that it understood the demand side and what caused certain people to buy certain types of our client's apparel products. As a result of dividing Wal-Mart's customers into six demand segments, we were able to divide Wal-Mart's stores into six clusters on the basis of who shopped in those stores and then align the merchandise carried in each store with the people who shopped there most often. By linking the demand of customers who came to the stores with the supply Wal-Mart had on its shelves, sales for these apparel items increased across all of Wal-Mart and most of that gain was enjoyed by our client.

THE PRICE SQUEEZE

The repercussions of these changes pose a major challenge for business: despite the fact that demand has been strong, most producers have been unable to raise their prices (as I describe below). The result is a viselike squeeze on profit margins. After implementing the easy, cost-cutting measures, there are fewer and smaller improvements to be made on the cost side.

The inability to raise prices in what has been an unprecedentedly strong economy is a phenomenon not widely understood today. But it can be explained clearly with a few statistics.

On the demand side, the news at first glance looks dim. Population growth in the United States has dropped to less than 1 percent per year over the past decade, about 20 percent lower than in the previous thirty-five years. Since about two-thirds of the U.S. economy is driven by consumer spending, this is an ominous sign. A lowered population growth translates into fewer consumers, which in turn portends lower demand. But in fact, another contingency offsets the grim outlook. Though there are fewer shoppers, each is buying enough to compensate for that. The result is that personal consumption has continued to grow by 3.3 percent annually. This means that demand is growing at the same pace as gross domestic production, the recent economic downturn notwithstanding. (However, it is not likely to remain this way. In the long term, an aging, slow-growing population would definitely diminish demand.)

Supply, which has been growing more strongly than demand, poses the big problem. In order to increase their manufacturing capacities, producers invested capital at a sizzling annual growth rate of 7.8 percent throughout the 1990s. The growth in capacity jumped to 4.4 percent annually in the 1990s, reflecting a 13 percent increase over the average rate between 1948 and 1989. Moreover, actual industrial production rose by an average of 4.1 percent per annum in the 1990s.

Since the growth in capacity exceeded that in production and, in fact, grew nearly 25 percent faster than demand, it seems clear that some facilities and equipment were standing idle. Indeed, there is overcapacity in most industries across the United States and most of the industrialized world, from food and apparel to electronics and chemicals.

In the steel industry, for instance, experts believe that there are 200 million metric tons of excess capacity worldwide. In 1999, the auto industry produced 54 million vehicles worldwide; however, it had the capacity to produce 23 million more, for which there was no demand. By 2002, analysts predict, the demand for cars will be 60 million, but the industry will have the capacity to supply 70 million. The results of a recent study conducted by the American Marketing Association found that this is a worsening trend: "As large multinational companies tend to seek a presence in virtually every major global market . . . managers will likely confront the difficult challenges of trying to deal with even more intensive competition for resources and customers."

Plant capacity is only one measure of the general surplus. The Federal Reserve Board's study on productivity conducted at the end of the 1990s reported that the productivity of labor, which had grown by less than 1.5 percent annually since 1974, jumped to an average annual gain of 2.6 percent—a 73 percent increase—from the mid-1990s.

In an attempt to elicit demand for the goods and services that make up the supply surplus, sellers increased their advertising by an annual rate of 6.2 percent. They also built more stores in which to peddle the goods: the space in which retail goods are sold has grown at a 13 percent faster pace than the population. If your supermarket aisles and shopping malls feel less crowded, it isn't because people are buying less; it is because they have so many more places to shop in.

In addition, imports exceeded exports during the 1990s by an average of 2 percent, exacerbating the problem by flooding the market with even more goods.

Simply put, supply has vastly outstripped demand; it is impossible for either the United States or the global economy to absorb this massive degree of surplus. This is why businesses no longer have the power to raise prices. When consumers are confronted with a price increase, they can almost always find a similar or cheaper alternative elsewhere.

THE CHALLENGE OF PRICE ELASTICITY

Economists gauge the price sensitivity of demand by assessing its *elasticity*. When demand is highly elastic, even a small price hike will cause a significant drop in unit sales and dollar revenues. On the other hand, when demand is highly inelastic, a price hike has little effect on unit sales and dollar revenues.

Scarcity, or *nonsubstitutability*, another concept discussed by Adam Smith, is a key driver of the inelasticity of demand. Differentiated products and services have few if any substitutes, making demand for them more inelastic and price premiums easier to obtain. One of the principal goals of Demand Strategy is to create differentiated products that your targeted demand segment will find indispensable, and for which they will be willing to pay more.

At the retail level, we can measure pricing power by comparing growth in the consumer price index (CPI) with growth in actual consumption. In the 1990s, for example, producers maintained only 70 percent of the pricing power they had enjoyed between 1947 and 1989.

On the business-to-business side, the effects of the demand economy were even more alarming: in the 1990s, business-to-business manufacturers held less than one-sixth of the pricing strength that they had enjoyed between 1947 and 1989, a loss of 85 percent compared to prior decades. (See the chart on page 20.)

Using different methods of analysis, Stephen Roach, chief economist at Morgan Stanley Dean Witter & Co., studied the shifts in pricing power and reached a similar conclusion. Observing a structural break in the U.S. economy starting in the mid-1990s, he wrote, "The conclusion is straightforward: There has, indeed, been a significant loss in macro pricing leverage in the United States over the past few years." Roach predicts that this is likely to become a global phenomenon. With the ongoing trends toward globalization, deregulation, and

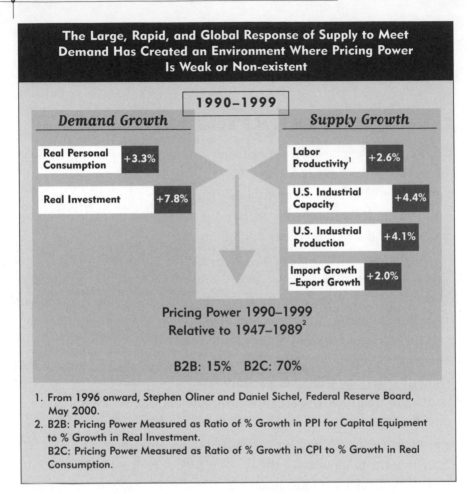

The Large, Rapid, and Global Response of Supply to Meet Demand Has Created an Environment Where Pricing Power Is Weak or Non-existent

1990–1999

Demand Growth		Supply Growth	
Real Personal Consumption	+3.3%	Labor Productivity[1]	+2.6%
Real Investment	+7.8%	U.S. Industrial Capacity	+4.4%
		U.S. Industrial Production	+4.1%
		Import Growth –Export Growth	+2.0%

Pricing Power 1990–1999
Relative to 1947–1989[2]

B2B: 15%   B2C: 70%

1. From 1996 onward, Stephen Oliner and Daniel Sichel, Federal Reserve Board, May 2000.
2. B2B: Pricing Power Measured as Ratio of % Growth in PPI for Capital Equipment to % Growth in Real Investment.
   B2C: Pricing Power Measured as Ratio of % Growth in CPI to % Growth in Real Consumption.

trade liberalization, "the American pattern of diminished pricing leverage should begin to spread to the broader industrial world in the years ahead. This implies that the rest of the industrial world is about to fall into step with America's no-pricing-leverage norm."

In this new environment, particularly with the loss of pricing power, companies realized quickly that their traditional approaches no longer worked. Because cost increases could not be passed on to customers, cost-plus pricing was no longer an option. Producers who were still reporting profits were earning them by cutting costs, an option that quickly reaches its limit and offers little promise for the future. Of course, what is preferable is rapid growth combined with pricing power. A recent study of one thousand large U.S. companies, for example, found a significant distinction between the ways they achieve earnings growth. Investors reward profits driven by sales growth with a 50 percent premium over profits increased through cost cutting.

One classic response to a profit squeeze is to churn out more goods, take a smaller profit on each item, and make it up in volume. But because of the already problematic supply surplus, that usually no longer works, at least for very long. FedEx's Fred Smith pointed out:

> In this supply-focused economy, manufacturers pushed mass production runs out the door to wholesalers, distributors, jobbers and others . . . but today it is very clear that pushing product out the door certainly will not create competitive advantage. Quite the contrary, it may often be a prescription for disaster. It won't even buy market share today. What it is very likely to get you is increased inefficiency and obsolescence.

Another way of responding to the squeeze on margins is to become the low-cost producer. But as Michael Porter points out in his work *Competitive Advantage,* this is very difficult to attain: "The strategic logic of cost leadership usually requires that a firm be the cost leader, not one of several vying for this position. Many firms have made serious strategic errors by failing to recognize this."

Many companies have tried reengineering. Authors Michael Hammer and James Champy, in their best-selling book *Reengineering the Corporation,* argue that the modernization of business requires that companies remove the barriers that separate people and departments and establish a new process-oriented approach to thinking about, managing, and operating their organizations.

In my experience, reengineering, though useful, does not sufficiently address the challenges posed by the demand economy. Typically used to redesign existing processes to reduce costs, shorten cycle times, or improve quality, reengineering is not intended to generate new platforms for growth, nor does it identify new insights into demand. Reengineering is most often used to cut costs, and like establishing yourself as the low-cost producer, it is not a long-term solution. In fact, so many companies have cut expenses and improved their efficiency ample, found a significant distinction between the ways they achieve earnings growth. Investors reward profits driven by sales growth with a 50 percent premium over profits increased through cost cutting.

One classic response to a profit squeeze is to churn out more goods, take a smaller profit on each item, and make it up in volume. But because of the already problematic supply surplus, that usually no longer works, at least for very long. FedEx's Fred Smith pointed out:

> In this supply-focused economy, manufacturers pushed mass production runs out the door to wholesalers, distributors, job-bers and others . . . but today it is very clear that pushing prod-uct out the door certainly will not create competitive advantage. Quite the contrary, it may often be a prescription for disaster. It won't even buy market share today. What it is very likely to get you is increased inefficiency and obsolescence.

Another way of responding to the squeeze on margins is to become the low-cost producer. But as Michael Porter points out in his work *Competitive Advantage,* this is very difficult to attain: "The strategic logic of cost leadership usually requires that a firm be the cost leader, not one of several vying for this position. Many firms have made serious strategic errors by failing to recognize this."

Many companies have tried reengineering. Authors Michael Hammer and James Champy, in their best-selling book *Reengineering the Corporation,* argue that the modernization of business requires that companies remove the barriers that separate people and departments and establish a new process-oriented approach to thinking about, managing, and operating their organizations.

In my experience, reengineering, though useful, does not sufficiently address the challenges posed by the demand economy. Typically used to redesign existing processes to reduce costs, shorten cycle times, or improve quality, reengineering is not intended to generate new platforms for growth, nor does it identify new insights into demand. Reengineering is most often used to cut costs, and like establishing yourself as the low-cost producer, it is not a long-term solution. In fact, so many companies have cut expenses and improved their efficiency

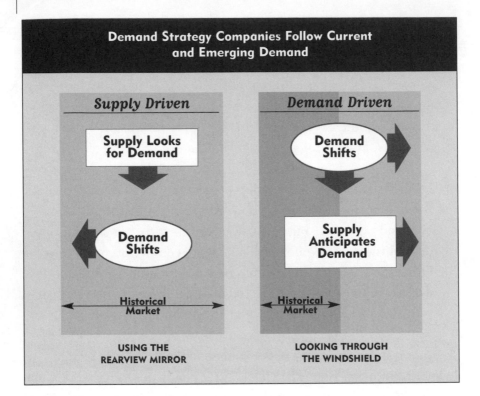

with the help of reengineering that the price difference between low-cost producers and their competitors has narrowed substantially.

HOW TO WIN IN THE DEMAND ECONOMY

The demand economy is a long-term phenomenon; businesses must consider how they will go to market in this new economic reality. Again, the first key is to understand what demand exists and, as a result, to be able to create differentiated supply that satisfies your customers more completely than your competitors' offerings. This is the point at which pricing power is restored to the provider.

The way to succeed in the demand economy is to compete on the basis of value-added differentiation rather than price. I want to introduce an uncomplicated economic formula that can help most companies earn back the capacity to raise their prices.

Each customer, at the moment of every purchase, determines that one product over all the others in its category meets his or her demand best. In the customers' eyes, that product provides the best value. And value is expressed this way:

$$\text{Value} = \frac{\text{Benefits}}{\text{Price}}$$

In this formula, only two macro factors influence value. The first is the product's benefits in the eyes of the customer. The second is the product's price.

A product's benefits include its performance, convenience, appearance, warranty, ease of use, and the trust consumers place in the brand, among other things. Customers in every product or service category will pay higher prices for products that they perceive as delivering more value. For example, millions of shoppers willingly pay billions of dollars for bottled water because they perceive it as healthier or better tasting, when they have unimpeded access to healthy, free water. Many people consider bottled water healthier than city water because it is free of chlorine and other additives. Conveniently packaged for portability, bottled water announces to those around us that we are intelligent consumers who select quality water over ordinary water or less healthy, sugary beverages. For many people, the physical and psychological benefits inherent in the product are so meaningful that they will pay top dollar to procure them.

Value, to repeat, goes up in one of two ways. You can either increase the benefits or lower the price. The Demand Strategist, rather than lowering cost, will always attempt to increase the benefits in ways that create more value for the target customer and more profit for the company. The Supply Strategist, on the other hand, will immediately attempt to create more value by lowering price.

Qualcomm Incorporated, a technology leader in the digital wireless communications market, provides a case in point. In the second half of 2001, demand in the technology sector dried up and prices for most high-tech products and components plummeted. But prices for Qualcomm's cell phone semiconductor chips were actually going up.

By adding features to its cell phone chips that made substituting another product nearly impossible, Qualcomm had successfully insulated itself from the rest of the market. According to a *Wall Street Journal* article, Qualcomm's treasurer, Dick Grannis, said that Qualcomm succeeded "by adding new features, such as faster data transmission and more information about a caller's location, into its cell phone chips" and that "the average price of the chips is rising." True to the economics of Demand Strategy, Qualcomm's chips, which were aligned with customer demand and meaningfully differentiated from competitive offers, commanded a price premium, while competitors were engaged in a price war.

The Demand Strategist attempts to thoroughly understand demand before creating supply. An understanding of demand enables you to plan and produce products and services that are sharply differentiated or scarce, which earn you higher prices and profits. By satisfying demand more thoroughly than your competitors, you will have more control over setting prices. Ultimately by aligning with demand to earn pricing power and increase profitability, the Demand Strategist comes closer to maximizing shareholder value in the demand economy. The Demand Strategist competes on supply but wins on demand.

To give you a better example of this, let's look at the histories of two telecommunications giants as they prepared to move to a new generation of products in the cellular phone market. The first, Motorola, employed a classic supply-driven approach; the other, Finland's Nokia Corporation, practiced Demand Strategy.

Managers at both companies recognized that a market for cell phones was developing. People's increased mobility created an unsatisfied need for wireless communication devices. At the same time, technological advances made such devices feasible, and government deregulation and common communications standards worked to encourage companies to offer wireless service. At this point, Motorola and Nokia, after analyzing the influential forces and factors in the market, had reached similar conclusions.

Nokia, however, approached the situation as a Demand Strategist. After thoroughly studying the demographics of its users and of the people most likely to adopt wireless services, Nokia's managers came to four key conclusions. They recognized that communication is a basic human need and that the demand for cellular service would grow well beyond traditional business users. In addition, the cultural trend toward customization and personalization, Nokia realized, would likely lead to a demand for personalized phones. They also recognized that the advent of digital technology would open opportunities for new value-added services, such as Web access. Nokia, with its deeper understanding of emerging demand, further realized that opening multiple channels of distribution would broaden its consumer reach.

Motorola, failing to grasp the full implications of these factors—the broader consumer market, and especially teenagers' telephone needs; the trend toward customization; the superiority and flexibility of digital technology; the advantages of multiple sales channels—maintained its traditional focus on supply. Having won the prestigious Malcolm Baldrige National Quality Award in the 1980s, Motorola had an unshakable belief in the inherent superiority of its products—an attitude that accompanied its executives into their discussions with cell phone service providers. As John Stratton, chief marketing officer for Verizon Wireless, recalls, "Listening, for Motorola, was waiting for you to stop speaking so they could tell you what to buy. It was endemic to their culture."

In addition to ignoring the emerging demand factors, Motorola made the shortsighted decision to protect and focus on its investment in analog equipment, delaying the introduction of digital technology as long as possible.

In sharp contrast, Nokia opted for Demand Strategy. Simply put, Nokia concentrated on giving its target customers what they wanted. Targeting the large, underserved low end of the market, it offered equipment with customized, personalized features that was easy to use. Instead of concentrating on business users, Nokia aimed its pricing systems toward recreational cell phone users. It chose to distribute through multiple channels in order to increase brand awareness and consumer reach. Furthermore, Nokia jumped into digital technology so that it could provide value-added services as quickly as possible.

The result was a resounding victory for Demand Strategy. In 1996, Motorola had a lock on more than 30 percent of the global wireless phone market, while Nokia's share was less than 20 percent. Four years later, their positions had neatly reversed: Nokia was up to 30 percent of the market, while Motorola's share had plunged to less than 15 percent. Moreover, according to an Interbrand survey conducted in 2001, Nokia had become the world's fifth most valuable brand, with an estimated brand value of $35 billion.

Striving for efficiencies before understanding the real nature of demand is like firing a gun before aiming. You hit the bull's-eye only by chance. As one of our clients ruefully noted in our first meeting with his company: "We carefully focused on building the most efficient supply chain in the industry. So now we deliver the wrong stuff to the wrong customers faster and cheaper than anyone else."

Costs are, of course, critical, but to create value for customers it is essential that you satisfy demand first. Only a thorough understanding of Demand Strategy, as well as the particular demands of your targeted customers, can lead you to long-term success in today's demand economy.

We are no longer in a supply economy, in which "How can I create large amounts of supply as efficiently as possible?" was the right question. Companies operating in that system were following the accepted economic theory that was first proposed by Adam Smith and continued to the present day by economists such as Paul Samuelson. They started by creating supply, and then went in search of the demand to absorb the supply they had already created.

We are in the midst of a shift of historic proportions. The changes in how we do business as we move away from a supply-driven world toward one that is demand driven will have repercussions for every manager, executive, and CEO. The significance of the demand economy cannot be overstated.

It is my intent to help you understand—and profit from—the demand economy, by helping you understand what you need to compete and win.

CHAPTER 2

DEMAND STRATEGY

How to Outperform the Competition and Create an Enterprise That Endures

o matter what type of enterprise you manage, you face a critical choice today: will you continue to do business in the usual way—perhaps the way that made your company successful in the first place—or do you have a great enough sense of the urgency of the economic changes taking place to adjust the way you do business, in order to successfully compete in today's demand economy?

Unlike recent management fads or movements, such as change management or reengineering, Demand Strategy doesn't require a bevy of outside consultants. What it does require is a change in how you think about your business, and a corresponding change in the sequence by which you run your business.

My central thesis is that a business must understand the demand in its market before it creates supply. It is the only way to understand and satisfy your targeted customers better than your competitors.

In this chapter I will suggest ways to compete and win in the new demand economy. I'll offer six specific steps for developing a Demand

Strategy that will virtually guarantee the success of your business, whether it is a multinational corporation or a small business.

When most companies face a problem with profits, their first response is to cut costs, reduce prices, sell harder, and squeeze their vendors. Demand Strategy offers a more effective alternative: when problems develop, businesses use their understanding of demand to differentiate their products so that they align as closely as possible with the demand of the customer targets in the marketplace from which they earn the most profit. Demand Strategy will help you anticipate demand and focus on the most profitable customer demand segments, to better align products before creating new products or services.

WHAT DEMAND IS—AND IS NOT

When Adam Smith first outlined the law of supply and demand, markets were basic and uncomplicated. This is far from true today. Yet writers of economics textbooks continue to oversimplify and unintentionally mislead their readers by representing demand as Smith did— that is, with monomarkets like wheat and grain. Demand is defined as the amount of a particular commodity or service that buyers are willing to purchase at a specific price. Many business leaders still view their markets as large and relatively undifferentiated, as they were taught in college, and lead their companies as if various kinds of demand were alike. As a result, they are fixated on the idea that price and market share are the overriding factors in beating their competition. First, some basic facts.

▪ *Demand Is Multifaceted*

Demand is a far more complex phenomenon than most economic textbooks portray. Demand includes consumers' desire or need for a product, its features, the availability of substitutes and their prices, the channels customers prefer, the availability of credit, and the convenience of purchasing the product. Of course, economists are fully aware of these influences, but, as exemplified by the way "demand curves" are drawn with price and quantity on the two axes, they underrate their importance relative to price. In practice, the other variables I've just described are equally important, if not more important, in influencing the customer's choice.

Economists also have a tendency to treat demand as though it were static. They recognize that tastes, technology, demographics, the information customers have, and culture can affect demand, but they tend to see these factors as "given," and unchanging for the purpose of their analysis—to the extent these factors have any influence, they will be felt in the long term.

But in today's global economy, where information flows instantly and technological change is almost continuous, demand is highly dynamic and subject to rapid change. The meteoric rise and total collapse of many Internet-based companies is but one dramatic example of the pace and scope of potential changes.

The telecommunications industry offers a critical lesson about the complexity and rapid pace of change in the demand economy. From 1996 to 2000, phone companies almost doubled their spending on telecom equipment, and for 2000, demand was forecast to grow by 15 percent. Equipment makers geared up to meet the demand. To keep up with booming customer demand, Nortel Networks Limited announced in the middle of 2000 that it would spend almost $2 billion and add nearly ten thousand jobs in order to increase production. A year later, as the anticipated demand failed to materialize, Nortel cut thirty thousand jobs and suffered a single-quarter loss of $19 billion. Industry demand forecasts were quickly revised from a strong, 15 percent increase to a 7 percent decline.

One of the key issues leading to the disastrous forecasts was a failure to understand customers within the broader context of demand. The equipment makers relied on discussions with their direct customers to build their forecasts. But their phone company customers were not really aware of what was happening to demand among their own end customers. As Lucent Technologies' forecaster Alex Bangash ruefully reported to the *Wall Street Journal* in the aftermath of the erroneous forecasts, "You can't just look at your customers, you have to look at your customers' customers."

Conducting a broader set of discussions within your customer's organization can also help determine how demand is likely to unfold. However, like many companies, the telecom equipment suppliers seemed to limit their discussion to their traditional buyers rather than understanding the perspective on demand from other parts of the organization. As former Nortel CEO John Roth told the *Wall Street Journal,* "All the conversations I was having with my customers were, 'John, you haven't shipped me enough equipment yet, when are you going to get the volume up?' The people we did not talk to in our customers' [companies] were the treasurers, who found out in January that they were having trouble raising the money" to pay for equipment.

Most economists seem to think of the demand for products and services as homogeneous: all customers are treated equally. In reality, no market is homogeneous. Every industry has many segments of demand. The customers comprising those segments have very different values and priorities, and understanding these differences is mandatory in the new demand economy.

A *segment* is a group of customers within a given business category who share a set of common demands. In other words, the value that any individual within the segment places on products or services will be very similar to that of other members of the same segment. Customers assess an item's benefits and prices to determine its value to them. Since Demand Strategy depends on a thorough understanding of demand prior to the creation of supply, it is critical that you familiarize yourself with all segments and select those that are most profitable to you as your primary customer targets.

Most industries have five to seven macro segments, which means that there are between five and seven different types of demand to be satisfied in most categories. The banking market, for example, includes demand among individuals who prefer to visit branches and transact business with tellers; people seeking the convenience of Internet banking; customers who value and want to make use of personal financial advisers; individuals who prefer to manage their own finances; and people who use banks for their checking and savings accounts, but not for loans or investments.

In the airline market, some vacationers scour the market for the lowest fares, while others pay for the added amenities of first class. Among business travelers, some with predictable schedules can plan trips in advance, while others have to purchase tickets at the last minute and pay a higher price. The higher price is acceptable because the real demand is flying to see a customer or to improve performance at one of your facilities.

Demand Strategists identify, then concentrate on, the segments that yield the most profit for their companies. You can target any demand segments you choose, as long as you understand the nature of their demand and build a cost-effective supply to serve them.

In fast food, McDonald's Corporation concentrates on the demand segment that looks for speed, consistency, and cleanliness. That leaves room for Wendy's International, Inc., to focus on the segment that wants heartier, customized meals. Of course, McDonald's will be happy to sell to Wendy's customers, but the success of McDonald's is attributable, in large part, to its concentration on the demand segments from which it receives the bulk of its profit.

International Business Machines Corporation (IBM) learned about demand segments painfully at the hands of Dell Computer Corporation. Surely there were people who wanted the sophisticated, cutting-edge technology of IBM's personal computers. But while IBM tried to sell its product to the entire market, Dell brilliantly understood that there was a demand segment comprised of customers who were confident in their knowledge of PCs and wanted a direct channel that supplied them with quality PCs at a lower price, thus offering better value.

Choosing your demand segment is crucial, and I will discuss this point in more depth later in the book.

■ Demand Can Be Either Current or Emerging

In addition to market segments, which vary from industry to industry, there are two basic categories of demand: *current* and *emerging*.

While current demand *should* be easy to identify, we at The Cambridge Group have repeatedly found companies so myopically focused on daily business and quarterly results that they miss obvious changes in demand. For example, when GEICO insurance began direct telephone marketing, the company's property and casualty competitors assumed this was a temporary phenomenon that would not adversely affect their industry. Only later did they recognize that a significant number of current buyers of automobile insurance viewed insurance as a commodity and were delighted to purchase what they perceived to be the same quality of insurance for less money through GEICO. By the time the other companies responded, GEICO was firmly entrenched and had changed perceptions of value in auto insurance, especially the role of the insurance agent.

Demand is organic and constantly evolving, sometimes incrementally and sometimes in large leaps. I strongly believe that every business manager should regularly determine whether or not his or her product is still in alignment with demand every six months to a year. Being behind the demand curve carries significant penalties, especially if your competitors have kept pace while you are still responding to yesterday's demand.

We are currently working for a client who created what is now a $25 billion worldwide business category. By anyone's judgment, the company would be viewed as having one of the great brands in the world. But for the past several years, it depended upon the brand to sell products and rarely, if ever, reviewed changes in demand. About three years ago, as a result, it began to experience a steep decline in sales, profits, and retail accounts. As the company's leaders themselves admitted, there had been no meaningful changes to their product lineup in five years, while competitors' offerings had changed significantly. The overall marketplace had changed significantly as well, with new major private label competition.

After determining how demand had changed in their category in the past five years, it was clear to us what the problem was. Because the company's managers hadn't kept track of demand, they were out of alignment in terms of their product design, their distribution channels, and their pricing. Moreover, their products weren't engineered for the age and gender of their category's fastest-growing customer group; finally, their mix of products offered to retailers was several years behind the category's evolution.

If you don't have a firm grasp of current demand, it's very unlikely that you'll recognize emerging demand—demand that will generate revenue and profits in the months ahead.

In most cases, current demand is less difficult to spot than emerging demand, which I define as a recent, still small, but growing demand for new and different products. But since emerging demand can transform an existing industry or even create an industry that will render your product obsolete, it is critical that companies not miss it. There are many ways to quantify emerging demand, any one of which can give you a prediction of the eventual size of the emerging demand.

Emerging demand can be seen from several vantage points. There is the predictable, logical shift that evolves from obvious trends. For example, you know that 31 percent of the U.S. population consists of baby boomers. Since that cohort is aging, you can deduce with some precision just what businesses and services are likely to grow significantly to meet their emerging demand. In this case, the beneficiaries will be companies that provide investment advice, eyeglasses, retirement communities, and health care—products and services tailored to an aging population.

Another kind of emerging demand requires constant contact with your target demand segments so you can detect changes in wants, needs, or behavior that are at the forefront of emerging demand.

In the early 1980s, for example, The Cambridge Group was hired by Harry Lees, then the vice president of marketing at Nabisco, to see whether there would be a market for high-fiber cookies. After conducting qualitative research across the country, my partner Kevin Bowen reported that, indeed, there existed enough demand for a high-fiber cookie to make it a small success. Of greater importance, though, was Kevin's and the Nabisco team's recognition of an emerging demand for food products that had lower fat. Armed with this insight, Ellen Marram, president of Nabisco Cookies and Crackers, led her division to a brilliant introduction and ongoing management of SnackWell's. The company's SnackWell's division grew to sales of $700 million a year.

Had Kevin and the Nabisco team not observed the marketplace with an open mind, they might easily have missed the significance of customers' positive attitudes toward lower-fat products, which was just beginning to emerge. The forces and factors analysis that we took the Nabisco team through enabled Nabisco to seize the market and launch SnackWell's long before the competition was able to respond.

One of the most famous cases of spotting emerging demand and developing an entirely new product in response to it was Sony Corporation's creation of the Walkman portable tape player. At the time, one of Sony Corporation's core competencies was its ability to miniaturize virtually all of its electronic products. What Sony noticed around the world was that music was moving away from being strictly entertainment and was becoming a way to express one's lifestyle. In addition, the jogging craze had hit the United States and other countries, and runners were desperate for something to relieve the tedium of long runs. The creation of the Walkman was a strategically planned and timely business decision based upon an understanding of changing consumer patterns and emerging demand.

Insurance used to be considered a stable and predictable business, but it has recently begun to undergo a transformation directly related to an emerging demand for a life insurance product that allows customers to participate in the historic growth of the stock market. Once that demand was recognized, industry leaders developed the variable annuity to meet it.

Today, businesses are engaged in a constant search for innovations that will bring fresh products and services to fill the needs of customers. The most important innovation successes, I have found, are achieved by companies that use a formalized business system dedicated to identifying emerging demand early.

Among companies with these processes are:

- *EMC Corporation.* EMC organizes its business into two groups. The first group focuses on products that will reach the market within eighteen months. The second group methodically searches for the next big thing—products worldwide that will be introduced in eighteen to sixty months—to tap into emerging demand. As I will discuss in more detail later, EMC involves its smartest customers in an eighteen-month process in which customers offer constant feedback and interaction at every stage of the development of EMC products, from invention to product introduction. By having customers directly involved, they are able to offer the critical insights and changes that virtually guarantee the success of the reinvented storage products.

- *McDonald's Corporation.* The very existence of McDonald's is the result of its founder's ability to identify emerging demand. The original McDonald brothers restaurant in California ordered many more malted-milk machines from sales representative Ray Kroc than any other restaurant in the United States. When Kroc went to see their operation, he saw that they had created a business system that could serve hamburgers faster and more consistently than any other restaurant. He spotted what he believed was an emerging demand for similar restaurants all across the United States. He was right. At last count, 46 million people per day go to McDonald's.

  McDonald's managers and leaders have systematically developed proprietary techniques for understanding emerging demand. They were the first to use traffic patterns and geodemography to understand where suburbs were going to be built. They then bought real estate and built restaurants two to three years before the housing around the restaurants was complete.

  They were the first to understand that children were the demand lever for families, which led to the creation of Ronald McDonald. They also identified an emerging demand for drive-throughs as more and more people wanted a fast and convenient way to get a meal without leaving their cars.

  The McDonald's obsession with identifying emerging demand can be found in its corporate structure. Rather than having product managers, McDonald's organizes around specific consumer targets—kids, tweens, teens, families, and so on. By focusing on these target demand segments, McDonald's knows more about its customers than any of its competitors.

- *Medtronic, Inc.* A manufacturer of cardiac pacemakers and other medical devices, Medtronic has an annual research and development budget of more than $500 million. It asks surgeons in hospitals and research centers to suggest new product ideas and help direct their development. Moreover, one or more Medtronic engineers attends 70 percent of the medical operations in which the company's products are used. By doing so, they learn more about current deficiencies in existing products, as well as identify new product opportunities. Such diligence helps to explain why Medtronic controls more than half of the intensely competitive cardiac pacemaker market.

- *Gatorade (the Quaker Oats Company).* One of the most important decisions Gatorade made in its history was to stay in very close contact with dozens of people daily through an ongoing survey of Gatorade consumers called Gator Base. This simple and inexpensive technique enables them to immediately identify emerging demand, and permits them to be the first to create products and programs that aligns with this emerging demand (as I will outline in more detail later in the book).

Emerging demand can ramp up quickly; you need to be prepared to move rapidly once it has been identified. The bulk of the profits generated by this new demand will flow to the companies that *spot* these opportunities first, *understand* them best, and *design* their supply accordingly. Such organizations are the only source for early adopters—customers who are willing to pay more to satisfy their demand. By the time other companies recognize the demand and race to meet it, the market has moved to a broader group of people, who tend to buy established products and who aren't willing to pay the higher prices for the product that early adopters pay.

In 1998, for example, 85 percent of EMC Corporation's revenues came from products that didn't yet exist at the beginning of that year. How did they accomplish this remarkable transformation? By having a firm grasp on emerging demand for storage systems that provide anywhere, anytime availability of information. From the very inception of product development, EMC involved fifty to sixty of its customers' chief technology officers (CTOs) in the design, operating system, and software application development. By involving these CTOs, EMC was certain it understood the demand the company had to satisfy. These customers interacted with EMC constantly during the eighteen-month development process. Anticipating this demand and involving key customers led EMC to introduce revolutionary storage products in 1998 and catch its competition completely by surprise.

EMC is an example of a company that pays heed to its leading-edge or heaviest-user customers—those who are ready to spend extra for the latest and best products. Inevitably, they are the most profitable demand segment you can target—much more so, all things being equal, than the average customer.

WHO'S WINNING ON DEMAND

There is often a substantial gap between what a customer wants and what a company thinks a customer wants. The gap can often be traced to a manager's obsession with supply—with the design, production, and marketing of a product that fits the company's core competencies or that allows management to utilize existing assets in order to avoid capital expenditures. As a result, managers fail to anticipate demand. A more certain way to succeed is by understanding demand and then creating a product or service that can be differentiated from the competition and is better aligned with what your highest-profit demand segment wants and needs—something that you alone understand and can provide. As the late shipping magnate Aristotle Onassis put it: "The secret of business is to know something that nobody else knows." The more you know about demand, the easier it is to differentiate your product or service from your competitors'. This enables you to charge a higher price and leads directly to top-line growth and increased profits.

I am far from alone in advocating these ideas. In fact, some of our leading companies have begun to apply strategies that put demand ahead of supply. Before I introduce the specific steps involved in putting together a Demand Strategy, let's look at the ways Demand Strategy has been used by successful companies in a variety of industries.

- Between 1995 and 1999, *Ford Motor Company*'s market share dropped by almost 2 percent, from 25.7 to 23.8. Was this cause for alarm at Ford? No—in fact, it was part of a carefully orchestrated plan, based on the principles of Demand Strategy, that helped the company post earnings of $7.2 billion in 1999, the highest in the industry.

  Before 1995, Ford's in-depth data on market demand was limited. Salespeople were rewarded according to the number of cars they sold, and they paid no attention to profit margins. As a result, salespeople concentrated on moving low-end, low-margin vehicles—it was easier, since they were less expensive.

  In 1995, Ford decided to identify its most profitable customers. Aided by market research, it determined what features customers were willing to pay extra for that the industry didn't yet provide. Ford's controller for North America and global marketing, Lloyd E. Hansen, cited more comfortable supercabs for trucks as an example.

  Next, Ford turned its sales units into businesses with their own profit targets, and told them which cars and trucks delivered the highest margin.

  Finally, the company redesigned its price structure, trimming the cost of its high-margin items, such as Explorers and Crown Victorias, just enough to increase sales without losing substantial profits.

  The effect of these moves dramatically affirmed Demand Strategy. There was a drop of 420,000 units among low-profit vehicles—such as Escorts and Aspires—and a rise of 600,000 units for high-profit vehicles. As a result, Ford's earnings on North American car and truck sales more than doubled from 1995 to 1999. Hansen called the company's plan "probably the biggest driver of Ford's profitability."

- *Amazon.com, Inc.,* was established as a lower-priced alternative to bricks-and-mortar bookstores. Then more cut-rate booksellers appeared on-line, offering substantially lower prices.

  But Amazon didn't attempt to match them on price, betting that Amazon's reputation, the variety of its offerings, and the convenience of its one-click Web page would keep its best customers from defecting. They gambled that customers would not switch for a lower price, because customer demand valued the benefits of reliability, variety, and convenience over price. Therefore, they were creating value by increasing the benefits in our value equation, Value = Benefits/Price.

  In 1999, two researchers at the Massachusetts Institute of Technology—Erik Brynjolfsson and Michael D. Smith—studied the on-line book market and found that Amazon.com's price structure was, indeed, holding firm, maintaining higher prices than other on-line discounters. Books.com, for example, undersold Amazon 99 percent of the time, yet it garnered only 2.2 percent of the traffic. Discouraged, its owner, Cendant Corporation, closed the company down and sold the name to barnesandnoble.com.

  For a time, pundits theorized that on-line discounters were going to drive prices and margins through the floor. Amazon demonstrated that understanding demand can enable a company to sustain its margins by offering its best customers what they want most.

  The formula for business success is to recognize what your high-profit demand segment needs, then work with your leading-edge customers to bundle the supply into a marketplace proposition that will satisfy it. I focus on how to develop a business system that is closely aligned with the demand you are serving in Chapter 7.

- Another dramatic example of Demand Strategy at work—and of grace under pressure—involves the *Ritz-Carlton* of Kuala Lumpur. In the Asian financial crisis of the late 1990s, the price of Malaysian hotel rooms dropped with the currency. But travelers were few. Luxury hotels in Malaysia joined the price war and room rates there plunged.

But James McBride, general manager of the Ritz-Carlton, saw a better way. He set out in pursuit of that segment of foreign travelers who wanted luxe treatment and could now afford to buy it with devalued currency. McBride arranged to meet arriving flights with music, mimosas, and more. The Ritz had its guests' baths drawn by butlers, and offered drinks and snacks served to the bathers. Technicians were available to fix ailing laptops and other electronic gizmos. In other words, the Ritz pampered its high-paying guests.

To offset their lower rates, the Ritz's rival hotels had been cutting luxuries, such as fresh flowers, lavish supplies of towels, and extensive staffs of personnel eager to please. The Ritz went the other way, keeping its charges high enough to pay for all the extras it offered. It did so because it knew that was the element that its targeted demand segment valued—in fact, treasured—the most. As a result, its occupancy rate in 1999 rose to 60 percent, up from 50 percent the previous year.

- Tom Freston, chief executive officer of *MTV Networks,* has to stay in touch with the notoriously mercurial musical tastes of teens and preteens. Yet for more than a decade, Freston has kept MTV near the top of the ratings. He says his success is due mainly to his relentless efforts to understand demand.

  "If we can be totally connected with our viewers," Freston said recently, "get inside their heads . . . their closets, their CD collections, and translate [what we find] . . . into a product, everything else in our business will fall into place." That is the motto of a true Demand Strategist.

  Freston spares no pains. "We actually in some cases put people under hypnosis," he recently said. "We will videotape their lives. We do a lot of quantitative stuff. But coupled with that is having an employee staff and culture that is inherently interested in our customers and what they do." This is an exceptionally good example of Demand Strategy: first understanding your target customer, and then (and only then) turning those insights into supply that effectively satisfies the ever-changing demand of teenagers.

MTV also knows that it must change as demand emerges— quickly. "Just as you get accustomed to serving one group and their particular attitudes, they have [moved] . . . along," Freston said. "And a mistake is to move along with them. There is a whole new generation coming in the pipeline that is quite different."

Again, Demand Strategy recognizes two basic categories of demand—current and emerging. Emerging demand is just beginning to take shape and form. Freston is ultimately responsible for making sure that his company spots the *emerging* demand and accurately predicts and adjusts for its developing shape. So far, he and MTV have done just that, but they take nothing for granted. If MTV can understand and satisfy the constantly changing demand of teens, it should be the goal of every business in America to understand and satisfy its demand segments.

WHAT DEMAND STRATEGY IS

Demand Strategy is, broadly speaking, a new way of thinking about the role of demand in running your business. The last two hundred years of a supply-driven economy have given way to a demand economy. Understanding the human and market forces that drove this historic change enables you to use your current skills and business acumen and simply apply them differently. What changes is the sequence— how to think and then act so that you can prosper. Demand Strategy includes a set of specific steps companies can take to identify the forces and factors that drive demand in their most profitable demand segments. By understanding current and emerging demand, they can build a differentiated supply that meets that segment's needs better than their competitors can.

I want to emphasize that Demand Strategy isn't a quick-fix marketing scheme. Once you recognize the primacy of demand, your organization needs to examine the whole of its business in terms of the demand it serves. By putting demand before supply, you will obtain a far clearer picture of what you can successfully supply that will earn the highest rate of profit and the greatest return on your organization's assets and invested capital.

Applying Demand Strategy gives your business four distinct advantages that will increase profits: First, you will be selling what your customers actually want. Second, you will be able to differentiate your company and its products from its competitors. Third, you will be able to reduce costs by eliminating products for which there is limited demand. Fourth, you will be able to sell your goods or services at a premium price. Why? Because a differentiated product that better satisfies demand earns inelastic pricing.

Here is a snapshot picture of the six basic steps of Demand Strategy that The Cambridge Group, working with many of the world's top organizations, developed.

Step 1. Analyze the Demand Forces and Industry Factors Impacting Your Business

Demand forces and industry factors are the causal elements that create or change demand.

These forces and factors can include demographics, the economy, competitors, legislation, societal trends, and technology, as well as other drivers that have an impact on demand and help to determine supply and pricing.

Companies must analyze all of the demand forces and industry factors that have the capacity to change demand within their industry. In studying the past and current forces and factors that drive demand, you will find patterns and important anomalies will emerge. By recognizing the patterns and finding answers to the anomalies you can begin to develop actionable new insights into current and emerging demand.

Industry factors are often obvious and easy to determine: new competitors, new technologies, additional channels of distribution or supply, and changes in the industry's structure. Industry changes could include modifications in the supply chain—distributors being elimi-

There are six very complete and easy-to-understand steps by which any company can leverage Demand Strategy

1	**Analyze the demand forces and industry factors impacting your business**	Create propriety, actionable insights into the drivers of changes in past, current, and emerging demand. **RESULTS:** ▸ Allows you to capture the highest profit demand and the greatest possible returns ▸ Demand shifts are anticipated rather than reacted to ▸ Earnings surprises due to demand shifts are avoided
2	**Select your most profitable demand segments**	Identify specific demand segments you can satisfy that yield the highest profits for your company. **RESULTS:** ▸ Products and offers targeted for specific market segments, versus mass market offers ▸ By satisfying specific demands well, your competitors are less likely to appeal to the same customers ▸ Efficient targeting of budgets maximizes sales at lower cost, resulting in higher profits
3	**Build enduring value propositions to differentiate your offers**	Collaborate with your best customers to build your enduring Value Proposition. **RESULTS:** ▸ A Value Proposition that **differentiates** and **insulates** you from the competition ▸ Allows you to charge more, and avoid discount pricing ▸ Increased loyalty as products/brands deliver on customer expectations
4	**Identify the strategies and business systems needed to meet your demand**	Leverage supply chain and channel sales expertise to achieve superior execution. **RESULTS:** ▸ Improved efficiency and effectiveness due to alignment with demand ▸ Enables a company to create a portfolio that appeals to multiple target segments ▸ New products/offers benefit from the company's superior distribution, sales, and marketing
5	**Allocate your resources**	Use demand insights to align resources behind best growth/profit opportunities. **RESULTS:** ▸ Allows companies to align with and satisfy demand at high levels of profit ▸ Shareholder value remains at consistently high levels
6	**Execute your demand strategy**	Follow a disciplined, proven process that directs your supply to customers who most want what your products deliver. **RESULTS:** ▸ Total organizational alignment ▸ Superior execution that trumps competitors

nated, for example, so that manufacturers deal directly with customers. An industry consolidation is another example.

Demand forces are external to your industry. They include new legislation, a change in the economy, and developments in the cultural and social spheres—a push for greater privacy in the Information Age, for example.

In virtually every company, market analyses are limited and center on fairly obvious, narrowly focused characteristics and performance. The Demand Strategy approach operates at a much broader level. By focusing on demand forces and industry factors, it goes well beyond the issues of the moment to produce a realistic snapshot and real-time understanding of the factors that have modified demand in the past and the factors that are creating future demand in your marketplace. When properly done, an analysis of past and present forces and factors in virtually every instance reveals clear patterns of cause and effect. Recognizing these patterns is key to gaining a critical head start in identifying emerging demand. By understanding the causal factors changing demand at their earliest stages, you can preempt your competition, differentiate your products, and have an excellent opportunity to earn higher prices because your supply outperforms your competitors in satisfying demand.

Step 2. Select Your Most Profitable Demand Segments

Academics continue to discuss supply and demand in terms of mono-markets, such as wheat and sugar. In fact, every market can be segmented from a variety of focal points, such as lifestyle, life stage, and behavior. The object is to become thoroughly familiar with the unique demand of particular segments so that you can identify those that will best fit with your own skills, resources, channels, and business systems.

When you choose target demand segments, you must do so by finding those that align best with your infrastructure and capabilities and allow you to differentiate your products or services in ways that lead to increased profitability. In doing so, you must consider your distribution channels, competitors, price points, product design, core competencies, and anything else that helps you get as closely aligned with customer demand as possible. You may find that the most profitable customers are currently out of your competitive reach, or you may see an emerging demand that your company isn't currently suited to meet. It doesn't make sense for an organization geared to producing low-price products to try selling luxury furs, no matter how extraordinary the opportunity. In many cases, some of the most profitable customers may already be buying from you. But you can encourage more of them to buy more goods or services at higher prices if you understand them better and attempt to satisfy their demand better than your competitors.

Step 3. Build Enduring Value Propositions to Differentiate What You Sell

Combining Step 1 (analyzing the forces and factors driving demand) with Step 2 (identifying the most profitable customers) enables companies that use Demand Strategy to connect three very rich fact bases: their customers, their industry, and their own company.

Unfortunately, most business plans change very little from year to year because companies are focused to a large degree on current sales and profitability. The broader analysis pursued by demand strategy allows them to determine not only how best to meet current demand, but how to begin preparing to meet an emerging demand ahead of competitors.

It is an intensive process. Each strategic option has its own risks and rewards, investment and technology requirements, staffing imperatives, supply-chain, timeline, and competitive implications. Each of these options must be thoroughly considered. Create hypotheses and use fact-based analysis to clarify how the forces and factors impact and relate to each demand segment.

After narrowing your options, a cross-disciplinary leadership team should be assembled to make the final strategic decisions regarding where and how to compete. But companies should not rush to that point. Debate within the organization should be full, open, and passionate. It is important to work to build shared ownership, confidence, and enthusiasm, rather than imposing a strategic judgment upon a business without a full understanding of goals and expectations. When department and functional leaders are fully committed to the strategic option chosen, its execution will have a far greater chance of success.

Once agreement is reached, it is vital that you develop an enduring *Demand Value Proposition*. In doing so you are essentially telling your customers, "I understand what you want; here is the set of benefits, the proposition we are offering to satisfy your needs and provide true value." It is the Demand Value Proposition that differentiates you from your competitors—differentiation is essential as supply proliferates and more and more products are in danger of becoming commodities.

An effective Demand Value Proposition typically has several *planks,* or facets, that form the basis upon which you have chosen to compete. For example, McDonald's has at least four planks that can be found in every McDonald's in the world: the restaurants are fast and friendly, they are clean, they cater to kids, and they provide consistent food.

As Chapter 1 explained, Value = Benefits/Price. Each McDonald's plank addresses a specific need of its target segments. By delivering their benefits McDonald's is satisfying more of its primary target's requirements than its competitors do. McDonald's has become the world's largest restaurant business because its benefits and its superior execution combine to create great value for billions of customers.

Demand Strategy ensures that a company's leading-edge customers—rather than its average customers—are guiding the creation of its Demand Value Proposition.

Step 4. Identify the Strategies and Business Systems Needed to Meet Your Demand

No strategy can be successful unless it is well executed. You need a finely tuned business system. In many cases, your business system will offer an opportunity to drive both differentiation and competitive advantage.

EMC Corporation, for example, entered the computer storage market in 1990 at a time when IBM had an 80 percent share of the market for mainframe storage. By developing better data storage hardware and software, over the next few years EMC came to dominate the market. Moreover, it developed a business system in which EMC works with its smartest and most visionary customers in order to reinvent the storage business every two years, and thus maintain its commanding lead in the market. EMC identifies the fifty to sixty people within its customers' organizations who know the most about data storage. After signing nondisclosure agreements covering a period of eighteen months, these fifty to sixty people then become intimately involved with EMC's engineers in reinventing existing storage technology, allowing EMC to leapfrog its competitors. This interaction with its customers helped to drive EMC's stock up 80,575 percent in the nineties; it became the greatest-gaining stock on the New York Stock Exchange during the decade of the 1990s (only Dell Computer, traded on the Nasdaq, had a higher gain over the same period).

In its earliest days, the Gatorade company decided to follow a "point of sweat" strategy, making Gatorade available in gymnasiums, fitness centers, and convenience stores where people were most likely to go after they had finished their workout or game. Gatorade established a presence at virtually every imaginable point-of-sweat outlet.

In doing so, they built a proprietary channel of distribution in which they preempted and outperformed competition. While the task seemed overwhelming several years ago, it is the commitment to this type of differentiation which makes the difference between a company that is merely good versus one that achieves greatness.

Sometimes business systems are defined not only by how employees act but by how they think and feel about themselves. The Walt Disney Company, for example, uses this concept superbly in its amusement parks, where employees are referred to as cast members. The ambiance of elegance at Four Seasons hotels is due, in part, to the signs placed everywhere employees congregate: "We are ladies and gentlemen serving ladies and gentlemen."

Step 5. *Allocate Your Resources*

One of the CEO's most important responsibilities is the proper allocation of resources. A strategy or a business plan has no value unless it is well executed. To be well executed means that appropriate resources are allocated to ensure success. It has always amazed me that corporations frequently lose focus by being in too many businesses at one time and then failing to have sufficient resources behind them.

The assessment of capabilities must be determined by senior management, which should provide resources where they will achieve the highest returns and earn the most loyal customers.

Business leaders frequently feel that the grass is greener on a competitor's lawn. In response, they plunge into multiple lines of business, each of which inevitably draws upon the company's limited resources. As a result, organizations permit their strongest human resources to be scattered in several directions. Yet as management guru Peter Drucker once said, "The scarcest resources in any organization are performing people."

Such companies have trouble providing enough financial resources to allow each line of business to become a vigorous competitor and a high-growth operation. While a few such conglomerates flourish in their various businesses—General Electric and Johnson & Johnson are notable examples—they are the exception. Much more commonly, companies with multiple lines of business have insufficient resources to consistently lead in their categories, and so they earn lower rates of return. One of my most difficult tasks as an adviser to senior managers of client companies is to reduce the broad range of businesses they are in so that they can concentrate on larger commitments and better performance from fewer businesses and product offers. I encourage them to sell mid- and low-performing businesses so that the resources of the parent organization can be given to the star performers or divisions.

Step 6. *Execute Your Demand Strategy*

One of Harvard Business School's most popular professors, the late Thomas Bonoma, taught his students that while strategy is important, superior execution is imperative. Professor Bonoma provided count-less examples of companies that had superb strategies that were undermined by mediocre execution, and he contrasted them with companies with average-to-good strategies but superior execution. In almost every case, the latter turned in the better performance.

Demand Strategists will fail if they are not scrupulously attentive to every detail of executing their strategy. That includes procuring timely information on the business's performance. Superior execution can be difficult: new channels and the Internet have made managing businesses more complex; products have shorter life cycles today, and communication is virtually instant. It is essential that the Demand Strategist remain acutely alert and responsive to unexpected activities from competitors. When these attacks come, there must be sufficient corporate resources available to immediately and decisively meet them head-on.

Mike Ruettgers, executive chairman of EMC, might be expected to consider strategy or innovation the most important parts of EMC's success. Not so. Ruettgers believes that its success is due 90 percent to execution and 10 percent to strategy.

WHAT DEMAND STRATEGY IS NOT

The preceding pages have explained in brief what Demand Strategy is and how it works. But it is also important to be aware of what it is not. Demand Strategy does not just treat customers as the target of a sales approach after a product has been developed—it engages customers much earlier by involving them in the actual creation and development of products to ensure that demand is being fully satisfied.

While in some cases demand is easily seen, in today's highly com-petitive business environment, demand, as we define it, is the set of underlying and often unspoken wants and needs of customers. In ef-fect, demand *creates* customers. With accurate knowledge about de-mand, you will be able to predict who your optimal customers are and will be. Most often "customer strategies" are efforts that aim to per-suade customers to buy what a company can supply. Using Demand

Strategy, companies are committed to a sequence in which they create products and services that customers already have a desire to buy. It is precisely because Demand Strategy brings together several benefits being sought by customers that it can achieve pricing inelasticity. The more differentiated your product is and the closer you come to fully satisfying your customer, the more you enhance your opportunity to achieve premium, or inelastic pricing.

Demand Strategy listens to and is guided by leading-edge customers. Companies that are continually leading and shaping their industries do so based on their keen insights into demand. Even the information from leading-edge customers is tested and put into context to ensure the accuracy of demand expressed by customers. In true Demand Strategy, leading-edge customers are intimately involved in envisioning, creating, and shaping the product to fit their articulated demand. This involvement of the customer from beginning to end is the critical link which ensures that you accurately understand and create supply which is being sought by the customer.

Customer strategies are used to sell a product; they pursue share of market. Demand Strategy, on the contrary, pursues a higher share of targeted demand; it produces highly profitable volume with inelastic prices because the strategy results in unique products that come closest to fully satisfying demand. As a result, Demand Strategy is the most profitable way to run a company.

No doubt some of the elements in Demand Strategy sound familiar: terms like "segmentation," "most profitable customers," "resource allocation," and "business system." I am sure you will find, however, that unlike other approaches—which focus on supply or begin with the customer—our starting point is demand, which is what truly starts and stops market behavior.

I've often read, and even more often been told, that the truly important ideas are frequently those that are the easiest to describe and understand. So it is with Demand Strategy. We have taken the world's oldest and most accepted law of economics, and by turning it around have changed most business enterprise so that its growth and profitability are faster and more certain.

While some of the basic terms like segmentation, resource allocation, and business system may sound familiar, our processes, our methodologies, and our analytic procedures are vastly different from what you've seen or used before. Part of the joy in practicing Demand Strategy is its straightforward logic and simplicity. Whether your business is manufacturing jumbo jets or children's toys, high technology or life insurance, the processes and the principles of Demand Strategy remain simple to follow. And by following a demand approach, every business issue becomes markedly easier to understand, solve, and convert to a continuous source of high profit.

Demand Strategy provides new methodologies and tools for many of its most critical steps. Our first step, a forces and factors analysis, is one that only a minority of companies attempt, and even fewer do so with the breadth and depth required to develop genuine insights into demand. Our approach to segmentation is entirely different, more analytical, more predictive of behavior, and more actionable than any other type of segmentation. In addition, our proprietary Customer Demand Analysis™ tools will determine which combination of benefits will enable you to sell the most volume at the highest prices based on your total proposition versus that of your competitors.

As the book will make clear, many of the most successful companies in the world use a demand approach. This underscores one of our key points: Demand Strategy can help any company compete more effectively and win. It is not the case that only certain kinds of companies can benefit from Demand Strategy. It does not require an army of outside consultants to implement. It does require a commitment to build a knowledge base about demand and to use that understanding to identify and more profitably serve those customers with the highest potential for loyalty, volume, and profit for your company.

In the next chapter, I show how Sears, Roebuck and Co.'s credit unit parlayed its grasp of Demand Strategy into a truly amazing business success.

CHAPTER 3

SEARS CREDIT WINS ON DEMAND

I magine for a moment that you are faced with losing a near monopoly, and that the product that will be competing with yours will cost nearly 25 percent less. How would you react? That was the situation the people at Sears Credit faced when they were told Sears stores would begin accepting MasterCard and Visa in a year's time. Up until that point, no card other than the one Sears itself issued was accepted in its stores. (Discover card, which Sears owned then, was also allowed.)

Yet early in the 1990s, Sears, Roebuck and Co. virtually defied the laws of business physics: it gave up its effective monopoly on credit cards in its stores, and did so without losing its key credit customers. In fact, profits, margins, and share of transactions went up for the Sears Credit Card, protecting its role as the primary contributor to Sears's overall profits.

As consultants in the case, The Cambridge Group had a ringside seat as well as a hand in the outcome. The case turned out to be a model of applied Demand Strategy.

Jane Thompson—the executive vice president in charge of Sears Credit—deserves the accolades for this coup. The former head of strategy at Sears, Jane became Credit's executive vice president shortly before the announcement was made that the stores would begin accepting MasterCard, Visa, and American Express.

Prior to coming to Sears, Jane got her MBA at the Harvard Business School, worked at the Procter & Gamble Co., and most recently was a partner at McKinsey & Company. It was at Procter & Gamble that she learned the importance of understanding customers as a critical part of running a business. I found that her training and natural instincts helped her lead the group in discovering the true value that customers received from the Sears card, and that understanding the whole of customer demand was second nature to her.

The Cambridge Group had been called in because the future of the Sears credit division was suddenly uncertain. Sears had budgeted over $400 million in profit in 1993 from its hugely successful credit card. But that goal was in jeopardy now that Sears stores were about to accept other cards. Using their Sears cards had become second nature to most of its customers, and it was a major part of the retailer's profit. But competitive pressure made the credit division's executives wonder how long such profitability could last in the face of opening Sears's stores to Visa, MasterCard, and American Express.

The first step in Demand Strategy, and in our view the best way to address Sears's problem, was to understand the forces and factors that would affect demand.

Retail credit cards and bank credit cards were proliferating. Affinity cards, issued by organizations like the Audubon Society, were making a dent in the market as well. Even big companies, such as Shell Oil Company and General Motors Corporation, were issuing their own cards. These giant enterprises weren't expecting to make money from the cards; they viewed them as marketing tools to make buying their products easier and more attractive. Sears Credit's competition was driving up marketing costs: total spending on advertising such credit cards increased 51 percent in just one year.

Even worse for Sears Credit, its competitors charged lower interest than Sears and other retailers did. Given these factors, retail cards' share of the credit card business had dropped by nearly 50 percent in retailers across the country. Retail customers across most major chains were decreasing their use of the stores' brand cards and using their bankcards instead. What the Sears corporation realized was that if its Sears stores would not accept other credit cards, its customers might well migrate to other merchants. Sears finally decided it had to start accepting American Express, MasterCard, and Visa.

The downside was that, to our large team, there was not an obvious economic reason for Sears customers to continue using their Sears cards. Sears charged an annual interest rate of 21 percent on its revolving credit, while the mean rate on other cards at that time was approximately 16.5 percent. Furthermore, customers had a new and substantial incentive in 1993 to give up their Sears cards altogether. Balance-transfer plans and low-interest "teaser" rates were taking the industry by storm: shifting your debt to a card offering one of these plans gave you an introductory rate of 8.9 percent for ninety days. In effect, for the next three months you saved more than half of your interest payments. Saving money didn't stop when these cards reverted to their regular rates, because even those rates were considerably lower than those offered by Sears.

Sears Credit was in a bind because it could not afford to lose its card customers, particularly its heaviest users. With further analysis it became clear that the best customers for Sears Credit were also among the best customers for the Sears stores. Moreover, these Sears Credit customers accounted for more than half of Sears Credit's profit. Indeed, the need to understand the demand of these critically important customers went well beyond credit cards—doing so was vital to the company's overall success.

In the organization's most optimistic forecast, profit from the card would drop by 9 percent within two years. The pessimistic view was that it would plummet by more than 40 percent. Competing card companies could easily procure credit bureau data revealing who Sears's heaviest card users were in order to pursue them: Sears was vulnerable to losing its heaviest card users. The Cambridge Group's task, along with John Delaney (the vice president of marketing) and a large Sears team, was to identify a demand that only Sears could satisfy. Jane Thompson, from the very beginning, was firm in her belief that by building the card benefits around Sears we would have a value proposition no one else could match.

Prior efforts to uncover a hidden demand had been unsuccessful, in large measure because Sears's interactions with customers had focused mostly on supply-driven issues, such as card pricing. The situation looked bleak.

Surprisingly, in the months ahead, despite the Sears card's 21 percent interest rate, Sears customers continued to use the retail company's card. Although by this time we understood many of the industry's forces and factors and we had some strong hypotheses on why customers continued to use their Sears card, we could not satisfactorily explain this.

My partner Kevin Bowen reviewed an analysis that divided the millions of Sears credit accounts into deciles so that we could more deeply understand these shoppers. The top 10 percent of the company's revolving credit card users represented almost three-quarters of its gross profit and were the demand segment that Sears had to retain and pursue. The team knew it had its work cut out for it because lowering the interest rate was simply not an option.

But our work had just begun and we needed to complete Step 2— understanding the high-profit customer—before we did anything else. Completing that step would enable us to decide on our strategic options.

When we looked more closely at the data we had assembled on our target segment, we found an anomaly. It was generally accepted by all credit card experts and issuers that a low interest rate was the most compelling reason to use one card over another. However, very few credit card users actually paid the lowest rate. We felt certain that if we could explain this aberration, we could discover new options for Sears.

Despite the enticements of competing cards, including low teaser rates, we discovered customers using Sears's card were slower than other retail cardholders to abandon ship. Perhaps, we thought, the low annual percentage rate (APR) and the balance-transfer option weren't as important as we had assumed.

When we looked at all Sears credit card customers, we reached one set of conclusions, but when we studied just the top 10 percent, from whom the company made the most profit, we got a very different picture. If we could discover something about that high-user-segment demand that the competition didn't know, and gain a proprietary grasp of that demand, Sears would potentially have a major competitive advantage.

John Delaney shared the opportunity his team had identified with the top decile of credit card customers, who represented well over half of the division's profit, with Jane Thompson. Thompson was enthusiastic about the Sears-based opportunities and she agreed to let the group take some limited action immediately.

First we asked salespeople and cashiers to encourage customers to use their Sears cards by asking what we called the "May I" question: "May I put this on your Sears card?" If a customer without one presented a rival card, the cashier would offer him or her the option of opening a new Sears card—which could be approved in ten seconds after the rival card's system had approved the purchase.

From studying our forces and factors analysis, we knew that customers felt loyal to Sears. It had one of the strongest brands we had ever seen. The company had a relationship with its customers that in many cases had been going on for generations. People grew up with Sears. Their parents furnished their first house or apartment at Sears, and bought their children's first school clothes there. They trusted Sears.

People had good reasons for shopping at Sears, including convenient locations and the perceived value of the merchandise. But the most important factor was the Sears guarantee—100 percent satisfaction.

Whenever customers anywhere purchase something, they are taking a risk, the significance of which is directly proportional to their income. To the Sears customer—middle American, neither poor nor rich—the guarantee matters. When that person buys an $800 water heater, which is a major commitment, he or she needs to feel confident that Sears will stand behind it completely.

In fact, we found that the 100 percent guarantee was more important to the high-volume demand segment than it was to Sears customers in general. We created demand focus groups around the country, bringing together hundreds of customers in this segment. Demand groups resemble focus groups but are conducted very differently, in that they interview only one target segment at a time. For example, if we are conducting a demand group about the cookie business, we would not mix people who preferred full-fat cookies with those who ate only cookies with reduced fat. Such groups are made up of only one target segment in order to understand the demand and the behavior of individual targets. Working with a single group makes it easier to form hypotheses that apply to that targeted group because the members share common demand, motivations, and behavior.

We talked with the group members extensively about how they lived, shopped, and made decisions about products. We also discussed how they selected the credit cards they used.

The demand groups proved to be profoundly important to our conclusions about credit card behavior. Had we just applied the generally held ideas, we would have been led astray in our analysis of Sears. We discovered that Sears customers were not hard-eyed, aggressive consumers, calculating their APR and switching their balances. They had numerous other concerns. People make choices for a variety of reasons; demand, too, is made up of myriad elements.

We discovered that the people with revolving credit with whom we spoke were among the least financially secure of Sears's customers. Every dollar that came in went out, and still, that usually didn't cover all their bills. If they were behind in their Sears accounts, they were likely behind on other bills as well, perhaps including their mortgage. They needed more control over their financial lives.

The desire to experience control over all aspects of one's life is inherent to the human condition. And our key Sears customers were among the people who felt the least control over their financial lives.

Late one night in a demand group, we were discussing the possible reasons that these customers stuck with the Sears card. A man about fifty-five years old said that while he and his wife were raising their family, they had more bills than they could handle. He said that each month they made the minimum payment on each bill so that they didn't fall behind. Since his Sears card required lower monthly payments, he used it whenever he could. This factor—Sears's low monthly payments—turned out to be critical to the Sears card's success, and a major difference between Sears's and other cards.

As we probed into what minimum monthly payments meant to people, many pieces of the demand puzzle began to fall into place. Another of the reasons these customers continued to use their Sears card was that they had to keep room on their MasterCard and Visa cards, which they could use at most other stores. If they maxed out those cards and the refrigerator broke down, only the Sears card stood between them and no refrigerator.

If, every month, all the money that comes into a household also goes out, then the interest charges are nearly irrelevant. What matters to this target segment above all else in a credit card is the minimum monthly payment.

The more we met with Sears credit customers in our target demand segment, the more we found that keeping monthly payments at a minimum was far more important than the rate of interest.

For the first time since they learned that Sears was going to accept MasterCard and Visa, Jane Thompson and John Delaney understood the demand of their core customers far better than their competitors did.

Many of the customers in the target segment used the card as a kind of budgeting tool, timing their purchases to keep the monthly payment the same. When they finally paid off the sofa at $15 a month and the payment dropped from $25 to $10, they could buy a television set that would bring the payment back to $25.

Also, Sears cardholders were reluctant to use the balance-transfer offers. They saw them for what they were: teasers, even tricks akin to bait-and-switch tactics. Frequently they asked, "How stupid do they think we are?" This was another reason they stayed loyal to Sears.

In addition to the economic and lifestyle demands we identified, we also found that people felt a strong emotional attachment to their Sears cards. It became clear that they felt that Sears was "their" store, a place on which they could rely.

Much of the emotional attachment to the card was the result of the fact that Sears consistently treated its customers well. The Sears Credit policy was sympathetic when its customers fell behind in payments. The message conveyed was: When you get into trouble, we will help you; if you fall behind, we will help you catch up. Customers felt reassured by Sears. Whatever APR it charged, its customers considered Sears to be a good company that treated people fairly.

This is the magical moment that all businesspeople hope for—discovering what creates customer demand, and at the same time understanding their customers in a way that none of their competitors do.

The only means to achieve this advantage is to look beneath superficial behavior and supply-based questions until you uncover the underlying cause of the demand in question. Usually there are demands in addition to product demand; often there is a psychological demand or some sort of reinforcement that creates value for customers. Feeling the prestige of driving a certain car is one example; belief that a company won't abandon you if you run into rough financial waters is another.

Having identified our target demand segment and learned what motivates it, we were ready to step into the third stage of Demand Strategy—creating strategy options. While lowering APR certainly remained an option, our new familiarity with demand opened many other options.

As we entered Step 3, Thompson directed our efforts toward the benefits that only shopping at Sears could provide. One of our options was to create a points program wherein people could earn free gifts, free air miles, and the like. This was a popular option in the early 1990s. But Thompson's insight into Sears customers led her to insist that the benefits relate explicitly to Sears—an insight that proved crucial.

The elements that combine to enable you to satisfy customer demand are usually multidimensional. Rarely will a single factor, such as low interest rate, satisfy demand. McDonald's, for example, meets its target's demand by providing a speedy, clean, kid-friendly restaurant, and consistently good food. Were it to focus on any single demand, its success would be greatly diminished. Similarly, Wal-Mart Stores' remarkable success can't be attributed to low prices alone. Its logistical operations enable the smooth replacement of fast-selling products, and information technology gives its employees far better information about their customers than other companies have. Were Wal-Mart Stores, Inc., to rely on any single demand factor, it too would be much less successful.

At Sears we created a mosaic of everything we knew that motivated our demand segment. While we wanted to build on Sears's relationship with these customers, we also wanted to attract more of them, which was our incentive to evaluate again what they really wanted from a retailer.

With limited money to spend, these customers were looking for value and financial flexibility. We also knew that these customers felt vulnerable to being laid off. They had little if any economic cushion. Financial security was their highest priority.

Though lowering the APR was one option, we were convinced that doing so was not inevitable. In fact, we were confident that if Sears Credit could focus on and meet the underlying—that is, the true—demand, it could hold the price line.

Let's return for a moment to the definition of value: Value = Benefits/Price. Our work revealed that Sears had an opportunity to substantially enhance the benefits it was offering without reducing the card's APR or the price of merchandise. Members of our customer segment were asking for certainty and flexibility. Above all, they wanted to feel in control of their lives; they wanted to be recognized as valued customers because that helped them feel more valuable overall.

Based on both our in-depth qualitative and quantitative research, we recommended to Sears that it could safely hold off on cutting the APR on its credit card. Instead, our whole team recommended a Demand Value Proposition that would offer heavy users a proposition that could satisfy both financial demand and emotional demand. This demand target wanted certainty, payment options, a relationship with Sears, and savings that would be earned by becoming members of Sears's "best customer club." They would receive special values and special discounts available only at Sears, which would make the value of the card very much worth its higher APR. Jane Thompson, John Delaney, and their colleagues agreed, and chose not to lower rates.

We then entered the fourth stage of Demand Strategy, identifying the systems and mechanisms that would facilitate delivering on our recommendation. We held meetings with department managers and associates across the country in order to reinforce the "May I" strategy—having salespeople ask customers for their Sears cards. Signage in stores was appropriately placed, and card applications were available at the entrances to all stores.

In the fifth stage, Sears Credit allocated the limited resources that were needed to enact the proposition. And finally, in the sixth stage, the Demand Strategy was executed.

Hypothesized Sears Credit-Card Demand Value Proposition
SEARS CARD CASE

DESIRED BELIEF: *THE SEARS CARD IS THE BEST WAY TO GET THE MOST FROM THE MANY SIDES OF SEARS*

Customer Situation	DVP	Features Delivered	Customer Belief System
Low Financial Self-Esteem	Recognition	▸ Sears Family Member Recognition ▸ Sears Best Customer Program	▸ "Sears appreciates my business, and they show it in tangible ways that say 'I'm important.'"
Goals Beyond Reach	Value	▸ Bonus $ ▸ Special Discounts ▸ Advance Sales Notification	▸ "I make a smart choice when I shop at Sears. There are lots of ways I benefit beyond just quality merchandise and a fair price that let me realize real savings."
Cash Flow Concerns	Flexibility	▸ Pick Due Date ▸ Skip a Payment ▸ Low Minimum Payment ▸ Pay at Register	▸ "Sears gives me options that make it easier for me to manage my money. As a result, I have greater control over my finances."
Vulnerability	Protection	▸ Satisfaction Guaranteed ▸ Personal Payment Assistance ▸ SCPP (for fee)	▸ "I feel comfortable and confident when I shop at Sears. I know if anything happens, they'll take care of me."

Suddenly, customers in the demand segment we focused on were hearing their core needs specifically addressed: more certainty, payment options, control, selecting the monthly due date that worked best for them, and more economic value in what they bought. The result was that these very important customers felt special and highly valued.

This strategy was not intended to mimic the standard relationship between a seller and a buyer, which ends with the customer's purchase. Rather, it aimed to understand the basic demand, and then to put in place whatever steps were necessary for Sears Credit to meet that demand. In Demand Strategy we view each purchase as a segue to the next interaction. The endless loop of purchases that is created acts to encourage the customer to shop with the card regularly and steadily.

In the end, the Sears Credit team accomplished the impossible: it gave up its monopoly and yet increased business performance. It raised the Sears share of credit card transactions in its stores, and its margins actually went up. Over three years, its profits on the card rose by 44 percent.

Sears Credit learned something about its customers of which its competitors remained unaware. By studying its customer base, the team achieved a proprietary understanding of the multifaceted demand among the customers it valued most, which allowed it to create a Demand Strategy that gave Sears Credit a remarkable victory.

Of course, the solution that worked for Sears won't necessarily work for every product, service, or company. The particular methods used to identify and serve the customers that yield the highest profits will vary from company to company and industry to industry. You may find it profitable to focus on more than one demand segment, or on a tiny slice of your customers. Perhaps you will find, as Sears Credit did, that the segment bringing you the most profit is comprised of people who are already your best customers. What is crucial is a thorough and thoughtful analysis of selected demand segments that will enable you to design a successful Demand Strategy. In the following chapters, we will examine each step in depth, so that you will be equipped to do precisely that.

THE FIRST PRINCIPLE

Analyze the Demand Forces and Industry Factors That Have an Impact on Your Business

he vast majority of business analyses focus on a particular activity or event: What has or has not sold? Has market share changed? Are new product introductions working? And most important, do the financial results align with the expectations? In most cases, the analysis includes a series of hypotheses that attempts to explain the events. Conspicuously missing, however, is a rigorous fact-based analysis of *why* product sales have occurred or changed and what factors and issues are at the root of these changes.

In fact, the need to develop such an analysis is why most consultants are hired. Consultants, of course, also solve existing problems, and they bring a fresh and independent viewpoint to a client company. Consulting has grown rapidly because the managers, who are busy planning and executing the functions and processes that keep a company operating, rarely have sufficient time to perform exhaustive analyses. With Demand Strategy, however, conducting such an analysis is the first step toward becoming a demand-driven company. Once that rigorous, fact-based analysis is in place, it is easy for internal managers to update it periodically; in addition, doing so diminishes the need for consultants to update your fact base. Still, it is rare for companies to spend the required time and manpower to understand and prepare for emerging demand.

The companies that consistently win are those whose leaders understand that business plans must include fact-based explanations for why specific phenomena take place. Demand Strategy involves a rigorous process to analyze demand forces and industry factors. In combination, demand forces and industry factors are the causal elements that are responsible for changes in demand. We look at what has created demand in the past, what is causing it now, and what is most likely to influence emerging demand.

The purpose of forces and factors analysis is twofold: first, to identify and understand the causal factors that create demand; second, to identify the context within which a business operates. This includes the economics of a company's business category as well as the economic realities that directly affect its business. It also includes changes in pricing, legislation, existing and near-term technology, new channels, new competitors, changes in an industry's structure, and the price of materials. In addition, the process focuses on social megatrends and demographics that will potentially affect the demand for goods and services into the future.

It is imperative that companies understand the forces and factors that drive demand in their business categories. Having a deeper, more accurate understanding of your industry and of important cause-and-effect relationships can lead to proprietary knowledge regarding how demand has been and will be created. Armed with such information, you can build a Demand Strategy that will increase your profits on a consistent basis.

Demand Strategy requires, first and foremost, a broader, more complete perspective than most businesses currently have. Using the knowledge it will give you, you will know more than your competitors about what will and won't sell. It is an approach that will lower the total costs of producing goods and services, while increasing your revenues, margins, and profits. It is the ideal approach for leading and managing a business successfully in the fast-paced twenty-first century.

Demand forces and industry factors provide an invaluable tool for understanding customer behavior more thoroughly. Within this context, you can identify and analyze the particular forces and factors that affect the demand for and sales of your products, today and in the future. The ability to identify emerging demand is what enables some companies to enjoy year after year of increasingly improved results.

The Starbucks Corporation, for example, has used a forces and factors approach to stunning success. In the several years before Starbucks opened its first store, coffee consumption was falling by almost 2.5 percent a year in the United States (based on cups per person per day from 1962 to 1985), and it seemed that the only way to increase sales was to offer coffee less expensively than the competition. Most people assumed it was absurd to open a coffee business in that environment. But Howard Schultz—founder, chairman, and CEO of Starbucks—analyzed the market in the context of forces and factors. Armed with an analysis of the popularity of coffee bars in Europe, where the relaxing environment and superior coffee made them ubiquitous, Schultz discarded conventional wisdom and recognized the potential to give customers in the United States an experience they didn't currently have, and charge a premium for doing so. Convinced that his data was correct, he approached 242 potential investors; twenty-five of them agreed to invest in his business idea. That Starbucks has become one of the world's most successful companies makes it likely that the other 217 now pay attention to forces and factors.

The demand forces and industry factors that are operating in your industry at any particular time will create, alter, increase, or reduce demand. Therefore, they affect supply and pricing.

An analysis of the demand forces and industry factors that have an impact upon your business will tell a coherent story that explains changes in demand, prices, profit, and performance. It will indicate what is driving current demand and accurately explain and quantify emerging demand at its inception. Ultimately, the results of such analysis provide a platform from which you can clearly develop an advantageous strategy in addition to managing your business and allocating resources successfully.

Our work with one of the world's largest beverage companies, for example, identified an unexpected anomaly related to one of its soft drinks. Over many years the company spent tens of millions of dollars on promotions, which one of their main competitors matched almost dollar for dollar. Yet the promotions resulted in no increase in market share or total consumption. As we investigated further, we found that consumers develop a strong taste preference for a particular brand of soft drink by age seventeen, after which very little will entice consumers to change brands. Yet it is common practice for these companies to spend tens of millions of dollars annually to win exclusive rights to sell their beverage at major adult venues. It seemed to be one of the best ways to get consumers to try the product, while also building brand recognition. But although people bought the drinks at ball games and concerts because that was all that was available, they continued to buy their preferred brand when they had a choice. As a result, most promotion money was wasted.

Once we understood this dynamic, we realized that the process of establishing a preference at a young age was key to shaping demand among soft drink consumers for decades to come. As a result of our findings, the company developed two new strategies to meet demand better, financed in part with funds previously allocated to procure "pouring rights." First, we focused more attention on "gatekeepers"— the parents who shop for groceries and determine which soft drinks come into their homes. Second, the operating plans and budget were changed to make the brand available at places and events that kids attend frequently—Little League, movie theaters, and malls. They created sponsorships for kids' leagues and made sure the drink was available in vending machines and snack spots wherever kids spend their free time. Once we knew how the forces and factors worked that shaped demand, we could more directly influence the demand of millions of people for a lifetime.

Since some forces and factors are more relevant than others, depending on the industry, companies must tailor their assessment to their specific situation. For example, interest rates clearly influence the demand for mortgages. But so do other forces, such as demographics, the overall state of the economy, developments in technology, and trends in lifestyles and tastes.

A forces and factors analysis is easiest to perform for *current* demand. Marketing executives will spot many of the forces and factors immediately. OPEC's resurgence and the resulting high oil prices affected a host of products, ranging from sweaters and kerosene heaters to used cars and tourist motels. Similarly, doctors, hospitals, and pharmaceutical companies are directly affected by even the smallest change in federal Medicare policy.

Certainly, these more obvious forces and factors influencing current demand are important. But if your analysis is limited to only the obvious, you will be unlikely to develop new insights that your competition is unaware of. To reveal the hidden, subtle, or seemingly tangential forces and factors that underlie current and emerging demand, your analysis must move beyond the superficial.

FORCES AND FACTORS ANALYSIS

Constructing a proprietary forces and factors analysis consists of three critical steps. First, you need to discover what has shaped demand in the past. Next, you need to examine your current situation to see if those forces and factors are continuing to influence demand, or if they have been replaced or modified by new ones. Finally, you must develop hypotheses about emerging demand based on the forces and factors that have the potential to shape or influence demand and are becoming more visible in your business category. Let's look at each in turn.

1. Understand Past Forces and Factors

You can understand present demand more thoroughly if you examine it in the context of how demand was shaped in the past and then determine how it has changed—and why. As Winston Churchill once stated, "The farther backward you can look, the farther forward you are likely to see." Significant changes might include the expansion or constriction of your product or service category, or the growth or contraction of your existing competitors.

By reviewing previous patterns, a manager might be able to see that the set of forces and factors she is confronting now is, in fact, a recurrence or repetition of forces she has experienced previously. This knowledge can give her a head start in planning for and meeting current and emerging demand. Unfortunately, virtually all companies are susceptible to "institutional forgetfulness." The people who coped with similar changes in demand the last time may be in other jobs within the company, or may have left the company entirely, taking their experiences with them. Creating an annual forces and factors analysis database can be an invaluable tool for subsequent managers. That way the company's past experience can continue to help shape success in the future.

For example, a few years ago we worked with the executive vice president of a large cereal manufacturer who was angry about a significant drop in sales and profits from the company's cereal group aimed at kids. He told me, "We learned ten years ago that kids' cereals have to be relaunched every two or three years because so many kids come into or leave the group that eats these cereals." But as I explained to him, "we" didn't learn that: he and his former team did, ten years ago. Because it was never committed to writing, that important piece of information was never passed on to newer managers. The dip in his cereal business, as well as the erosion in his share price, were avoidable—had the current managers possessed the knowledge and benefit of the company's past experience.

In addition, analysis of past forces and factors is an invaluable tool for senior managers who are managing many businesses simultaneously. An annual summary of forces and factors (usually a document of two or three pages) studied by business managers and shared with the senior managers relieves the latter of having to keep track of every detail of each business. There is a tendency in business to manage based on what made the company, division, or product successful back when the previous president ran that division. Several years of forces and factors analysis can function as reminders of the influences that cause demand to evolve.

A few years ago, a company in the apparel industry took a serious look at its forces and factors analysis and discovered a disturbing pattern. In this business, demand is driven by style, price point, the customer's age and gender, and the channel through which the product is sold. And this company was not in step with any of these forces and factors. Its prices were not aligned with the lower-priced competitors that had flooded the category over the past five years. It was still trying to command a premium for basic entry point products that it had not differentiated in ten years.

We did the analysis illustrated in the chart on page 70 for the clothing company's new chief executive. After examining it, he knew exactly what steps were necessary to turn his business around.

The company was sinking because, over the course of several years, its designers grew out of touch with what men and women in various age groups were wearing, what channels would be most appropriate to sell its clothing in, and what price points would give its products a chance to compete meaningfully. As the company's supply made painfully clear, it had either ignored or misunderstood the demand in its industry. The analysis highlighted the company's problems so that the new chief executive was able to take remedial action immediately. Within a year of his arrival, the company's gross margins increased significantly and its bonds increased in value by 85 percent.

2. Assess Current Forces and Factors

Many companies begin—and sometimes end—their analyses of the marketplace from the perspective of supply (see Chart 4B). Demand Strategists begin with demand, though they may work simultaneously on parallel paths (see the charts on pages 72 and 73). For example, companies may examine how the structures of their own and comparable industries evolved, and at the same time assess their competitors.

Among the most significant findings to look for are anomalies, or unexplained discrepancies, in the data. For example, comparing the assumption that Sears's credit-card customers were primarily swayed by interest rates with the actual interest rates on their Visas and MasterCards, we found that more than 90 percent of customers were paying well above the lowest interest rate available. That's precisely the

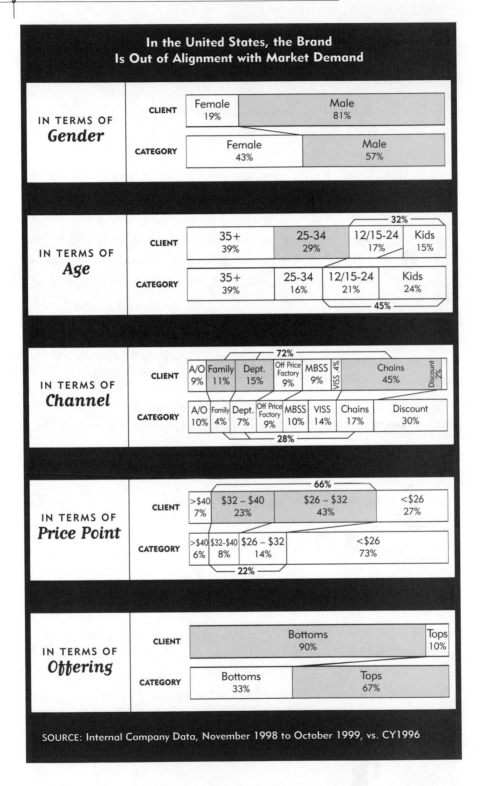

In the United States, the Brand Is Out of Alignment with Market Demand

IN TERMS OF Gender

CLIENT: Female 19% | Male 81%
CATEGORY: Female 43% | Male 57%

IN TERMS OF Age

32%

CLIENT: 35+ 39% | 25-34 29% | 12/15-24 17% | Kids 15%
CATEGORY: 35+ 39% | 25-34 16% | 12/15-24 21% | Kids 24%

45%

IN TERMS OF Channel

72%

CLIENT: A/O 9% | Family 11% | Dept. 15% | Off Price Factory 9% | MBSS 9% | VISS 4% | Chains 45% | Discount 2%
CATEGORY: A/O 10% | Family 4% | Dept. 7% | Off Price Factory 9% | MBSS 10% | VISS 14% | Chains 17% | Discount 30%

28%

IN TERMS OF Price Point

66%

CLIENT: >$40 7% | $32 – $40 23% | $26 – $32 43% | <$26 27%
CATEGORY: >$40 6% | $32-$40 8% | $26 – $32 14% | <$26 73%

22%

IN TERMS OF Offering

CLIENT: Bottoms 90% | Tops 10%
CATEGORY: Bottoms 33% | Tops 67%

SOURCE: Internal Company Data, November 1998 to October 1999, vs. CY1996

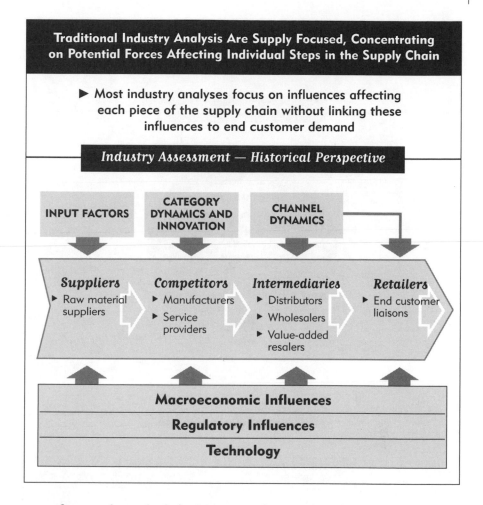

Traditional Industry Analysis Are Supply Focused, Concentrating on Potential Forces Affecting Individual Steps in the Supply Chain

▶ Most industry analyses focus on influences affecting each piece of the supply chain without linking these influences to end customer demand

Industry Assessment — Historical Perspective

| INPUT FACTORS | CATEGORY DYNAMICS AND INNOVATION | CHANNEL DYNAMICS | |

Suppliers
▶ Raw material suppliers

Competitors
▶ Manufacturers
▶ Service providers

Intermediaries
▶ Distributors
▶ Wholesalers
▶ Value-added resalers

Retailers
▶ End customer liaisons

Macroeconomic Influences

Regulatory Influences

Technology

sort of anomaly we look for because when it is explained, the findings will lead to a deeper understanding of the causes of demand.

It was an anomaly in the telecommunications industry that allowed us to find answers to one client's problem. At the time, telecom companies were spending hundreds of millions of dollars on telemarketing efforts to compete for new customers. Though our client was winning more households than its competitors each month, the competitors' sales and profits were growing faster. To understand why, The Cambridge Group and our client's team conducted a forces and factors analysis.

We discovered through our analysis that the competition concentrated on households with heavy users of telecommunications; our client was focused on adding every household it could, regardless of its

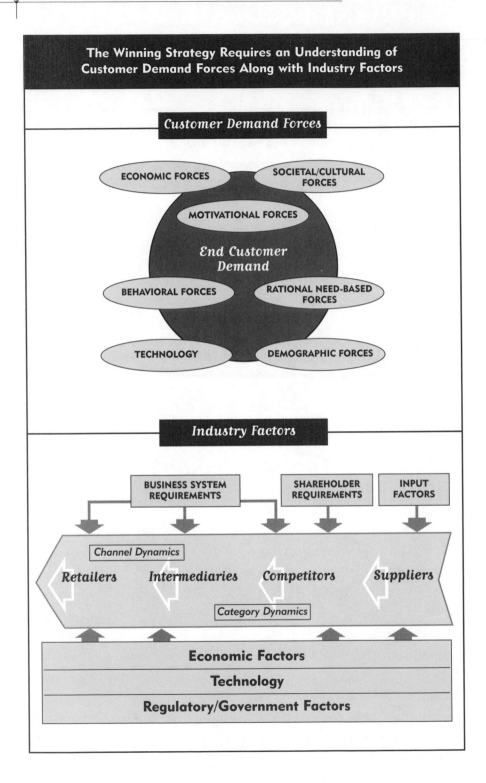

The Winning Strategy Requires an Understanding of
Customer Demand Forces Along with Industry Factors

Customer Demand Forces

ECONOMIC FORCES

SOCIETAL/CULTURAL
FORCES

MOTIVATIONAL FORCES

End Customer
Demand

BEHAVIORAL FORCES

RATIONAL NEED-BASED
FORCES

TECHNOLOGY

DEMOGRAPHIC FORCES

Industry Factors

BUSINESS SYSTEM
REQUIREMENTS

SHAREHOLDER
REQUIREMENTS

INPUT
FACTORS

Channel Dynamics

Retailers   Intermediaries   Competitors   Suppliers

Category Dynamics

Economic Factors

Technology

Regulatory/Government Factors

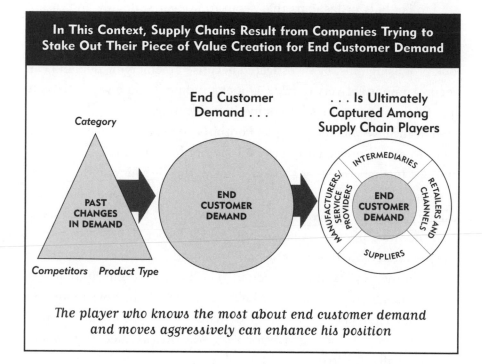

In This Context, Supply Chains Result from Companies Trying to Stake Out Their Piece of Value Creation for End Customer Demand

Category

End Customer Demand . . .

. . . Is Ultimately Captured Among Supply Chain Players

PAST CHANGES IN DEMAND

END CUSTOMER DEMAND

INTERMEDIARIES

MANUFACTURERS/ SERVICE PROVIDERS

END CUSTOMER DEMAND

RETAILERS AND CHANNELS

SUPPLIERS

Competitors   Product Type

The player who knows the most about end customer demand and moves aggressively can enhance his position

potential profitability. We discovered that competitors had targeted the roughly 16 percent of U.S. households that move each year, and designed specific offers and programs to solicit that group. As we explored further, we found that movers spend, on average, 40 percent more than the general population per month on telecommunications, in order to stay in contact with families and friends from whom they moved away. In other words, moving was a critical force and factor that drives demand in telecom. Our client was losing valuable customers because it had been unaware of this profitable segment's unique demand.

3. Identify Emerging Forces and Factors

Emerging forces and factors are those just beginning to affect demand and show potential to play an extensive role in shaping it over time. Often, past as well as current forces and factors can serve as a base from which to project how demand is likely to change.

Unlike fads or fashions that seem to appear suddenly and disappear almost as quickly, most shifts in demand that endure are rooted in observable, though not necessarily obvious, factors. Patterns that look promising must be investigated because an emerging demand can become important very quickly. Understanding it can give a company significant opportunities for competitive advantage.

Let me give you one example. For thirty years, Pentagon analyst Andrew Marshall projected forces and factors for the military, using his findings to shape military strategy. During the Reagan administration, Marshall, by studying obscure demographic and economic data, was among the first to recognize that the former Soviet Union, as *Newsweek* reported, was "in crisis—and spending a far bigger slice of its national income on defense than anyone had suspected." Marshall's answer was to spend the Soviets into the ground. The Reagan administration pursued Marshall's strategy, and as Marshall predicted, the Soviet empire a few years later collapsed trying to match the Reagan-era defense-spending spree. According to *Newsweek,* "Marshall seemed clairvoyant."

Marshall's "clairvoyance" was, of course, his ability to identify emerging patterns and systematically draw conclusions from his findings. Not every manager is able to see these patterns, even when presented with irrefutable data. Managers need to learn to identify the patterns in order to seize any opportunities to align their company's supply with the new, emerging demand.

Fred Smith of FedEx Corporation first presented the idea for his overnight package delivery business in a term paper written when he was a student at Yale. In the paper, he accurately anticipated today's fast-cycle service economy (his professor, famously, gave him a C). The result: one of the great success stories of modern business. Success depends on the ability to accurately detect emerging demand opportunities.

Early in 2000, Medtronic's chief executive officer, Bill George, laid out a ten-year vision for the highly successful medical devices company. The company had traditionally focused on cardiovascular products. Medtronic's founders had developed the first external, battery-powered cardiac pacemaker in 1957, and until recently, pacemakers accounted for about half of the company's total sales. Medtronic also produces mechanical and tissue valves, stents, guide wires, and catheters used in angioplasties and defibrillators. Outside of the cardiovascular sphere, it makes products used to treat neurological conditions, such as Parkinson's disease, and products designed to alleviate chronic pain.

In his ten-year plan, George identified five major industry factors that, based on his company's research, he believed would affect demand in the health care market profoundly. All are related to the emergence of chronic-disease management, a market that George wants Medtronic to lead by 2010.

George identified the following industry factors: First, almost 80 percent of current U.S. health care costs go to managing chronic diseases. Second, the elderly population is likely to increase as baby boomers age, thus increasing the prevalence of chronic diseases. Third, the biological sciences are unlikely to develop cures for such diseases within the next decade. Fourth, the important need to improve the quality of life for people who suffer from chronic diseases has not yet been met. Finally, integrating information technology and medical technology offers new opportunities for managing chronic diseases.

Medtronic used a fact base that helped the company to identify the forces and factors that would change demand in health care for the next ten years. In a clear and decisive message to his shareholders, Bill George explained that Medtronic had anticipated a demand it is committed to meet, and is now developing the supply to do so. Its goals are immeasurable gains for people living with chronic diseases, and financial profits for itself.

While it is relatively easy for a manager to be *alert* to emerging demand, it is difficult to gauge it accurately. There are, however, many companies that have developed predictive research instruments. You have to be careful not to let any individual or set of forces and factors preoccupy you; you can't afford to ignore other factors that might blindside you. On the other hand, while changes in demand pose a threat to complacent managers, they are opportunities for Demand Strategists who are equipped to seize the advantage.

Of course, reliable information upon which to base forecasts can be difficult to procure, especially in emerging or rapidly changing markets. There has never been a better example of this than the extraordinary boom and bust of the Internet. We now know that projections calling for the Internet to rewrite the rules of business and make "old economy" companies obsolete were wildly overstated. In retrospect, the projections of revenue for many of the dot.coms seem absurd because an enormous percentage of existing off-line transactions would have had to move on-line in order to even approach some of these projections.

Taken in isolation, it is possible to understand how responsible and sober-minded business people got caught up in the euphoria of the Internet and truly believed their own sales projections. However, the only way to accurately predict on-line sales was to calculate both on-line and off-line sales so that the total of the two different channels bore some resemblance to total category spending before the Internet. For example, some of the on-line mortgage companies predicted numbers that were so high that the best business analysts started to question the source of these numbers, because if you added the on-line and off-line projections together, it would have meant that housing sales in the United States would have more than doubled in a single year. Once again, the accuracy of the predictions required that they be seen in a larger context.

Now most business leaders have properly planned for the Internet as being an additional channel alongside retail and direct mail. The Internet won't transform the world overnight as once thought, but it will continue to grow as a channel for reaching customers with your message, providing detailed product information, offering customer support, and conducting transactions. As a result, companies should explore how to leverage the Internet going forward rather than ignoring it altogether.

Managers at Iridium, the highly publicized satellite phone company created by Motorola, believed that millions of people around the world wanted mobile phones that could be used from even the most remote locations—places well beyond the range of existing cellular phone towers. Iridium and its investors poured $5 billion into the development of its satellite-based service to meet the demand it was projecting. But the customer demand it had counted on never materialized. Instead of attracting millions of customers, Iridium gained only 55,000. As a result, the company went bankrupt less than one year after launching its new service.

While customers are obviously critical to demand, you are vulnerable to making serious mistakes if they are the only source for your demand and supply projections. This underscores one of the primary problems with processes that advocate customer intimacy or customer centricity. Of course, customers are key to your understanding of demand, but they should not be your only source of information. To understand demand thoroughly, you must have a context within which you can assess what customers tell you. Without it, you leave your company as financially exposed as Iridium and the many failed dot.coms were.

Today it is mandatory to understand forces and factors first. You have to be selective in deciding which customers to talk to because the concept of "customers" is far too broad. Does it include those who buy the most from you today? Does it include former customers? For insightful information, you must define which customers are likely to be the most useful.

Moreover, in today's multichanneled, rapidly changing business cycle, you must also include your own customers' end customers. In a supply-driven economy, this depth of information and market understanding wasn't always necessary, because supply was frequently absorbed by existing demand. In today's demand economy, however, you must get information from competitors and from original equipment manufacturers (OEMs) or other shared suppliers before you make decisions about your products. A forces and factors analysis will provide the context that will enable you to make sense of the information you've assembled and to develop an ongoing method of estimating demand.

Several forces and factors affect virtually all businesses: the general economy; the structure of a company's specific market; competition; market growth and profitability; technological and other innovations; demographic changes; and societal megatrends. Of course, like fingerprints, the forces and factors underlying changes in demand are unique to each industry.

The General Economy

A few years ago, the Harvard Business School stopped offering its course on business cycles, which had once been among its most popular. Former U.S. Treasury secretary Robert E. Rubin mordantly commented, "I don't think anybody has repealed the business cycle. You can believe the experience of the last few years, or you can believe all of economic history. I choose to believe all of economic history." He was proven correct in 2001.

With today's global economy, business cycles now transcend national borders. As a result, we have to pay attention to macroeconomic trends that extend far beyond the U.S. coastline and involve far more than tracking U.S. interest rates. Unexpected developments ranging from the depletion of the world's fisheries to the collapse of the Mexican peso can affect businesses throughout the United States and the world. The devaluation of Thailand's baht not only can trigger a general economic crisis in Asia but also can have serious repercussions for investors and businesses in the United States. While the euro may or may not threaten the dominance of the U.S. dollar, it certainly can't be ignored.

Many events, however, can be anticipated. For example, as this is being written, we know that U.S. imports from China in 2001 are at an all-time high. In 1999, electronics, toys, footwear, and apparel accounted for almost half of those imports. We can safely project that U.S. imports from China will increase when the World Trade Organization (WTO) reduces current trade barriers and tariffs in 2005.

Yet some companies studiously ignore these changes. They may see the individual data points, be aware of current trade with China, perceive key categories of imports, and acknowledge the WTO agreements, but still fail to see that together they weave a connected tapestry.

The Structure of Your Market

The structure of your market is the process by which your products move from manufacturing to delivery to customers. Your upstream and downstream channels are not unchangeable and can always be thought through anew. For example, to earn its share of the total profit on a given product, the average wholesaler carries a lot of inventory. On the other hand, Dell Computer Corporation, which builds computers to the customer's specifications, bypasses both wholesalers and retailers, reducing inventory substantially. A company's market can be structured in a myriad of ways.

When we worked with United Airlines' cargo division, United Cargo, our first task was to learn how shifts in demand had changed the fundamental structure of its market. United Cargo primarily serves large freight forwarders, which consolidate freight traveling between smaller shippers and their recipients. To understand how demand among freight forwarders would evolve, we needed to know how demand among the shippers they serve was changing.

For a variety of reasons, key segments of shippers had become more sensitive to time and more interested in integrated logistics services. For instance, many redesigned their supply chains in order to provide just-in-time (JIT) delivery and to provide a greater degree of customization by completing assembly after shipping. As a result, shippers needed more certainty and logistical support than ever before. As their needs grew more complex, the shippers wanted to partner with fewer freight forwarders. Clearly, to win this emerging demand, freight forwarders would have to do more than just move freight.

Based on what we learned, as well as on the existing structure of the freight forwarder industry, we were able to anticipate how the industry was likely to move forward. Demand for commodity shipping would still be strong, and some freight forwarders would continue to focus on it, competing primarily on low price and availability. Others would offer greater reliability at higher prices. A third segment would differentiate itself by managing all of the information related to its shipments. Finally, a fourth group of forwarders would invest in building the differentiated logistical skills that would enable these forwarders to be value-added partners with leading-edge shippers.

This was, in fact, how the freight forwarding industry evolved over the years. The shippers' changing demands generated a corresponding change in the structure of the forwarder industry. Our forces and factors analysis made it possible for United Cargo to align with these changes, target the companies that invest the heaviest in forwarding, and therefore align with the most profitable shipper demand. This targeted strategy led to specific changes in United Cargo's service offerings as well as in its business model. The outcome of these changes was both higher margins and higher volume levels.

Sometimes an entire distribution channel can be endangered by a new one. When Amazon.com, Inc., opened for business on the Internet, its low overhead and rock-bottom prices posed a threat to conventional bookstores—a process that economists call *disintermediation*. But the stores fought back by adding coffee shops and comfortable chairs that invited browsing. They differentiated themselves by making shopping at their stores a pleasurable experience.

Usually, a change in market structure is the brainchild of an alert manager who is responding to a new pattern of demand. The retail mail-order catalog, for example, became a distribution channel in the nineteenth century, aiming to reach rural communities with few if any stores. Catalog shopping surged again in the 1980s, serving people who need or like to shop but have no time to do so.

Competition

In any market, profits are limited by the extent of competition, which is always subject to change. In 1999, when Mexico unexpectedly teamed with the then ineffective Organization of Petroleum Exporting Countries (OPEC) cartel in order to restrict oil production, the reduction of competitors boosted oil prices around the world. New competition can emerge unpredictably. The popularity of the relatively new facsimile transmission, which grew to prominence in the early 1990s, was hurt severely by the coming of age of the Internet.

It was always important to pay attention to your competitors' new products or production techniques. Today it is absolutely vital. As little as half an hour a day devoted to perusing your competitors' Web sites will yield astonishing quantities of data.

Of course, competitors can find out just as much about your operations, which is why you must protect your business by giving it a differentiating edge that your rivals can't easily match. You are fortunate if you have a unique process or patent, or a powerful proprietary brand name. In some cases you can protect yourself by becoming indispensable to distribution partners. Increasingly, competitive insulation is developed through a set of partnerships, joint ventures, or working relationships with customers, suppliers, or former competitors.

That you need to watch out for your direct competitors is obvious. But indirect competitors, which may be able to meet customers' needs adequately with new technologies and completely different cost structures, are equally if not more dangerous.

Xerox Corporation provides a striking example of the importance of tracking competition from the perspective of demand, rather than supply. Xerox has suffered huge financial losses in recent years in part because it defined its market by what it offered, that is, its supply— copiers. Instead, it could have addressed the demand for products to facilitate information sharing, a need that can be satisfied in many ways.

From 1959 to 1973, Xerox's patented 914 xerographic copier acted as a money machine for the company. The best-selling industrial product up to that point, the 914 yielded Xerox gross profit margins of 70 percent. In addition, for every machine sold, Xerox could project additional and ongoing profits from toner, paper, and service contracts. Finally, Xerox's 95 percent market share was virtually guaranteed due to its patent-protected technology.

Clearly, Xerox's patents were a major industry factor that held competition at bay and granted the company a virtual monopoly. Incredibly, as it turned out, Xerox didn't plan for the expiration of its patents in the early 1970s and the wave of competing products that were waiting to emerge. Without patent protection, Xerox's market share was cut severely; it dropped to a mere 13 percent by 1982, primarily due to low-cost competition from Japan.

To survive, Xerox undertook dramatic cost cutting and quality improvement programs. With its costs and quality back in line, it was once again winning business and gaining market share. The company introduced Document Centre, the first digital copier, in 1994. Document Centre was a highly successful innovation in copiers and quickly became a $3 billion per year business for Xerox.

Ironically, Document Centre's success may explain why Xerox was blind to a new competitive threat: the ink-jet printer. While it was focusing on the copier market's high end with the digital copier, a new set of forces and factors was driving enormous sales of ink-jet printers. A new segment of demand, the rapidly growing small office–home office (SOHO) market, had emerged, which was all but ignored by Xerox. Xerox's machines were not appropriate for the SOHO market—they were too expensive, large, and difficult to maintain. And so the small, relatively inexpensive, and easy to use desktop printers dominated by Hewlett-Packard Company and others became the staple for the SOHO market.

Eventually, Xerox realized that printers were reducing the need for copiers. With a few keystrokes, people easily print multiple copies of documents without leaving their desks. Although HP was not one of Xerox's direct competitors (HP didn't make copiers), its printers took significant share from Xerox. Xerox finally invested heavily to enter the printer market, but did so too late; HP's dominance was firmly established. Xerox made a "crippling strategic error . . . [by] belatedly challeng[ing] HP," according to *Business Week,* and as a result suffered a serious reversal in fortune.

Market Growth and Profitability

Typically, profit margins are highest in expanding markets, where businesses are on the leading edge in problem solving or technology, and lowest in mature markets, where the products trade like commodities. This means that the inherent growth and profitability of a market or market segment is a critical industry factor. Though it is possible to prosper in either expanding or mature markets, the skills and organization required are very different.

Industry growth and profitability not only influence demand; they also shape ways to develop the supply that will meet it. For example, if your people do not have the skills to identify production-line detail that cuts a penny from costs, you should avoid a commodity market or one in which pricing is trending down. If your company can't make intuitive leaps to creative new solutions or services, neither information technology nor advertising is the right place for you. This is why it is crucial that companies analyze their talents and skills clearly and objectively before targeting specific market segments.

The bottom line is always profitability: you must always choose the business and the demand that will bring the best return. Some companies prefer to relinquish market share rather than participate in a price war. For example, one of 3M's core strategies focuses on new product development. In five years, roughly 40 percent of its revenue will come from new products. On occasion, it has walked away from a price war. In the 1990s, as competition from high-volume, low-margin suppliers drove down the cost of videotapes, 3M (which invented videotape) dropped out of the business. And it doesn't regret the decision. Likewise, Schwab chose to avoid a price war with its competitors on the Web and found other ways to add value. As a result, its stock took off.

Technological And Other Innovation

In 1965 Gordon Moore proposed the "law" that computer processing speed doubles, and costs are cut in half, every eighteen months, and so far that has been true. Although technological progress isn't limited to computers, they set the pace at geometric rather than arithmetic rates of change. And now researchers are on the verge of miniaturizing circuit technology literally to the molecular level. This could create a new computer era, in which quantum computers revolutionize information technology and deliver mind-boggling computing speeds and power.

Though computers facilitated it, the Internet is now its own revolution, with whole new ways of doing business. And since technological progress isn't synonymous with computers, innovation can include more than technology or product development. In the past twenty years we have developed new ways of analyzing markets, running companies, and planning our own careers, and each involves the forces and factors of the marketplace. Innovation becomes easier and less risky once you understand that demand must precede supply. Perhaps the most useful definition of innovation is that of Alvaro de Souza, former president of Citibank North America, who said, "It's not an innovation if there's no benefit to the customer."

In order to realize their full potential, your innovation efforts should address all three major categories of innovation: product line updates, new platforms, and business transformations driven by internal or external factors. If you focus entirely on product line updates, you are probably overlooking longer-term options that might have greater impact. On the other hand, if you concentrate exclusively on transformational opportunities, you may ignore relatively easy options that are close at hand.

Our experience with innovation work has led us to conclude that everyone across the organization should focus on the innovation opportunity for which he or she is best skilled. A brand manager may readily identify ways to extend, improve, or update his or her brand. However, transforming the business may require people with different skills, perhaps research and development technologists from within or even from outside the company.

Microsoft Corporation's innovation efforts cover all three areas. It periodically improves and updates its ubiquitous Windows operating system and the applications it supports, then distributes new releases. While Windows 95, 98, and 2000 revise and enhance one another significantly, none is considered a new growth platform.

But the company has recently introduced a new growth platform, Xbox game technology, giving Microsoft the potential to win a new market, the $7 billion game console market, which is skewed primarily toward preteen and teenage boys. Sony Corporation, Nintendo Co., Ltd., and Sega Enterprises, Ltd., have dominated this segment for the past several years. Microsoft hopes that Xbox will change that.

Though Microsoft's initial response to the Internet was practically to ignore it, Bill Gates realized that it could transform the entire information technology industry, and he pushed Microsoft to develop products for the Internet as quickly as possible. After playing an unaccustomed game of catch-up, Microsoft is now recognized as a leader in Internet access and Internet software.

Innovation takes place outside of technology's sphere, as well. We often find opportunities in relatively sleepy categories that have not experienced significant change in a long time. One of my former partners at The Cambridge Group, Peter Klein, did just that by helping Oscar Mayer develop Lunchables.

For generations, parents have been packing lunches for their kids who go to school, day care, or camp. In hundreds of thousands of houses across the United States, the weekday morning routine was familiar. Generally, Mom made the lunch, which was typically a sandwich and a piece of fruit. When Peter began to work with Bob Drane of Oscar Mayer, two very strong forces and factors were at work, both of which related to the moms' frustrations with this task.

The first issue was time. For the most part, mothers work, and packing lunches was frequently one job too many in the morning. The second issue related to the kids' responses. Kids often complained about the lunches their moms packed; they wanted something that tasted good and was more fun than just sandwiches.

A clear demand for a win-win alternative was begging for a solution. And Oscar Mayer's significant cold cuts business motivated it to solve the problem. When Lunchables were introduced in 1988, the fast, fun, ready-to-eat meals looked very promising.

A typical Lunchable is a portable single-serving combination of meat, cheese, and crackers that comes with a beverage and a snack. As such, Lunchables allowed Oscar Mayer to tap into two brands owned by its parent corporation to provide cheese (Kraft) and drinks like Kool-Aid and Capri Sun (General Foods). Not only was this volume helpful to the corporation, but these well-known brands attracted parents and kids. Leveraging the brands provided Lunchables with a unique point of differentiation. In addition, by leveraging its proprietary refrigerated distribution system and selling the product in the supermarket's refrigerated section for both actual and perceived freshness, Oscar Mayer was able to lock out competitors. Finally, Lunchables created a new platform for convenient meal solutions. Today, the concept has been extended into variety packs, fun packs, low-fat versions of foods, pizza, and more.

As a convenient meal with trusted name brands that kids look forward to, Lunchables addresses both of the forces and factors issues—benefits that may be worth paying a little extra for. For kids, they are fun, different, not boring, and they taste good. For Oscar Mayer, Lunchables is more than a line extension or product update. Reflecting innovative, out-of-the-lunch-box thinking, Lunchables are a lucrative new growth platform that is now worth almost $1 billion and commands 85 percent of the market for prepackaged children's lunches.

Innovative products or services can lead to spectacular success. But innovation should not become a mantra that ignores other factors. You can't compete in the demand economy's rapid life cycles on the basis of innovation alone: products are too easily copied or imitated. Innovation as a strategy won't work, since it is, by definition, unpredictable. In fact, unless it grows out of Demand Strategy and satisfies an actual demand or need, innovation on its own is rarely effective. In fact, a more accurate definition of innovation in business is a new and better way to meet demand—whether the demand is among customers, manufacturers, retailers, or others who are critical to your success.

Demographic Changes

The baby boom following World War II has helped to shape the economy in general, and certain markets in particular, since 1946. It has caused successive ebbs and flows in businesses as diverse as diaper service, school construction, wedding gowns, housing development, and financial consulting. Leading the population shift from cities to suburbia and to the Sunbelt, boomers—who are responsible for the success of minivans and now sports utility vehicles—have fed markets for furniture, barbecue grills, minicams, and VCRs. As they age, they will make use of retirement homes, elder leisure activities, long-term care insurance, and nursing homes.

Today, businesses are trying to get a grasp of the newest generation in the U.S. population. Sometimes referred to as Millennials, this generation includes anyone born in or after 1985. There are about 80 million Millennials, who are poised to influence U.S. society as much as, if not more than, the baby boomers.

Despite their importance, the baby boomers and Millennials only partially explain the demographic upheaval the world is now experiencing. To quote Peter Drucker, demographics is "the single most important factor that nobody pays attention to, and when they do pay attention, they miss the point."

The trend that will profoundly change the world and, quite literally, all of its markets is one that is being overlooked: the rapidly shrinking population. The gross number and percentage of births in developed countries has decreased significantly. In southern Europe, including Portugal, Spain, the south of France, Italy, and Greece, the birthrate is down to one live birth per woman, less than half of the 2.2 births per woman that would simply replace the population. In Germany and Japan, the birth rate is 1.4. In the United States, immigration from countries with high birthrates has maintained the replacement level, but demographers predict that the U.S. birthrate, too, will be falling by 2010.

Though it is impossible to calculate the effects of this on the economy, it is easy to say they will be dramatic. In Japan, if the trend continues, the total population will drop from the 135 million that it is today to only 50 million in a century. In southern Europe, the repercussions will be even more drastic. Without an adequate number of young people to keep the economies running, developed nations will rely on their older populations, who will be healthier and living longer, to prolong their work lives because of the need for temporary workers, tutors, and consultants. And by 2020, despite the drop in Japan's population, the Asia-Pacific region will be home to almost 55 percent of the world's population.

Megatrends in Society

Some sea changes evolve gradually and are observed and analyzed as they occur. The sexual revolution of the 1960s and 1970s is one such example. Others arrive overnight, such as the surge of anti-Japanese racism that transformed the United States after the bombing of Pearl Harbor in 1941, or the radically heightened security concerns around the world in the aftermath of the 2001 terrorist attacks against the World Trade Center and the Pentagon.

However they come about, social megatrends are forces and factors that profoundly affect markets everywhere. A very simplistic example is the effect of World War II on the workforce of many countries. Men went to battle, women took their places in the workforce, food and supplies were rationed, and the availability of many consumer goods dried up for the duration. As a result, a postwar explosion fueled by pent-up demand drove mass production and created a postwar society marked by consumerism, suburbanization, and the eruption of the middle class.

The advent of the birth control pill led directly to the sexual revolution, to unmarried couples openly cohabitating, to decisions to defer starting families, to the third wave of the feminist movement, to more women in the workforce, and to the evolution of the child care industry, among myriad other repercussions.

Dozens of other megatrends affect demand by shaping people's needs and desires. For example, beginning in the mid-1980s and extending through the 1990s, a steadily increasing trend toward "active life enjoyment" and a move away from sedentary leisure have taken shape. Feeling isolated from the natural world, people felt a need to interact with nature more directly and experience life more boldly. Station wagons and minivans were replaced by rugged SUVs that opened the possibility of off-road adventures or just the feeling of being more adventurous. Vacationing at the beach or touring other countries was replaced by adventure travel. People wanted to experience an African safari, trek around Mount Everest, or scuba dive at the Great Barrier Reef. X, or extreme, sports—mountain biking, snowboarding, heli skiing, and bungee jumping—evolved as a means of flirting with danger that seemed to satisfy the desire for excitement that people sought.

Feeling disappointed in and betrayed by many of the U.S. institutions they had always trusted and relied on—the government, corporations, schools, churches, even the family—baby boomers over the last two decades have become less trusting and more self-reliant as well. Public officials have been besieged by scandals; lifetime employment at corporations is a thing of the past; employment itself is often tenuous.

As a result, people seek lifestyles in which they can exert greater control and depend less on others. This megatrend manifests in an increased demand for home schooling and in home offices, and perhaps even explains some of Home Depot's appeal—doing it yourself instead of counting on a plumber or contractor. Other megatrends include a growing appreciation of racial and cultural diversities in the United States as well as an increasing desire for individuality.

The inherent nature of megatrends makes them difficult to predict. However, when companies observe one in progress, it is essential that they use it to improve their understanding of demand and their communications with target consumers. Only if companies are alert to the megatrend's impact on forces and factors and then on current and emerging demand will they be prepared and be able to use the megatrend to advantage.

ADDITIONAL FORCES AND FACTORS

I have discussed in general terms seven of the most salient mega forces and factors. Of course, I can't tell you which are the most important in your industry, company, and particular situation, but here are some additional forces and factors to keep in mind as you think about your specific business:

Forces and factors that affect your supply chain, including
- suppliers
- supply capacity

- supply base shifts to new regions
- manufacturing technologies
- cost of adding capacity
- OEM material costs
- outsourced manufacturing rather than vertical integration
- disintermediation
- distribution changes
- Internet exchanges
- new substitutable suppliers or products
- private label products
- sales force skills, coverage, and incentives

Forces and factors that affect the nature of your interactions with customers, including
- demographics
- geographic location
- income level
- ethnicity
- gender
- lifestyle and life stage
- working women
- time impoverishment
- use of media
- new communications technology
- channels from which to shop, from mass merchants and category killers to the Internet and catalogs

Government-related forces and factors, including
- government spending
- legislation
- regulation or (increasingly) deregulation
- equal employment laws

The crucial question is, how can your organization understand and work with these and other forces and factors? It is important that managers and executives keep an open mind and conduct a realistic and objective assessment of where their company stands in the market-place. Every organization must build its own fact base with the forces and factors pertaining to its unique current situation. Train everyone in the company to consider it so that doing so becomes an automatic checkpoint in your company's culture. A fact base will enable you to alter your company's procedures and strategies as it makes clear what important changes have taken place or are taking place.

The forces and factors in the fact base coalesce to form a mosaic that represents your business from a perspective that you most likely haven't yet fully considered. As you examine the relationships and interactions between the various forces and factors, you will see possibilities to strengthen your business that you probably never imagined. Although you may have recognized each individual facet, you likely had little perspective on how the forces and factors interacted and influenced one another, enabling you to preempt changes and lead your market rather than accept the consequences of following your competitors.

This process is intended to provide an objective reference point. In today's demand economy, events move more rapidly and are more interconnected than ever before. When events are moving quickly and people are working amid commotion and confusion, a manager with a firm grasp of the forces and factors that drive demand in his or her market has a much better sense of how to lead and respond.

In Chapter 5, I will focus on the next step in this process, how to identify and target the customers who will be most profitable for you. In Chapter 6, I will show how you can combine different responses to forces and factors along with the needs of your target demand to create a Demand Value Proposition—something that will become an enduring part of your Demand Strategy.

CHAPTER 5

THE SECOND PRINCIPLE

Select Your Most Profitable Demand Segments

Thereare two ways to run a business. On the one hand, you can believe that your customers are similar to one another regarding what they want or look for from your products; therefore you have one giant, mass market. On the other hand, you can recognize that customers have different wants, needs, and demands, whether the category is cookies or cars, banks or dog food. Demand Strategy is predicated on the latter approach.

One of the central premises of Demand Strategy is that *every* business category must be divided into segments so that you can understand how customers in each segment are motivated and why they make decisions. Only after knowing that can you practice Demand Strategy.

In every industry, total demand can be divided into segments: groups, or clusters, of customers who buy for similar reasons. Across segments, the needs that underlie specific purchases may vary widely, which is why the concept of breaking markets into segments is so important to Demand Strategy.

Each industry can be segmented in several different ways. The auto industry, for example, can be segmented according to the vehicles customers have bought in the past: family sedans, sports cars, SUVs and minivans, new cars or used. The market can be segmented based on consumer demographics, such as age groups or income levels. Or it can be segmented by what motivates a person from a particular segment to select a car based on auto attributes—for example, good gas mileage or safety. Knowing as much as you can about each segment allows you to create supply that will satisfy its specific demand.

Let's stay with the auto industry for a moment. Every car company believes that its business divides into segments. As a result, car makers offer very different types of cars to satisfy their different segments of demand: demographics, patterns of use, needs, and demand are a few ways of segmenting the market. When car makers look at demographics, they find that minivans skew to young families, while singles prefer sports cars and older drivers prefer the comfort and power of large sedans. Alternatively, by examining patterns of use, a car maker might discover that the heaviest users of pickup trucks cross all age groups and live in rural communities. Or an assessment of needs could reveal a market for a small commuter car or one that can haul a boat trailer. Consumers' demand can be used to determine who wants what: that is, some people want the prestige of a luxury car, while others focus on the car's cost, and still others want only a fuel-efficient car.

Although there are many ways to classify or segment an industry, we find that *demand* segmentation is the most useful for a business. Because it clarifies existing demand, such segmentation identifies immediately actionable opportunities to improve a business by focusing on high-priority demand segments. Most approaches to segmentation describe *what* happened in the past; because they don't analyze the motivations that underlie demand, they don't identify the *why* that can help companies plan the future.

As we discussed in Chapter 1, the most important demand teenagers around the world have for the cars they will buy five to ten years from now was very surprising to our automotive client. The managers at a large automaker that we worked with believed the teens would want speed, sleek designs, and excellent stereo sound systems. After all, that is what past generations of young adults looked for in cars. Yet when we segmented the market using demand segmentation, we found that the majority of teenagers prioritized safety—protection from physical harm, and a car maker providing emotional security—as being most important to them. This hugely valuable information could not have been revealed by any other approach to segmentation. In retrospect, teens' need for safety is less surprising, given school shootings, the presence of gangs, high levels of injury and death among teenaged drivers and passengers, and other factors that increasingly threaten their physical safety.

While autos can be divided into fairly obvious segments, the majority of business categories cannot. Yet selecting the segments to focus upon is a *critical* decision. Demand segments are the central nervous system of Demand Strategy because no further steps can effectively be taken if the wrong segments are targeted.

Despite the critical role that targeting plays in business success, we continue to find companies operating as they did decades ago with only a vague notion of who their target is, broad demographic targets (for example, women aged twenty-nine to forty-five), or targets that are simply wrong. For example, we recently worked with a well-known beverage company that had always targeted the consumers it thought were its heaviest users—women aged fifty-five and older who lived in affluent communities located primarily on the East Coast, where this company had been founded a century ago. In fact, we learned that the heaviest users of this category are large families with an ethnic skew living primarily in rural communities in the South. As is so often the case, this targeting insight was the key to unlocking profitable growth for our client. With a deep understanding of the demand among the most valuable target, the company was able to create new products, packaging, advertising messages, and distribution strategies to deliver on the demand of the largest and most profitable segments.

In my experience, targeting is even more critical for business-to-business companies, because an individual sale or contract—which often hinges on the depth of understanding of the customer—can be worth millions of dollars. In the case of a newspaper publisher that we worked with recently, they were approaching all advertisers in exactly the same way they had for fifty years: with one basic offer. In fact, the ability to produce color ads in their newspapers was the only real change in their approach to the market for decades. When we conducted a demand segmentation for them, we found that their most important advertisers had very different demands and therefore responded differently to specific offers. Some advertisers focused on building their brand image, some wanted to drive traffic to their stores on the days the ads appeared, some wanted to generate a phone contact, and others were trying to generate awareness and trial. By creating specific advertising offers for the very different segments of demand, the newspaper increased the efficiency of the sales force by 40 percent. The sales force was much more knowledgeable about the needs of different types of customers and tailored its offers accordingly.

With another business-to-business client, dramatic changes among its customers required a new approach to the market. In part because of its siloed, divisional organization, this equipment and service provider did not realize that reengineering and rapid consolidation among its customer industries was creating a new set of demands among them. Due to the changes and cost pressures of both reengineering and consolidation, the largest customers now wanted fewer strategic suppliers to which they could outsource broad sets of needs. Until they realized how important this growing demand would become, the internal divisions of the equipment and service provider had become a significant barrier to working with the large customers that were most profitable to serve. These customers wanted one point of contact to outsource all of their needs, not six separate divisions to deal with.

The goal is to select the segments that are likely to yield the highest profits, considering your business system, infrastructure, competition, and core competencies. Once you have done that, you have taken an enormous step toward seizing control of your company's performance and profitability.

While there is much overlap, every segment will have something which separates it from other segments. Understanding what is valued by each segment gives you a substantial competitive edge. Furthermore, it allows you to match your supply to what that segment values.

In so doing, you gain pricing power—because you have the opportunity to create differentiated supply that earns relatively inelastic pricing.

The best way to segment any market is by considering the types of demand it includes. By that I mean knowing for certain what motivates people in each segment to buy.

Segmenting begins with *qualitative* research. Quantitative analysis can tell you how many people are in each segment, how much they spend, and how they rate different options. Managers who are more comfortable with quantitative research are sometimes anxious to skip the qualitative stage. But the qualitative stage is crucial because it is here that you form your hypotheses regarding what people want. Time and again we see segmentation work in which managers skipped the qualitative step, and thereby lost an important opportunity to learn something new about their customers and their motivations.

Before the Coca-Cola Company introduced New Coke, for example, it conducted thousands of taste tests across segments of cola drinkers in which New Coke was the decisive winner over the original Coke, now known as Classic Coke. Had the company completed the necessary qualitative research first, it would have discovered that people thought the new drink was in addition to, rather than a replacement for, the old Coke. Though consumers liked New Coke, they were concerned and even angry when they discovered it was intended to replace the original drink they had come to love.

One of the largest ready-to-eat cereal companies, as a result of its hasty quantitative research, failed to introduce a highly profitable adult healthy cereal. Their quantitative research showed that introducing the proposed granola product would be a financial disaster.

Several months later, a competitor with the same idea conducted qualitative research among various demand segments. The results clarified the fact that there were two large segments of health-conscious, ready-to-eat-cereal users (out of a total of seven cereal segments) that embraced the idea. When the quantitative piece was performed among the segments that already purchased healthy cereals, the results were overwhelmingly positive. On supermarket shelves six months later, the new cereal was more popular than any other introduced in the ready-to-eat category for the past several years.

The first company erred by having its quantitative researchers ask members of all ready-to-eat-cereal segments to react to the healthier product. The problem was that more than half of these consumers ate presweetened cereals, never read the ingredients listed on the box, and weren't at all interested in finding a new, healthier, good-tasting cereal. The researchers failed to focus on demand segments of people seeking healthier cereals. It was a serious mistake.

Viewing the market through the lens of demand segmentation allows you to reach three crucial ends. The first is a better understanding of the volume and economic value of various segments. In turn, this data can enable you to focus and allocate resources on the specific demand segments that can give you the most profit. Finally, you can get wonderfully rich direction for innovation, differentiation, and communication in simple preference comparisons.

Allocating your resources to the segments that can earn the highest returns doesn't mean that they are your only source of business. But by fulfilling the demand among one or two segments better than any other competitor, you will not only win a larger share of their business, you will also gain some portion of adjacent segments' business. They might be attracted to your offer because they use it when they want some variety, or because it most closely aligns with some of their needs despite having been designed for other demand segments. Your targeting efforts should be inclusionary, not exclusionary, because segments reflect skews in behavior, not absolute behavior. Segments are not hard and fast, black or white; they are often different shades of gray.

Demand usually breaks into five or six macro segments; depending on the nature of the business, it may divide again into a number of subsegments. For each segment, it is critical that you determine the size and nature of the demand and whether or not you can earn a profit serving it. As you begin to target a demand segment, it is also important to consider how the category might change in the future.

Let's look at an example of demand segmentation in a single, seemingly uncomplicated market: the dog food industry.

Before World War II, when rural life was still the norm in many parts of the United States, the relationships between adults and their dogs was friendly but distant. "When the focus of American life became urban," Dr. Michael Garvey, a New York City veterinarian, remarked not long ago, "pets moved indoors and people started to spend more time with them. As modern life got quicker and more impersonal, the pet moved in to take the place of friends and family."

As the elderly population grew and more people were living alone, the pet food industry began a marketing campaign that emphasized the beneficial effects of having a pet companion on the health and overall quality of humans' lives.

Several years ago I was asked to help a pet food company that was steadily losing ground. We found that its senior managers couldn't answer basic questions about segments, channels, or the changing mix of products their customers were purchasing. As a result, I suggested that the managers perform a demand segmentation. Up until then, this market was segmented by the type of food—canned or dry, with many segments in between.

The broader demand segmentation results were remarkable. They showed that in the dog food industry, demand segments are determined by the relationships owners want to have with their dogs. The first segment, called "loving indulgers," is in general composed of mothers whose children have left home and for whom the dog becomes, either consciously or unconsciously, a child substitute. The primary demand for members of this segment is to be loved by their dog. They don't care what the food costs as long as buying it makes them feel they are pleasing their pets.

At the other end of the spectrum, both in attitude toward the dog and sensitivity to price, are the owners we called "tolerating functionalists." They are what remains of the prewar farming community and they view a dog as a farm implement or tool, not a pet. They buy the cheapest brands of food in the largest sacks they can find.

Between those two poles are three more demand segments. "Caring companions" accept dogs as part of the family; they want quality food and are willing to try new brands they think the dogs will enjoy, but they would balk at expensive delicacies.

People in the "active nutritionist" segment see their dogs as running partners or travel companions. These owners are concerned about their dogs' health, thus demand that they have nutritious food. They are ready to shop at a specialty store that provides the food that meets their high standards.

The final demand segment, the "budget conscious," love their dogs but have limited financial resources. They buy basic dog food as part of their routine shopping.

The Three Dog Bakery, founded in Kansas City, Missouri, in 1989, focused almost exclusively on the loving indulgers demand segment. They produce luxury treats for pampered pets. Dedicated to serving fresh-baked treats like Beastro Biscotti ($1.75 apiece) and Pet-it Fours (two for $1.50), it now boasts more than thirty franchise shops around the United States. The stores also offer special holiday treats—Champ Pagne (a sparkling water for New Year's Eve) and Halloween costumes ranging from giraffes to Vikings, meant to be worn by dogs. Clearly, concentrating on the loving indulgers demand segment, although a relatively small group, can be very profitable.

The dog food industry has to supply owners in every price range who encompass every level of attachment to their pets. All else being equal, how owners perceive their dogs and what roles they want the animals to fulfill in their lives—that is, the nature of the relationship between owner and dog—is the most important factor in determining what humans are willing to pay for dog food.

I recommended that the company I was working with closely track the emerging demand for healthier dog food. Iams, for example, had just introduced its very healthy food, and early responses were positive.

Which segment should a Demand Strategist in this industry target? At first glance, it would seem that the loving indulgers care the least about cost. But making segment targeting decisions is more complicated than that. Demand Strategy requires a company to consider all the relevant demand forces and industry factors before selecting segments to focus on.

First, companies need to align their core competencies with the demands of the different segments. The core competencies also have to align with the strength of a company's distribution and supply channels in the areas preferred by each segment.

The aging of the baby boom generation, for example, is sure to increase the number of people with empty-nest syndrome who may be potential "loving indulgers," or "caring companions" of their pets—a measure that would dramatically alter the economics of the industry. On the other hand, an economic downturn could make people more budget conscious and potentially shrink the top tier of the industry.

It is equally vital that you determine which demand segments your competitors are focusing on, and then choose the one that gives you the best chance of differentiation. Has a rival come up with a manufacturing or distribution innovation? Can you match it or even find a way to improve it?

Finally, your company will need to align its production capacity, infrastructure, resources, sales, and marketing strengths with the demand segments it selects. If you always have been a mass-market operation known for budget prices, for example, you probably don't want to target the loving indulgers. Likewise, it would take an enormous infusion of capital to turn a manufacturer of upscale canned dog food into one that makes ordinary dry kibble that sells in fifty-pound sacks.

Since all industries have more than one demand segment, there is room for companies to pursue several different Demand Strategies. In a given neighborhood, one dry cleaner may specialize in leather and technically difficult cleaning, while another does equally well focusing on same-day service. Both shops are needed because they appeal to different segments of demand.

Obviously, no single formula will enable every company to identify its most profitable demand segment. But there are fact-based methods for researching the economics of different segments to determine which segments you can best serve profitability.

Southwest Airlines Company and UAL Corporation had been, until the September 11, 2001, terrorist attacks, two of the country's most profitable airlines. UAL's United uses major airports, hires union employees, flies seventeen different types of planes, and caters to the business traveler. Southwest, on the other hand, uses secondary airports and a point-to-point route system, does not hire union employees, flies only 737s, and caters to the traveler on a budget. These airlines serve entirely different market segments. Each is ideal for its market, and neither could successfully compete in the other's realm.

There is no single correct answer regarding which segments to target in demand segmentation. Each company and each business manager must assess its strengths, infrastructure, and business system and choose to compete where it has the most expertise and can make the most money. As the Internet, direct mail, and today's superstores make clear every day, consumers have more shopping choices than ever before. As I will discuss later in the book, the mass-market audience no longer exists. It has been replaced by demand segments whose needs can be met only by different benefits and offers. Whether or not particular shoppers choose you will depend upon how well you understand and select your demand segments and, of course, how well you create products that benefit them.

Ask yourself and the people who run your business this question: What do you know about your most profitable demand segments that your competitors don't know? In my experience, only a tiny fraction of business managers around the world can answer that critical question. Yet selecting your demand segment is usually *the most important decision you can make*—to let fate decide what that segment will be, or to choose unwisely, will almost surely doom your business. When you and your managers have several good answers to the "What do you know" question, you should be on the verge of a big upswing in profits.

In recent years, retail banks have struggled as the financial services market has become increasingly complex and more competitive. In this new environment, banks have lost considerable deposits to competitors, such as brokerage and mutual fund companies. Previously, banks were the primary providers of financial services for the majority of consumers, offering services from checking accounts and credit cards to mortgages. Today, the areas that typically generate the most profits for banks have been cherry-picked by focused, monoline competitors such as Countrywide and Norwest for mortgages, and Capital One and MBNA for credit cards. In addition, the artificial protection that was provided in the United States by interstate banking laws (which prevented banks from merging across state boundaries) and the Glass-Steagall Act (which kept banking, insurance, and securities businesses separate) has disappeared. Now, local and regional banks are fighting to preserve their customer relationships against attacks from resource-rich national and global competitors, such as Citigroup and J. P. Morgan Chase. Meanwhile, serving bank customers has become more complex than ever before. Most banks have been forced to maintain traditional branches while simultaneously investing in new channels, such as ATMs and the Internet.

Through our work with the Bank Administration Institute (BAI), a large industry group for retail banks in America, The Cambridge Group has been helping banks identify and understand changes in demand so that they can develop more successful strategies.

As one of the preeminent associations in banking, the BAI wanted to determine the emerging challenges confronting banks. Its own research indicated that one challenge was the fact that the competitive dynamics in the industry were changing rapidly, and that the vast majority of banks needed a new strategy to maintain their current business and grow further.

The objectives of our work, simply put, were to develop "a new understanding of demand and a new go-to-market approach" that would allow banks to compete effectively in the rapidly evolving financial services marketplace. The primary goals included

- Benchmarked learning from companies that are thriving in mature categories similar to what the banking industry is now experiencing
- Developing an in-depth understanding of the new definition for consumer financial services
- Delivering insights and tools to make the findings more actionable or immediately actionable than those realized through traditional studies

My partner Navtej Nandra led the effort, out of which came a demand segmentation that we call the "Demand DNA." With it, we can see differences in attitudes, motivations, and demand in five key areas that drive consumers' decisions in financial services. The first is the consumer's primary financial goal, which can range from making ends meet today to accumulating funds for purchasing a home, financing their kids' educations, or retiring. The second demand factor relates to customers who work with financial advisers, versus those who prefer to plan and manage their finances themselves. A third issue that distinguishes the segments is tolerance for risk: some people are more willing to accept risk than others. A fourth factor distinguishes between people who are comfortable using new technology, such as the Internet, to manage their finances and conduct transactions and those who are not. Finally, some segments strongly prefer personal service at the branch level, while others prefer transactions through ATM machines and by phone.

From the differences between consumers in these five areas, the Demand DNA revealed eight distinct demand segments. The segments' names are intended to give you a capsule view of their distinguishing characteristics.

1. *Confident asset managers:* People in this group have the highest median net worth, are both financially and technologically astute, and focus on equity investments.
2. *Satisfied plan followers:* Members of this group are financially secure and stick to the financial plan they have developed over time, often with the help of a professional adviser.
3. *Established traditionalists:* These are people who have few financial worries, are focused on retirement, and strongly prefer dealing with people rather than technology.
4. *Family asset builders:* These tend to be young families planning to buy homes and who are saving for their kids' education; they have a strong affinity for technology.
5. *Bewildered boomers:* These are concerned with their finances, particularly regarding retirement, and have little confidence in their own ability to plan and manage them.
6. *Time-driven transactors:* This group uses technology to minimize the time and effort required for managing their finances.
7. *Striving borrowing families:* They aspire to meet family focused goals but feel significant financial stress.

8. *Overwhelmed survivors:* These individuals or families have relatively limited financial resources and feel overwhelmed by both finances and technology.

Now, imagine for a moment that you are a bank manager who wants to improve how you serve your customers. With this segmentation information as background, you can ask a customer a short series of what are known as *predictor questions.* Based on the five motivations, you can estimate which of your customers fall into which segment. You might use customer information, perhaps from loan applications or the forms used to open a checking account, to model answers to the predictor questions. You could get more accurate results if you asked customers to fill out a brief survey—at the branch, on-line, or in their monthly account statements—in which you included the predictor questions.

Once you have this information on your bank's customers, you can develop offers and align your activities to ensure that you boost your customer acquisition, penetration, retention, and profits by aiming the right offer at customers whose demand you know. This is made much easier by meeting the individual demands of your customers by aligning products, customer care, and cross-selling activities based on knowing what your customers' demands are.

In effect, an understanding based on demand allows you to answer the following crucial questions:

- Who should you target in your marketing campaigns?
- With what offer (products, services, channels, price)?
- What is the best way to communicate (brand architecture, positioning, media, messages)?
- How can you best deploy your resources (people, technology, R&D, alliances, acquisitions)?

Let's look at a bank that is trying to sell products to its affluent customers, demographically defined as households with over $150,000 in investable assets.

On the surface, these customers look alike. All fit a high net worth criterion, and most use a wide array of investment products; they buy insurance and are not heavy users of debt (as compared to their assets). By developing some information on their life stages, the bank may be able to target some products and services more successfully.

But this is a static view of demand, restricted to what the customers own already. It does not tell you if they are interested in another product or what benefits will attract particular customers. If a bank offers "me too" products, only serendipity could account for why a customer buys another product from the bank.

If you look at what is motivating their demand, you may draw insights that will profoundly affect what you sell to them and the growth you can attain from these customers.

Ninety percent of these customers fall into five of the segments that I defined earlier: Confident Asset Managers comprise 25 percent of this group, with another 65 percent almost evenly divided between Satisfied Plan Followers, Established Traditionalists, Family Asset Builders, and Bewildered Boomers. The remaining three segments account for the remaining 10 percent of customers.

Let's say that you were targeting Confident Asset Managers and Established Traditionalists for the first salvo.

Confident Asset Managers are looking for an investment-oriented company that enables them to use leading-edge tools to manage their assets. You would emphasize that they retain control, have access to research, gain easy execution, and can choose from your specific set of offerings. Given their channel preference, you would never invite them to a branch or a seminar, but instead would refer them to your Web site. In fact, they ought to be on your mind when you design your Web site, since they will be by far its heaviest users. Because this segment does not believe that banks are capable of serving their needs, you may have to consider alliances or cobranding with asset management companies in order to build your brand equity.

Established Traditionalists, on the other hand, are looking for a trusted institution that treats them respectfully and offers them access to products with which they are comfortable. They are, for the most part, risk averse and prefer investment products designed to help them maintain their capital. You would emphasize different benefits in your communications, including trust, stability, personal relationships, and security. This segment, which longs for the good old days when banking was more personal, would use your branch network. Therefore, you would use branches as a sales channel by inviting these customers to an in-person meeting to discuss savings planning and opportunities. You would also emphasize your own brand since this segment believes that the bank's brand equity is extremely robust and flexible.

To summarize:

Target	Confident Asset Managers	Established Traditionalists
Products	Brokerage, growth funds, money managers, variable annuities, variable/ universal life	CDs, value and bond funds, asset allocation, fixed annuities, whole life
Channel	On-line	In person, branch
Communication Emphasis	Control, equities, research, easy execution	Security, stability, trust, in-person relationships
Resources Allocation	On-line experience, alliances with asset managers	Training for relationship manager, simple asset allocation tool

Now imagine you are a bank manager using only demographic data to segment your market. Your information might help you understand the life stage differences between segments—say, the needs of young families versus those of retirement age consumers. However, as we have seen, demographic data would not help you understand important differences within segments. As a result, you might offer a one-size-fits-all solution to everyone aged fifty-five or over who has an income in the $50,000–$100,000 range. Meanwhile, a banker with a demand segmentation based on attitudes and motivations would align offers much more closely with the demands of specific segments.

Clearly, a company's most profitable demand segments never stand still. They are constantly evolving, growing, shifting, merging, and disappearing, which is why keeping a constant vigil over how demand forces and industry factors affect demand is imperative. Only with such diligence can you continue to understand demand before you create supply, and reap the benefits of doing so.

Your task throughout the life of your business is to ferret out the demand segments that promise the highest profit in the context of your company's infrastructure, culture, and competition. Your goal is to investigate further than your competitors do to discover the unmet needs of potential demand segments. Demographic data are secondary, and though useful for describing each segment, they are not criteria used in the segmenting process.

In the business-to-business sector, one demand segment might include customers who care most about the speed with which a project is completed; another could be comprised of people whose priority is quality; and still other segments could place reliability, innovation, or low cost as their priorities.

It is fascinating to see how the nature of demand changes as you move from business category to business category. We saw in dog food that the desired personal relationship with the dog was the critical factor. In technology, however, the best segmenting variable is very impersonal and relies entirely on performance.

In high-technology businesses, there are three demand segments: the leading edge, the competitive edge, and the trailing edge.

- *Leading Edge.* Individuals and companies in this segment depend upon technology and want it as soon as it is introduced. Leading financial institutions, computer software companies, and major airlines are examples of businesses that need the advantage that new technology provides. Without it, they couldn't meet the demand of their own leading-edge customers. Therefore, they are less price sensitive than some of their second-tier competitors.

- *Competitive Edge.* People and companies in this segment think technology is important, but they want it at a discount. They will wait until a product is in its second or third year, or even buy it in the secondary markets after the leading-edge companies have moved on to the next development. Mid-level banks, smaller airlines, and automotive suppliers are included in this demand segment.

- *Trailing Edge.* Individuals and companies in this segment need technology because no one can survive without it, but they are adopting it slowly and they are the most cost sensitive. This is largely because their businesses do not depend upon information technology for their success. Their requirements, whether they are consumers or executives in business-to-business transactions, are relatively straightforward.

An example of a company that chose one of its demand segments long ago and recently took an enormous risk to retain its loyalty is the Minnesota Mining and Manufacturing Corporation (3M). Because it understood demand segments, it was able to withstand stiff competition in the computer diskette market. When Kao Corporation brought out a low-priced diskette in the early 1990s, 3M resisted the urge to drop the price on its brand, knowing that doing so could pose a risk to its high-quality image, as well as to its profits. Furthermore, it might also provoke Kao to cut prices again.

Like General Motors Corporation, 3M developed its business as a portfolio of products that served many demand segments. Now the company decided to apply that concept to the diskette market in order to minimize risk and maximize return. As is true of all markets, this one had different segments of demand with varying degrees of price sensitivity. If one group chose diskettes based on price, another didn't consider cost. More important, the people who were indifferent to price considered the inexpensive diskettes to be poor quality. They avoided the low end because they feared losing their data more than they worried about paying a premium.

Instead of reducing prices, 3M launched a flanking brand of low-priced diskettes, called Highland, and made a substantial profit by pinpointing the most price-sensitive demand segment. At the same time, releasing the new line under a different name precluded the loss of its higher-profit customers.

The same insight—that markets with many demand segments will bear a variety of prices—underlies the strategies of many software companies. For instance, marginally different versions of the same voice recognition software range in price from $79 to $8,000, depending on the demand segment.

You should invest a lot of thought and research identifying the demand segments that will be appropriate for you. In addition to observing how people behave, you have to be able to understand that behavior. Though the detailed questions you ask will depend on the business you are in, a good demand segmentation will answer all of the following questions:

1. After examining the factors that motivate customers' purchasing behavior, what sectors of demand emerge? In a successful company, everyone understands his or her customers, products, and competition. Some companies, like McDonald's, organize around the segments they have identified to focus the enterprise. McDonald's segments include kids, tweens, and teens.

2. What is the potential of each segment to generate revenue and profits? What will it take to secure a large share of the demand segment? What groups use the product most?

3. To what markets are you currently offering products? What demand segment is your highest priority, and why? For our airline client, we discovered that 9 percent of flyers accounted for almost half of revenues. With this new insight, the company made that group its priority target.

4. Where might you find opportunities for growth that have not yet been developed or addressed? What are your secondary development targets and prospects?

5. Can you uncover additional opportunities to penetrate the market, deepen relationships, and keep customers?

6. What opportunities do you see for brand/product portfolio management and alignment? Under a given brand name like Ford or

Toyota, most car makers offer a portfolio of cars, including sedans, SUVs, minivans, and sports cars. Different models of cars in the portfolio are designed for different customer segments.

7. Considering their rational and emotional characteristics, their behavior, and demographic data, what do members of a particular segment have in common? What are the implications for your business in targeting those groups?

8. What can you hope to gain by allocating resources to those segments? Is your organization action oriented and prepared to take advantage of opportunities as they present themselves?

9. How will the market evolve over time? What are the implications for your business? From where might latent and emerging demand surface? For instance, we helped a technology provider divide financial services firms into segments. One primary reason we identified retail banks as highly attractive targets was that they were just beginning the wave of mergers and acquisitions that created a significant need to integrate technology systems.

10. What are the best distribution channels and opportunities of each sector? Are there opportunities that can be leveraged by working with partners?

11. Where are there arenas in which demand is not being met adequately or at all? Sears Credit capitalized on the fact that the demand its most profitable customers had for a highly flexible credit card with low monthly payments was not being met by existing offers.

12. Where are your competitors placed, and why? What are your options for increasing and defending market share? What is your most powerful strategy for differentiating your products? Once you successfully establish the organization's unique features, how can you insulate those distinctive elements from being replicated by competitors?

13. What features or benefits will enable you to have inelastic pricing?

14. How do your brand and product offerings stack up against your competitors' by segment? Do you see opportunities to optimize your brand and product value?

15. What's the best channel and message for communication?
16. How can you leverage the information you have accumulated so
    that your company continues to benefit from it?

As a result of addressing these questions, FedEx Corporation was able
to identify a demand segment, and then move aggressively to meet that
demand with an approach that has proven extremely successful. In the
very crowded and intensely competitive overnight shipping business,
FedEx dominates two demand segments that produce exceptional revenue. One cluster of customers targeted by FedEx, for example, is
shippers sending highly valuable and time-sensitive air cargo. Though
members of this group represent only 2 percent or so of total weight
shipped, this type of order accounts for half of the entire value of international trade. After selecting the customer groups that its research
predicted would generate the highest profits, the company made a serious commitment to serve them extraordinarily well.

FedEx's emphasis on high-end air freight contrasts with the strategy of its rival, United Parcel Service, Inc. (UPS). In 2000, UPS had
revenues of $30 billion, compared with FedEx's 2000 revenues of $18
billion, making UPS more than half again as big as FedEx. UPS's focus
is on ground shipping and delivery to individual customers' homes.
FedEx's research showed that delivering to people's homes costs far
more than delivering to their businesses. This is because residences,
which usually receive only single packages at a time, are scattered
throughout a wide area, whereas businesses tend to be concentrated
in fewer areas, and often receive multiple packages.

FedEx's other goal is to serve customers who use (or would like to
use) distribution as a strategic competitive advantage. For example, by
coordinating just-in-time inventory from component suppliers around
the globe, FedEx helps build-to-order manufacturers, like Dell and
Cisco, use speed and flexibility to their competitive advantage. Anticipating big profits from serving a demand segment that wants integrated
supply-chain solutions, FedEx is marketing itself as the company corporations should hire for supply-chain management, A to Z.

In the view of Fred Smith, FedEx's founder, chairman, and chief executive officer, his company's supply-chain solutions strategy is practically inevitable now that commerce, information, and goods must meet "a new standard of demanding customer requirements."

Smith claims that "the Internet is the neural system. We're the skeleton—we [FedEx] make the body move." As a result, the company reinvented itself as an integrated logistics partner for a variety of companies, including Cisco.

FedEx will spend more than $100 million creating the e-systems and services that will enable it to become the "conveyor belt" for Cisco, which transacts 90 percent of its sales via the Web. Eventually FedEx will coordinate all of Cisco's shipping and, in so doing, phase out the latter's warehousing.

In other words, FedEx has recognized an emerging demand segment that is more encompassing and far more lucrative than its air freight business. It is positioning itself to provide a full range of Internet-based supply-chain services, including e-distribution centers for today's largest corporations.

America Online, now a subsidiary of AOL Time Warner Inc., also owes much of its success to the fact that it continuously gauges customer demand more accurately than its competitors. Very early in its history, America Online recognized the large segment of Internet users that wanted, above all, simple, convenient access to all Internet services, buying opportunities, information, entertainment, and other content.

AOL supplies exactly that: it is the on-line service that gives breadth and substance without compromising simple, convenient, and unlimited access. It tapped a demand segment that continued to grow, and by the end of the 1990s, it was the largest, richest, and most influential company in the on-line industry. Furthermore, because it was so convenient and easy to use, AOL was able to charge a significant premium for its service, which its major competitors, some of whom provided Internet access for free, could not. In 2001, AOL charged $23.90 per month for unlimited on-line use, making it the price leader among Internet service providers. It enjoys a price premium of nearly 10 percent over rivals MSN, EarthLink, and AT&T WorldNet, and about 20 percent over Prodigy. Simultaneously, AOL's competitors are losing ground despite offering their services at much lower cost or even free. AOL's 31 million members worldwide make its customer base 4.4 times larger than MSN's, 6.3 times greater than Earth-Link's, 9 times larger than Prodigy's, and 22 times the size of AT&T WorldNet's.

In the 1980s, AOL CEO Steve Case was the first to figure out where on-line demand was heading. Although neither he nor his vision were taken seriously at the time, Case saw possibilities for the Web that transcended the vision of the technophiles who were developing the young industry. Its long-term value, Case thought, lay in the potential to hook PCs together. He imagined millions of ordinary people exchanging opinions, shopping, comparing prices, having opportunities to buy myriad items, and having access to unlimited information. In Case's view, the Internet's future did not lie with the technology nerds but with meeting the demand for, in his words, "easy ways to do online the things we do off-line, like communicate, get information, shop, socialize, and fall in love."

What Case foresaw was the democratization of the Web. The realization of that, he recognized, depended on the Internet and, by extension, America Online being easy to use. He knew, too, that realizing his vision would require offering content that was so encompassing and interesting, all kinds of users would return to the site again and again.

Case's next quandary was who, within the vast universe of potential customers, were those that America Online could most profitably serve. Here he bet on intelligent, informed people who saw personal computers and the Web as tools and means to an end, rather than on the technologically sophisticated who viewed computers and the Internet as fascinating in and of themselves.

Such a demand segment was composed of people who, in some ways, were like Case himself. Unlike Bill Gates, Case was not a technical expert. In fact, he hadn't purchased a computer until he was working in the marketing department of Pizza Hut, years after he graduated from college.

It was when he finally got connected to the Source, one of the first on-line services, that he realized "something magical was happening."

The capacity to send and receive text to and from people all over the world, even at this rudimentary stage, inspired his imagination.

In 1985, Case joined with Washington investor James V. Kimsey to set up an on-line service for people who owned Commodore 64 computers. Before long, the service attracted users of other computer brands, and as subscribers swelled to more than a hundred thousand, the company renamed itself—America Online.

Though miniscule in comparison with America Online's current 31 million members, those original hundred thousand paying customers were evidence that Case and Kimsey had identified a demand segment worth pursuing. Significantly, this sector wasn't defined by their type of computer or software, by demographics, or by their technical expertise. America Online chose to serve a demand segment defined by their demand for a service that would enable people to explore and use the Web's capacities in their personal and professional lives.

Case thought that his targeted customers would stay with America Online as long as using it remained easy. They would be even more likely to remain loyal if the content was continuously enriched and the community of subscribers enlarged. Furthermore, Case believed that if America Online satisfied its customers' needs, those customers would not be particularly concerned with its cost. Thought through like a true Demand Strategist!

When America Online introduced a flat monthly rate of $19.95 for unlimited Internet access, skeptics called it a recipe for disaster. In fact, America Online did face a serious problem, but not the one it was warned about. The flat-fee subscription attracted such a torrent of new business that incoming phone lines were flooded for weeks. Delays multiplied and customers' temperatures rose. Case hired new operators and installed new phone lines by the thousands, and only narrowly averted disaster. Emerging from the crisis stronger and more popular than ever, America Online had signed up millions of new subscribers.

The company's key to survival in its intensely competitive industry has been its ability to create new services in response to new demands; its overall strategy has been what Case calls "AOL Anywhere." In his relentless pursuit of his goal, Case proclaimed in 1999: "You can already check e-mail on your Palm Pilot, and soon you will be able to chat with online buddies while watching your favorite TV show, or retrieve stock quotes over your smart phone." The remarkable and continuous success of America Online is due, in large measure, to its brilliance in framing and understanding demand and, based on that knowledge, building supply that aligns closely with it.

In 1999, AOL and Time Warner announced their intention to merge. In addition to vast new resources of content, the acquisition gave America Online an enormously expanded convergence capacity through Time Warner's cable system, which serves 20 percent of U.S. cable subscribers.

By leveraging its early grasp of the forces and factors shaping its industry, and by targeting and satisfying the sectors within those demand segments that are looking for simplicity and convenience, America Online has been able to sustain relatively high monthly fees. By providing unique benefits that millions of subscribers feel they can't find elsewhere, it has earned highly inelastic pricing power. In my view, this is the company's most impressive accomplishment. Now, when it makes exclusive partnership agreements with other companies, it often requires the prospective partner to pay a significant fee for the privilege of being associated with the America Online brand. And unlike many less successful companies, America Online remains unceasingly steadfast in its focus on and pursuit of strategies that align with its Demand Value Proposition of simplicity, convenience, and ubiquity. Indeed, now it is in a position to influence and shape additional demand forces and industry factors as they emerge.

Successfully implementing Demand Strategy requires that your company concentrate on the forces and factors that may precipitate even a slight change in your most profitable customers' demands. And the fact is, every company and demand segment is vulnerable to uncertainties—economic slumps, changes in government regulation, or alterations in popular fashion or taste.

For example, when consumers became concerned with the level of fat in their foods, ConAgra, Inc., introduced Healthy Choice frozen meal entrees. It became one of the most successful responses in several years to a change in demand in the food industry. The president of Healthy Choice, Jim Tindall, asked me to architect a three-year growth plan for his new product line. Applying Demand Strategy, we proposed an orderly way to introduce new Healthy Choice products. We thoroughly architected the products, the sequence of introductions, and the product attributes required in order to use the Healthy Choice brand. It's called the Healthy Choice gauntlet. Today, Healthy Choice dominates the low- and no-fat division of most of ConAgra's categories in the United States, from deli meats to popcorn to desserts, in part because the company recognized the emerging multibillion-dollar demand and immediately set out to satisfy it.

You must have a thorough understanding of your own company's operations, and its place in its industry and in the world, before you can accurately identify your most profitable customer groups. Among the questions you should ask yourself about each demand segment you consider:

- How will current and emerging forces and factors change my demand segment?
- What are the current and probable future growth rates of the segment?
- What channels of supply and distribution are important to this segment? Will they be important tomorrow?
- What is my company's strength in these channels vis-à-vis its competitors?
- Do I have the logistics required to compete profitably in these segments?
- What is the rate of innovation among companies serving this segment?
- What profit margins can I expect in this business or from this demand segment?
- How much capital will I need to enter or stay in this business?
- What new technologies are likely going to be required in the near future and beyond? Do we have them? Will our capital expenditure budgets make it possible for us to get them?
- Is the technology required already available, and do our current employees know how to use it?

- How would our company's cost structure compare with those of our current and potential competitors?
- Do our company's core capabilities align with the needs of this demand segment?
- How strong is our brand, and how valuable is it in the context of this demand segment?
- What will our marketing costs be if we select this demand segment? Is there elasticity in pricing? Are these customers likely to be loyal?
- What are the geographic opportunities if we select this demand segment?
- Is our product sufficiently differentiated so that it meets Adam Smith's rule of scarcity/nonsubstitutability?

Companies rarely invest the time and effort to perform this kind of analysis, which may explain their mediocre success.

If there is only one thing about your business that you can be absolutely certain of, it is that it will evolve and change continually in response to demand forces and industry factors. Therefore, you have to learn how to analyze your position in the business universe, and understand which of your potential demand segments are going to yield you the most profit.

These are just a few of the considerations involved in selecting demand segments for a relatively uncomplicated business. They are intended to help you think through how to identify and serve those demand segments that will be the most lucrative for you. Selecting the right demand segments can make the difference between the success and failure of your business.

CHAPTER 6

THE THIRD PRINCIPLE

Build Enduring Value Propositions Through Differentiation

nce you have established which groups of customers can bring you the highest profits, the next step is to convert that information and the insights you've developed into profit. That is the subject of this chapter.

In order to succeed, it is essential that you align your product or service with an unsatisfied need within your selected demand segment. At the same time, assess how your competitors are differentiating their offers.

Each step involved in building a Demand Strategy will, itself, provide a wellspring of information. And, as a company's fact base grows, so will its understanding of the marketplace.

Once you've completed the forces and factors analysis, you should be far more familiar with what creates and changes demand in your marketplace. As a result of the demand segmentation you conducted, you now know which customer groups have the potential to offer your company the highest profits, as well as a wealth of facts about the demand of these groups and how to satisfy them. Now you are ready to build your business's Demand Value Proposition, or DVP. The DVP contains the four to six specific strategies that define how you intend to compete.

Every Demand Value Proposition has multiple platforms, or planks; while the individual planks of the Demand Value Proposition are important in and of themselves, together they form an integrated picture of your proposition and the value you promise to deliver.

A DVP defines what customers can expect when they use your product or service; simply put, it is the promise you make to those customers, as well as a summary of the strategy you will use to compete. The DVP should offer many advantages and benefits to your targeted market or markets.

Companies tend to fall into one of two camps: those that have an enduring strategy and those that resort to episodic strategies. An enduring strategy is one that has proven to be successful in the marketplace over time. While it evolves along with the industry and is responsive to changes in demand, its key planks and promises change very little over the years regarding the benefits and value it offers customers.

A company with an episodic strategy is perpetually seeking the right customer proposition; toward that end, it attempts a different approach periodically—every two years or so—which can be confusing to customers. The downside to this is that customers may avoid the company's product or service because they can't be sure what to expect.

In my experience, companies with episodic strategies lack the information, the comprehension of the market, and the confidence that are required to create a successful, competitive proposition.

In almost every instance, highly successful companies use an enduring strategy. With companies such as Mercedes, the Walt Disney Company, McDonald's Corporation, GE, Wal-Mart, and Microsoft Corporation, the fact that their strategies are known to both competitors and customers doesn't matter, because their operations and execution are so superior. They are much like the legendary Green Bay Packers coached by Vince Lombardi in the 1960s. You knew Paul Hornung or Jim Taylor would run the ball to the left side of the field, but knowing what they were going to do didn't make any difference. The Packer running backs and offensive line were so exceptional that they succeeded anyway.

Companies with episodic strategies change their competitive formulas as well as their go-to-market strategies regularly in a ceaseless effort to discover a formula that will enable them to beat their competitors (competitors who, most likely, have enduring strategies). In twenty-five years of consulting with Fortune 500 companies around the world, I have never known a company with an episodic strategy that won consistently. Companies need an enduring Demand Value Proposition to have both the discipline to adhere to their propositions' principles and the flexibility to update them as times change. Employing and executing enduring strategies are fundamental to success. Every time a customer purchases something, he or she does so with a specific expectation of how it will perform. A well-executed, enduring strategy will meet or exceed expectations; an episodic strategy surprises customers, which is usually tantamount to disappointing them, since they had clear expectations for the product when they bought it.

All successful Demand Value Propositions have multiple planks. Why? First, because all products and services offer several benefits. In addition, the multiple planks, when taken together, create an integrated value proposition that is greater than the sum of its individual parts.

McDonald's, for example, doesn't win because of its playgrounds for kids, or because it is fast and friendly. It wins because its Demand Value Proposition combines several individual benefits to create a whole that is appealing to parents and kids.

The success of Wal-Mart Stores, too, is the result of its DVP. Wal-Mart leads on several planks: low price, availability of products, excellent quality for the dollar, and friendly service, just to name a few.

Appealing to a demand segment with multiple planks protects a company from its competitors. Although a competitor may imitate one or two of your benefits, it is nearly impossible to replicate all of them.

McDonald's enjoys market dominance because of its strong brand and compelling Demand Value Proposition. It might appear, at first glance, that fast food is a commodity business in which price is the customer's primary determinant. But that overlooks McDonald's clear differentiation: even if its hamburgers were more expensive than Wendy's or Burger King, its total value proposition—fast and good-tasting, family friendly, clean, part of the local community, and above all, fun—is what truly distinguishes it from the pack. Its DVP is tailored specifically to its target segment, parents and kids. McDonald's has a formula that, thus far, has been impossible to duplicate; many competitors have tried, and though a few succeed on some planks, none has been able to outperform McDonald's entire Demand Value Proposition.

Forty years after Ray Kroc started the company, McDonald's is still competing on its quick, efficient service. As a result of its superior operations, each restaurant strives to live up to its commitment to deliver fast, friendly, and efficient service.

The next plank is the restaurants' cleanliness, which is, of course, critical. If customers find a restaurant's facilities unclean, they will worry about the state of the kitchen and the care with which the food is prepared. Therefore, despite McDonald's enormous traffic every day, each restaurant is exceedingly clean.

Another feature of the McDonald's chain is its consistency. Whether you are in Frankfort, Kentucky, or Frankfurt, Germany, the products taste exactly the same. At McDonald's, customers know exactly what to expect, from the physical arrangement of the counter and tables to the food. And it is that consistency that keeps them coming back again and again, wherever they may be.

The next plank in the McDonald's hypothesized Demand Value Proposition is its commitment to children. Through Ronald McDonald and other McDonaldland characters, movie tie-in toys, in-store play areas, and Happy Meals, the company strives to win the hearts and minds of young customers, whose loyalty it may keep for life. By stimulating demand among children, McDonald's wins entire families because parents know both what to expect and that their kids will love it.

Few people are aware of the last plank in the McDonald's Demand Value Proposition: its community appeal. In addition to its national advertising agencies, the company has an ad agency in each of the 213 largest cities in the United States. It uses these relationships to keep abreast of local demand and to learn about that particular community. The agencies create advertising and develop promotions that are tailored to meet the specific needs and lifestyles of each local community.

Together, these five planks—quick service and good-tasting food, cleanliness, consistency, special attention to children, and community citizenship—are the premises upon which the McDonald's enduring value proposition competes.

The McDonald's Demand Value Proposition		
Customer Demand	*McDonald's Hypothesized Value Proposition ("The Supply")*	*Customer Belief System*
"My life is so hectic . . . when I need something done, I need it done quickly and painlessly."	Quick Service	"They're happy I'm there, but I can still get in and out."
"I like to deal with people who take pride in what they do."	Cleanliness	"The restaurants are so clean, I know they pay attention to quality in everything they do."
"I don't like surprises. I'm more comfortable with things that are familiar and consistent."	Consistency	"I know what I'm going to get every time. I won't be disappointed."
"It's important to do things as a family that my children are sure to enjoy."	Commitment to Kids	"I loved it as a kid so I'll share that same joy with my children."
"My neighborhood is important to me. We live here."	Community	"McDonald's knows me, they care about people, I know them. I feel comfortable with them."

Companies with enduring strategies win because once a customer has a positive experience with a company the first time, she has expectations for the next time, which, when met, reinforce her first perception. Although Demand Value Propositions are aimed at the customers who will bring the highest profits, they are not intended to exclude other demand segments. A company's high-profit target segments should deliver anywhere from 50 to 60 percent of its sales volume. The remaining volume will come from other demand segments that use its products occasionally or are widening their choices of products and services.

If I am working with an organization employing Demand Strategy, I need to understand the demand priorities and the needs of many different customers. But it is the high-profit-yielding customers who *select* the planks that make up the company's specific value proposition. We use groups of six to eight people from the high-profit-yielding demand segment to test different planks. The groups are encouraged to select the eight to ten best planks, as well as the five that they would most want the product to give them. Eventually, we are able to winnow the various planks down to those that are the most important to this particular demand segment.

Every product and business generates a belief system among its customers based on what customers experience, hear, or learn about the product or business. By building a value proposition around demand, targeted customer segments should develop a belief system in which your product/business best satisfies their demand.

What's surprising is how basic most of the winning combinations of value proposition planks tend to be. In most cases customers want what the company originally seemed to promise them—benefits that may no longer be delivered due to budget issues, changes in strategy, or failure to align with customer demand.

Among the actual perpetrators of unfulfilled promises are a worldwide bank with an intolerably high error rate in checking account statements, an airline where surliness seemed to be their middle name, and a food company that had cost-reduced all the taste out of their food. I've never encountered a customer group that asked for anything extra or out of the ordinary. For the most part, they want the product to "work well" and the customer to be treated well.

Once the Demand Value Proposition has been drafted, its planks should be reviewed by members of senior management to determine their practicality and profitability. If you find a substantial gap between where the company is today and where the customers want it to be, that gap most likely cannot be closed in a single year. Rather, you need to implement changes based on a logical sequence that often lasts two to three years. But you should be able to see the results of the changes almost immediately through improved sales, repeat purchases, and higher profits. The idea couldn't be easier. Give people more of what they want and they'll buy it—again and again.

Building a proprietary Demand Value Proposition is not complex. Having completed the forces and factors analysis, you already know much more about your high-profit-yielding customers than before. The next thing to do is to prioritize their demands.

Before I begin the process with a company, I ask the company's top ten to twenty executives to complete the value proposition that *they* believe is most desired by their customers. In reviewing the managers' results, I consistently find a 70 percent variance within the group.

In other words, even when executives who have worked together for years identify the demand in their market, there is little agreement on what demand they must satisfy and on differentiation versus competition.

From this exercise, senior managers can immediately see the differences that exist internally. It can be a powerful way to point out the gaps between what they think their customers want and what their customers say they want. Once they see the incongruity, management teams tend to become markedly more open to change and markedly more open-minded.

For example, The Cambridge Group asked the ten senior managers of a money center bank we were working with, including the CEO, to identify the five things their most valuable customers want from this world-famous bank. In essence, we were asking them to write out the Demand Value Proposition for their organization. When we reviewed the results, we found that no two managers produced the same version of the proposition. Moreover, they listed only a few items that coincided with the highest priorities of their targeted customers.

If the senior leadership of an organization doesn't agree on the proposition the company is offering to customers, it has a big problem.

When that same leadership is out of touch with its customers' priorities, it has an even bigger problem.

We recognized that phenomenon in our work with the Bank Administration Institute (BAI). The BAI realized that the nature of the demand for financial services had shifted so dramatically that banks needed to change the fundamental ways in which they compete. In light of that, at BAI's Retail Delivery Conference at the end of 2000, they focused on Demand Strategy. Hundreds of bankers were asked to vote on what they perceived to be consumers' highest banking priorities. While almost 50 percent of the bankers thought that consumers would pay a fee for ongoing financial advice and planning, only 20 percent of consumers were interested in doing so. And while nearly 80 percent of the bankers felt that consumers would be more likely to bank on-line if their privacy were guaranteed, only 28 percent of consumers felt that way.

Without a fact base, even the most astute managers cannot accurately predict what customers want. Many of the managers were promoted into the executive ranks fifteen or twenty years earlier, and as a result, few had any ongoing contact with customers. Many of them had lost touch with how demand was changing.

Whether the variance between senior management's views and the customers' is 25 percent or 75 percent, the company cannot maximize its results if it is not aligned with the demand of the customers who yield the highest profit. Furthermore, no company can achieve its full potential until all members of senior management are working together toward the same goal. When I first asked the senior managers to complete the DVP, I anticipated a much closer alignment between them. But these inconsistencies explain a good deal about why so many companies fail to fulfill the potential of their people and their products. One of the great benefits of the Demand Value Proposition is its use as a guide for aligning senior management.

To illustrate my point, let me relate an incident that occurred in the boardroom of a very large Midwestern food company. Our objective in working with management was to determine why the company's growth and profitability were less than its competitors'. I recommended to the chairman that each major business unit (there were five) send its top three or four people to participate in a Demand Strategy session. At the session, each senior officer described his or her own understanding of the current marketplace and what could be done to accelerate growth and profitability. At the end of the session, the chairman announced in a soft voice, "I think the answer is we're forging sideways."

The CEO realized that although the business was being run by excellent people, they were moving in separate directions, and on some very important issues in completely opposite directions. People in manufacturing attributed the company's problems to poor forecasting by people in sales. The marketing department thought more money should be invested in advertising in order to grab market share. The sales force believed their products were priced too high relative to the competitors' prices. And so on. The managers had different perspectives on what was causing the problem and each was trying to solve it in a different way. But in fact, the problem was inherent in the company's management processes.

In my experience, a business performs at its best when its people share common goals and strategies, and when its products or services are designed to address two particular objectives: *relevance* to the targeted demand segment and *differentiation* from what the competition is offering.

The importance of relevance and differentiation was confirmed by a comprehensive study of how businesses and brands fare, conducted by the advertising agency Young & Rubicam. Y&R's comprehensive study, the largest of its kind, looked at the responses of 185,000 people in forty countries and evaluated nearly twenty thousand brands, from snack foods to high-tech equipment. The bottom line: to succeed, you must make your product stand apart from the competition in ways that are meaningful to customers. Nothing, Y&R discovered, drives future earnings, future earnings growth rates, future margins, pricing power, and market performance more than relevance and differentiation.

By relevance I mean the benefits of a product or service that are meaningful to and hold value for your targeted demand segments. Simply put, relevance is a measure of how important a value proposition is to a given customer or segment of customers. It is the critical starting point for all customer relationships. If a product or service is not relevant, or gradually loses its relevance, it will fail.

Differentiation measures an offer's uniqueness, both in absolute terms and in relation to competitive offers. As I've stated before, undifferentiated products are, in fact, commodities that compete solely on the basis of price. Meaningfully differentiated goods, on the other hand, command a price premium in the market. What we call differentiation is what Adam Smith referred to as scarcity, or nonsubstitutability. Differentiated and relevant offers have greater price inelasticity: as their prices increase, their sales decline only slightly, if at all.

Interestingly, the Y&R study found that if a business or brand loses its differentiation, it will in all likelihood see a decline in profits as well as in the overall health of the company or its products. The financial consulting firm Stern Stewart, creator of the economic value added (EVA) framework, analyzed Y&R's data and reported that the most highly differentiated brands and businesses had, on average, 50 percent higher operating margins and 108 percent higher operating earnings.

The extent to which a product is differentiated from its competition can also indicate future shareholder value. Brands and businesses that were strongly differentiated grew in market value by 35 percent in 1998, compared with a 12 percent growth on brands that were less well differentiated. In 1999, the gap between the two was even sharper: highly differentiated businesses grew by 45 percent, while less differentiated ones grew by 20 percent.

Clearly, developing a Demand Value Proposition with and for your most valuable customers, one that is aligned to deliver to your targeted segment, is critical because it will enable you to achieve greater relevance and higher differentiation. You can be sure that if you are unable to articulate a DVP that is distinctive and compelling, neither will your customers.

Recently we consulted with a major high-technology company that needed help developing its Demand Value Proposition for its targeted business customers. We conducted demand qualitative groups with leading-edge customers to understand their needs and to test and refine potential value proposition planks. Once the qualitative portion was completed, we tested the whole new proposition quantitatively, and the client was delighted by the extremely strong results.

Once the company delivered on its Demand Value Proposition, customer interest (which we measured by assessing the likelihood of the company receiving repeat business) went up by 125 percent—indicating a corresponding market share increase in double digits. In this business, each share point is worth more than $1 billion.

These extraordinary results aren't limited to the high-tech industry. We have seen similar outcomes in service businesses and packaged goods companies. When the Demand Value Proposition is aligned with the targeted group's demand, relevance and differentiation increase dramatically, which triggers a jump in preference and usage. The consistency of these findings can be attributed to the economics at the core of Demand Strategy. When built and executed correctly, the Demand Value Proposition enhances value for the targeted demand segment by closely aligning a company's products and benefits with the demand the target is trying to satisfy.

As I discussed in Chapter 1, value is increased either by raising benefits or by lowering price. Being in tune with actual demand augments the product's benefits and relevance, which in turn increases the total perceived value. Of course, this is predicated on the assumption that you have studied your targeted demand segments closely. After all, without an extensive understanding of them, you cannot align with their demand effectively.

THE DEMAND VALUE PROPOSITION

At The Cambridge Group, we arrive at an organization's Demand Value Proposition by following these steps:

1. Agreement is reached on the most important demand present among our target segments. This is determined by the forces and factors analysis and the process of demand segmentation. To compile a thorough list, we include all of the demands, regardless of

how well or poorly the company is currently performing on those dimensions.

2. Each demand is described on a simple white set of boards and presented to the qualitative demand groups, which are composed of customers from the segments yielding the highest profits. Though other segments aren't involved in building the proposition, their views are included when the propositions are quantified and exposed to a full range of customers.

3. Eight to twelve demand groups are conducted with customers from targeted, high-value segments. Though demand groups resemble focus groups, they differ in important ways, including the fact that each group is made up only of customers from one segment. During each demand group, twenty to twenty-five possible enduring platforms are presented and discussed.

4. During the last half hour of a two-hour meeting, the ten platforms that received the most support are presented to the customers again. Then they are asked to select, in order of importance, the five or six platforms that form their ideal concept. It is always encouraging and invigorating for clients to see how uncomplicated it can be to design a highly differentiated winning proposition in their category. Since most companies are accustomed to driving their propositions from the supply side, they usually haven't realized how many important demands were not being addressed.

As a side note, we at Cambridge believe that most companies don't conduct qualitative or focus group research correctly. We have a hard-and-fast rule that in any demand group of eight customers, all eight must belong to the same target segment. If they don't, opinions and benefits sought are so different that the meeting becomes discordant and confusing, and the only way for customers to reach agreement is to water down and generalize concepts so that each target finds something desirable. For example, if one demand segment loves chocolate cookies and another loves vanilla, and they are both equally represented in a demand focus group, the only hope you have of reaching even a modest level of agreement is if you offer a Neapolitan cookie.

This is unacceptable if the goal is to learn as much as possible to differentiate your product as much as possible.

Let me give you an illustration. My partner Bruce Onsager recently created a demand segmentation for an airline client. One of the segments identified as most valuable was comprised of the 9 percent of the airline's passengers who were not price sensitive and represented 47 percent of its revenues. Senior management realized that building an airline that gave preferred service to this 9 percent—which represented 47 percent of the revenue—was a much better investment than aiming to fill all seats by offering discounts.

Before we began to work with this airline, they had conducted extensive research with a random selection of customers and discovered that one of the greatest unmet demands was for entertainment consoles installed at every seat. But when we asked the highest-profit-yielding 9 percent what they would most like to see the airline add or change, they wanted a more comfortable seat. Frequent fliers wanted a comfortable seat in which to work during the first leg of their trip and to rest or sleep on the return flight. They viewed entertainment units as unnecessary and were in the bottom quartile of what they wanted the airline to add to their planes.

Typically, when the customers finish designing the four to six platforms that meet their demand, we ask them to explain the rationale behind the particular package that they assembled.

The airline's most valuable customers helped construct a Demand Value Proposition consisting of six key planks. First and foremost, they needed access to their destinations across the country and around the globe. Second, unsurprisingly, they wanted their travel experiences, whether to the next state or overseas, to be seamless so they could focus on work. The third plank involved the need for airline employees to assume more responsibility and to address more actively the problems that arise when bad weather or faulty equipment leads to flight delays or cancellations. They also wanted the airline to provide more information so that passengers could evaluate situations on their own and make alternative plans. Instead—many felt—the airlines patronized them by withholding information and making decisions for them.

Fourth, these frequent fliers wanted to be recognized and treated as the important passengers they are. In their view, they had earned privileges that other travelers had not, such as early boarding, upgrades, and more frequent flyer miles. Fifth, having ample space was a high priority as well. And finally, these travelers wanted attentive, professional service from all airline personnel, from reservations agents and gate agents to the flight crew.

That clients are usually surprised by the fundamental nature of the customers' propositions has a disturbing implication. It means that most companies fail to deliver some very basic demands to customers and, as a result, have trouble establishing loyalty. Instead, these businesses are perpetually increasing promotional budgets in order to reach their sales objectives, without addressing what customers really want.

The obvious answer is to figure out which demand segments are the most valuable to you and to give these people what they need. They will pay a higher price, your promotion costs will decrease, and your customers' loyalty will increase significantly.

In the airline industry, we found management was focusing on the critically important *what* aspects: safety, efficient operations, flight schedules, and frequent flyer programs. But the most valued passengers were concentrating on *how*. Safety was expected; what they were demanding was better service and easier methods for making and changing what are frequently extremely complicated travel plans.

As businesspeople, we understand the complexities involved in making the operational changes that customers want. Still, it is worth underscoring that the demands themselves are quite basic. In virtually every industry—food, high technology, apparel, financial services—we find that customers' unmet needs are for the most part elementary. When companies make appropriate investments to satisfy them, pricing becomes more inelastic—that is, you don't have to lower prices— and revenues, customer loyalty, and profitability increase rapidly.

Over the years, my colleagues and I at The Cambridge Group have developed some principles, about which we feel strongly, regarding what constitutes an enduring DVP. To begin with, each plank is predicated on the assumption that a business can differentiate itself from competition on this platform. And each plank should be consistent with the core competencies and brand equities of the business. Before including a plank (which, after all, is a promise to your most important customers) make sure you can fulfill it. The plank should address an issue on which you can win, or at least demonstrate superiority. It must represent a goal toward which resources can be allocated, so it allows you to track and evaluate its progress. Finally, the plank should be part of an enduring and sustainable strategy that moves the company or product forward, as opposed to an episodic response to a market or competitive change.

Let's return to the proposed value propositions prepared by the members of senior management, which turned out to reflect very different demands from those actually expressed by their customers. We have found that management rarely has a clear and unified idea about what customers value the most. Putting the two—management's view and the targeted customers' view—alongside each other is called performing a *gap analysis*: specifically, it explains the extent of these differences, and explores how much of what customers need is lacking in a company's performance.

Helping senior managers see the discrepancies between their current market propositions and those that represent the demand of the customers who generate the highest profits is not easy. In effect, you are telling managers that significant issues are holding the company back from performing better. However, quantifying the qualitative results allows you to advance the discussion from one that can be rationalized away, and therefore dismissed. With the fact base, you have incontestable data derived directly from the customers' views.

Let me give you a brief example that illustrates my point. One of my partners at The Cambridge Group, Jason Green, was working with one of the world's largest high-technology companies. Though this company had been enjoying superior results, it missed some of its performance objectives. It was at that point that the company called us.

By the time we got involved, the company's senior management had already prepared and had preliminary agreement on a five-platform proposition that defined how they would compete in their increasingly crowded marketplace. The proposition that Jason and his team completed after working with our client's customers was dramatically different from the one designed and approved by the client's senior management. In fact, the quantitative research reflected that if the company adopted Jason's recommended Demand Value Proposition based on the customers yielding the highest profits, it could gain as many as 16 share points, worth roughly $16 billion.

The Demand Value Proposition is inextricably tied to the value equation. Since the value decision is critical to a business's long-term success, senior management often modifies the proposition created by its customers, while still trying to preserve the essence of the platform. The degree of inelastic pricing that can be attained frequently surprises senior management; feeling yoked to certain price points, they didn't consider offering benefits that would earn greater loyalty and higher profits.

With an accurate fact base of customer data, a company can model specific scenarios on an ongoing basis. Cambridge has developed one such tool, Customer Demand Analysis (CDA), which measures overall demand potential as well as customers' preferences for various product features and brands. Using it, we can identify the features that customers want most, and then measure the price premium they are willing to pay for them. The capacity to translate the sought-after benefits and features into an integrated Demand Value Proposition is crucial for delivering the right offer to the right customers at the right price. In addition, it can determine the potential payout for improving a particular aspect of the value proposition or key aspects of the brand's equity.

Although CDA is our proprietary approach, there are other tools available that are like it. The specific tool you use is, of course, less important than ensuring that you get the insights you need. The key is to make certain that the approach and the specific tool you use will generate an accurate picture of demand.

With both a structured understanding of demand and an enduring value proposition that satisfies that demand, you can significantly increase and sustain long-term profits. You will also be insulated from competition by making your offerings more relevant to your targeted customers and more differentiated in the marketplace.

COMMERCE BANCORP

Commerce Bancorp of Cherry Hill, New Jersey, is an excellent example of a company that has applied Demand Strategy to develop a successful Demand Value Proposition. A midsize regional retail bank with about 185 branches, Commerce has been outperforming its competition by defying the conventional wisdom of its industry. It targeted a demand segment that most other banks have ignored and built a unique Demand Value Proposition to satisfy it.

Retail banking has been affected by numerous demand forces and industry factors that have worked to decrease demand for its services. Among the most critical of these is government deregulation, which has allowed new competitors to enter the banking industry, including insurance companies, brokerages, and out-of-state banks. In turn, this has paved the way for the industry's consolidation through mergers and acquisitions. Moreover, by changing the fundamental requirements that traditional bricks-and-mortar banks now have to meet, as well as introducing new Internet-based banks, technology has altered the competitive landscape. As a result, most banks are focusing on how to increase their loan portfolios rather than on how to fund their loans.

The portfolios' growth has caused banks to rely increasingly on expensive wholesale sources, such as commercial money markets, to fund them. In doing so, the banks have in large part bypassed core deposits (funds from customers' checking, savings, and money market accounts), despite the fact that these funds are cheaper and the depositors who provide them are usually more loyal to the bank.

The forces and factors affecting banks have created significant profit pressures for many of them. After a wave of consolidation, many banks were forced to make their mergers and acquisitions—often justified in terms of creating new cost efficiencies and boosting profits—pay off. However, the spreads they earned between loan and deposit rates (the *net interest margin*) were squeezed between the intrinsically high cost of funds and competition to provide the best rates to borrowers. To improve profits, many banks turned to the "80/20 theory"—that 80 percent of bank profits come from 20 percent of banking customers.

Banks that have used the 80/20 theory have done so in two ways.

First, they concluded that they should lavish attention on the 20 percent of customers who generate most of the profit. Second, they believed they should find ways to make a profit on the other 80 percent by cutting services, adding fees, or dropping the 80 percent altogether. The 80/20 theory was convenient for the banks that wanted to cut costs in order to stimulate profitability and take advantage of the synergies that were necessary to make their acquisitions work. Many banks cut the services offered to the majority 80 percent of their customers while, at the same time, they added a host of new fees.

The individual branches, which represent a major cost to a bank, were among the first victims of the cuts. Entire branches were eliminated, employees were fired, and in the branches that weren't closed altogether, service hours were reduced. Banks pushed customers to use ATMs and call centers that could handle transactions for a fraction of the cost of a teller.

Given these changes, only the consumers' assumption that it was equally bad elsewhere kept many at their current banks. At this point, with a significant demand segment not being served, Commerce saw its point of entry. While most other banks wooed the sought-after 20 percent, Commerce realized that the 80 percent of customers who were growing more dissatisfied with their banks represented an opportunity.

In my discussion on the Bank Administration Institute (BAI) earlier, in Chapter 5, I identified eight fundamental demand segments relevant to retail banking. Each differs on its specific needs, such as financial goals, the level of personal service desired, risk profile, and confidence in new technologies. Two of these groups are particularly wealthy: the Confident Asset Managers and the Satisfied Plan Followers. Given their relative wealth, it is not surprising that they are often targeted by banks following the 80/20 rule. However, these segments are among the most likely to leave banks to pursue equity investments. They are also the most likely to value professional financial advice from nonbank providers.

The remaining six segments, which many banks overlook, are in fact potentially very attractive, for two reasons. First, with combined assets, they represent significant volume that exceeds what the wealthier groups generate. Second, and more important, four of the six use and need bank services frequently and repeatedly. In other words, members of these segments value banks, form relationships with their branches, and as a result are less likely to leave them in favor of other financial institutions. After identifying these demand segments, Commerce's next question was how to serve them. Despite the fact that the 80/20 theory shaped the strategies of most banks— or perhaps because of it—Commerce was convinced that it could successfully serve customers who valued personal service and convenience.

Vernon Hill, Commerce's chairman and chief executive officer, announced that his bank was "diametrically opposed to the 80/20 rule. It has destroyed more banks in this country than any other theory."

According to Hill, the 80/20 rule makes three fundamentally flawed assumptions: First, it assumes that you can perceive which customers are high profit and which are not. Second, it assumes that customers are static; those that yield high profits today always will. (One problematic implication of this is that you would avoid doing business with a young person who is just starting out, even if his or her earning potential is great.) Finally, it assumes that training employees to differentiate customers, then treat them differently, rather than provide high quality service for all your customers, is desirable.

Commerce's Demand Value Proposition, which describes how it serves its targeted demand, is both a set of promises and the value equation it offers. Built on five major planks, the proposition focuses on convenience, customer service, consistency, simplicity, and innovation. Commerce, modeled on the great power retailers like Home Depot and Wal-Mart, has built a consistent brand that brings the different elements of the value proposition together to deliver what Vernon Hill refers to as a "great retail experience."

In order to adhere to its billing as "America's Most Convenient Bank," Commerce offers seven-day-a-week banking services from seven-thirty in the morning until eight at night. As other banks close branches, reduce hours, and operate with fewer tellers, Commerce is offering more of each. The branches, replete with rest rooms for its customers' convenience, have extended hours, with tellers working on

Commerce Bank's Demand Value Proposition Enables It to Obtain a Price Premium from Its Target Customers	
Commerce Bank's Hypothesized Demand Value Proposition	*Customer Belief System*
Convenience	I truly believe that Commerce is "America's Most Convenient Bank."
Service	I know that Commerce's employees are trained and motivated to provide me with great customer service.
Consistency	At Commerce, no matter which branch I visit, who I talk to, or which channel I use, I will experience the same great retail experience.
Simplicity	I know that Commerce Bank is upfront about their charges and won't try to nickel-and-dime me with fees every time I deal with them.
Innovation	Commerce Bank is committed to finding new ways to make my banking experience easier, faster, and more enjoyable.

weekends, including hours on Sundays and even on holidays. With convenience in mind, it has several branches in each community, and also offers multiple channels, including drive-throughs, ATMs, a 24/7 call center, and on-line banking. Hill pays close attention to demand forces in delivering the plank of convenience. For example, when he chooses the locations for his suburban branches, he is influenced by the fact that women do 85 percent of banking in the suburbs, hence they decide where the family will bank. "So," Hill says, "you design sites that women like. For instance, women, generally speaking, do not like to travel on big, multi-lane highways. They would rather travel on secondary roads that have the local neighborhood commercial district. You put sites there."

Customer service is another cornerstone of its Demand Value Proposition, and Commerce executives monitor it closely by conducting surprise visits, quizzing employees, and offering incentives and awards for superb performers. The bank has established and invested heavily in Commerce University, its own training facility, which was designed with the express purpose of helping employees develop their customer skills. "Obtaining buy-in to the service minded culture is crucial," says Vernon Hill. The company's interest in service is an obsession that has been described as almost cultlike.

Consistency in the retail experience is another essential element of Commerce's value proposition. In conjunction with its high quality of service, all branches have the same look and feel; they have big display windows, distinctive metal roofs, and identical furniture and equipment. The message to customers is that they can always count on the bank to deliver the same excellent retail experience. Unlike those of other banks, Commerce's customers feel welcome at every branch, not just their customary one. In Vernon Hill's analogy to retailing, "A Home Depot is a Home Depot wherever you go."

While other banks have created complicated fees and hidden charges in the fine print of their offers, Commerce's goal is simplicity: free checking for the first year, after which a minimum balance of only $100 is required; free money orders and coin counting and no gimmicks. The trade-off is in the returns. The free checking accounts earn no interest, the savings accounts, money market accounts, and CDs are all 25 to 50 basis points below the market. As Vernon Hill phrases it, "We've learned to gather very low cost of funds, so we can re-invest in the business. We also don't nickel and dime our customers with fees. We basically say to customers, 'Give us your low cost deposits, and we'll give you convenience, no hidden fees, and a great retail experience.'"

Commerce's lower rates on deposits are the value equation that its target demand finds fair. Customers consider the lower returns a fair exchange for the benefits they receive, and the bank earns a premium for delivering them.

Its innovations, focused on improving customer service by speeding up transactions without sacrificing accuracy, have simplified many teller functions; for example, tellers have the capacity to create a deposit receipt with one-touch keystrokes. Commerce's highly successful on-line banking innovations also enhance customer service and satisfaction. Indeed, it was one of the first banks to offer on-line banking, not as an alternative to other channels but in addition, as part of a "clicks and mortar" policy to enhance customer convenience. That its development costs were very low did not stop it from receiving *Forbes*'s Best of Web award; moreover, its 28 percent on-line penetration rate is the highest of any bank in the United States. Interestingly, Commerce's research indicates that the average customer who banks on-line still visits a branch several times a month.

Commerce Bancorp's value proposition relies on the premise that the whole is greater than the sum of the parts. Because its success isn't driven by any single plank of the proposition, CEO Hill believes that he has insulated his bank from competitors. He asserts: "Our competition can't copy us—they could copy parts of what we do, but not everything. They would have to completely retool management, culture, fees, and delivery system. They would have to start all over."

Commerce's approach has led to spectacular results. By focusing on an underserved customer segment and offering them a compelling value proposition, the company has been able to attract and retain core deposits—checking, savings, and money market accounts—from loyal customers. This has translated into a huge funding advantage: Commerce's cost of funds is just 2 percent, compared to 4 percent for the many banks that compete for funding from wholesale deposits.

Offering cheaper funds enables Commerce to deliver the "great retail experience" promised by its value proposition. These funds also allow the bank to pursue less risky loan opportunities—which add stability to revenues and profits—and to reinvest in the business. The company's net interest margin (the spread between lending and deposit rates), at 4.8 percent, is 50 percent higher than that of competitors, such as Fifth Third Bank, which is certainly considered a high-performance bank.

In contrast to the near zero growth of its competitors, Commerce's strategic choice to focus on an underserved segment has created enormous growth and profits: between 1997 and 2001, revenues grew by 27 percent a year, net income grew by 26 percent, and earnings per share increased by 17 percent. These increases mean that Commerce's earnings are growing 78 percent faster than the industry's. In addition, deposits grew faster than those of any publicly held bank in the United States, with an average rate of 21 percent per year from 1996 to 2000. In 2001 deposits grew 33 percent. Wall Street has approved of Commerce's performance; its stock price has almost tripled from what it was in the years 1995 to 2000, while the average bank stock rose about 120 percent during that period.

More important for the long-term success of the bank, it has a large and growing account base and rapid deposit growth. Between 1997 and 2001, Commerce's deposits grew 26 percent annually; by comparison, First Union, a large bank that competes in the same geographic area, saw deposits grow at an anemic 1 percent per year. Commerce now has more than 1 million accounts, a figure that is being augmented by forty-five thousand new accounts per month.

Like the very successful retailers that it seeks to emulate, Commerce closely tracks performance at the store level. Its average deposits are $74 million per branch, versus $29 million per branch for its competitors. In the category of "same store growth," a critical measure of success among retailers, it is also strong. Among branches established for two years or more, Commerce's deposits grew 16.5 percent between 2000 and 2001.

Shareholders have been richly rewarded for investing in Commerce Bank. Its rapid growth earns it a price-earnings multiple of 22, versus an average of 10 for leading banks. Moreover, between 1991 and 2001 the stock rose nearly twentyfold. During this period, its total return was 30 percent higher than Microsoft's, 170 percent higher than GE's, 180 percent higher than Berkshire Hathaway's, and 660 percent higher than the S&P 500's.

As it looks toward the future, Commerce Bank is very open about its strategy and growth objectives. Vernon Hill explains, "Our growth rates continue to go up, despite the fact that they should flatten out based on our size. We are growing fast, even on a larger base." The bank plans to grow organically—rather than through acquisitions—by refining, then re-creating, its demand strategy. It seeks to establish twelve hundred new branches in the Northeast corridor from Washington, D.C., to Boston and generate $100 billion over a ten-year period. Observing that "no successful retailer has ever built itself based on M&A," Hill plans to leverage what he refers to as the "power retailer" model. If Commerce succeeds in its objective, it will become one of the ten largest banks in the country.

Commerce Bancorp's success illustrates the value of differentiation when the goal is to generate growth, profits, and shareholder value. It is a core part of its strategy. Says Vernon Hill, "We look at differentiation every day"; the bank is diligent in its relentless effort to ensure that the difference between Commerce and its competitors is always 180 degrees.

The list of differences starts with the business model. While traditional banks have high-cost funds, low-cost operations, and no growth, Commerce has low-cost funds, higher operating costs, and profitable growth. According to Hill: "Traditional banks try to cost-save their way to prosperity," while at Commerce, "we invest our way to prosperity." The cost-saving approach, he believes, degrades the retail experience as banks are unable to reinvest in the business. Moreover, once a branch is broken, it is often impossible to fix. Internal growth falls off, and banks have to resort to mergers, which only worsens the problem.

Traditional banks believe and act as though customers are rate driven. But Hill counters this idea: "We think customers are experience-driven, not rate-driven. A bank you like is the bank you'll use." To illustrate the point, he shows data from a 1997 survey by the *ABA Banking Journal*, in which customers were asked to rate their primary reasons for choosing their bank. Only 3 percent cited good rates, while 62 percent cited convenience in one form or another. Still, most banks ignore this finding and focus their advertisements almost entirely on rates. Hill bluntly points out: "They're all advertising rates, and we're advertising convenience. But they're working on 3 percent, and we're working on 62 percent."

Traditional banks view branches as cost centers that should be eliminated whenever possible. At Commerce, the branch is a competitive advantage that delivers convenience and service, not a weakness. Branches are where the bank can build and differentiate its brand, and Commerce Bancorp exploits this advantage fully. Its relevance and differentiation has earned Commerce Bancorp rich rewards in the form of growth, profitability, and inelastic pricing.

Given his achievement in a very, very competitive retail banking environment, Vernon Hill's performance is nothing short of brilliant. When you see his inelastic pricing working with a broad cross-section of customers, you can see the power of Demand Strategy. His use of forces and factors, demand segmentation, segment targeting, and differentiation via a unique value proposition all contribute to his superior performance. He's done this during a very difficult time for retail banks while competing against some of America's biggest and best-known bank conglomerates. Does this mean Demand Strategy is guaranteed to work? No, but it is guaranteed to work if you do it as well as Vernon Hill has.

At this point, we're ready to move on to the fourth principle of Demand Strategy—how to identify the strategies and business systems needed to meet demand.

CHAPTER 7

THE FOURTH PRINCIPLE

Identify the Strategies and Business Systems Needed to Meet Demand

trategy is, of course, critical to enduring business success. But even the most brilliant strategy is of little practical value unless you have the right business systems and operational skills to execute it. The most successful Demand Strategists depend upon their strategies to guide their business decisions in the same way architects depend on blueprints. The design and implementation of the four elements of their key business systems—(1) research and customer interface systems, (2) operational processes, (3) organizational functions, and (4) technological support—reflect the Demand Strategies they develop that drive product differentiation and create competitive advantage.

No company has done a better job aligning its strategies and business systems with demand than Capital One Financial Corporation. In fact, Capital One is frequently realigning itself; its systems are so refined that they ensure virtually flawless implementation of the enterprise's Demand Strategy. Capital One has successfully developed and refined all four of the critical business system elements I've outlined. This has given them distinct competitive advantages, as the detailed account that follows will demonstrate. Capital One's entire organization has changed so much that it is, in fact, a very different company from the one that first emerged in 1994.

Capital One was already a going concern when Signet Banking Corporation spun it off. Though its cofounders, CEO Rich Fairbank and President Nigel Morris, did not have a banking background—both had worked as consultants to banks—they were hired by Signet in the late 1980s to run the bank's credit card division, which primarily issued and serviced Visa and MasterCard accounts. They quickly had become innovative leaders in the card industry.

By the mid-1990s, the card business was in considerable foment (as discussed in the account of Sears Credit in Chapter 3). Among the forces and factors at work were rising promotional costs and increasingly heavy competition from new kinds of card issuers (phone companies, automakers, gasoline stations), which treated the cards as a loss leader to develop new purchases and establish ongoing loyalty. In addition there was the rapid improvement in information technology and the growing sophistication of database management and data mining. Capital One's data bank had information on approximately one out of every seven U.S. households—enough information to fill the hard drives of two hundred thousand personal computers. It held records on every customer's interactions with the company, as well as every purchase bought with a Capital One card. Only a few, including Fairbank and Morris, realized that they were sitting on a mountain of information that could be used to remake the world. Their vision led to Capital One's pioneering "information-based strategy."

At the time, two of the most conspicuous forces and factors in the industry—ones that had revolutionized the business—were two that Fairbank and Morris themselves had invented. The first was the teaser rate, which tempted a customer to switch to a new card by offering low introductory interest rates. The second, the balance-transfer option, invited the customer to move his balances from his old card at the new low rate. After two or three months, of course, the introductory rate gave way to a much higher permanent rate.

While these tactics brought a tide of new customers to Signet, by the time Fairbank and Morris began using them at the newly inde-

pendent Capital One they were proving counterproductive. Customers were switching to a card only for the two or three months of
the introductory rate, then switching to another. In effect, the card
companies had trapped themselves in permanently low and unprofitable rates, with the added paperwork costs of transferring accounts
every sixty or ninety days.

All of this made it hard to single out the most profitable customers,
let alone create strategy options for reaching them. The company
found it impossible to make tactical marketplace choices. But Fairbank and Morris were determined to better understand their markets
by using continuous market testing, and to change their product to fit
demand. "When we started this company, we saw two revolutionary
opportunities," Fairbank said. "We could use scientific methodology to
help us make decisions, and we could use information technology to
help us provide mass customization."

The first element of the business system, research and market testing, provided the first clue to finding profitable customers amid the
chaos: it showed that while people were adept at teaser shuffling, they
didn't much relish the hassle; a significant number expressed a preference for a simple card with no annual fee and a steady, relatively low
interest rate. Thus, demand had changed within a few years in this
fast-moving market.

For the next two and a half years, Capital One tested fixed-rate
cards to see if they appealed to those customers. The cards came in
more than a hundred different combinations of interest rates, credit
limits, and detailed terms, but they had eliminated teaser rates and
annual fees.

The most popular card in this competition would result in a high
degree of customer loyalty and low attrition, but it had one problem.
With its low interest rate and the mix of borrowers it would attract,
projections showed that the card would lose money. There would be
too many defaults.

Fortunately, there were strategic options that could save the day.
Working on the data, Capital One's analysts concluded that the one
thing the card needed to turn a profit was a customer base with better
credit risks, and the growing mountain of data in the company's com-

puters made such people easy to find. After more testing, Capital One offered a 9.9 percent card in 1998 to selected low-risk customers. It was an immediate success.

True to Fairbank's vision of mass customization, Capital One varies this formula with a slightly different offer for each customer, tailored to his or her circumstances. If you include every combination of interest rates, fees, credit limits, requirements, and decorations on the face of the card, the company offers six thousand different credit cards today. Its 33 million cardholders—a number that grows at the rate of twenty-five thousand a day—generated nearly $5 billion in revenues in 2000, up from $95 million in 1995.

It was necessary to establish a great deal of contact with the customers for this to work. Capital One had thirty-five hundred employees fielding more than 1 million calls per week from cardholders trying to activate a new card, find out their current balance, question their bills, report lost cards, negotiate an extension, and the like. By 1998, that system was breaking down, requiring Capital One eventually to adjust their operations systems, organizational structure, and technology systems. But first it had to analyze the problems.

First, Capital One discovered that customers' phone calls were simply taking too long. Customers would dial the lost-card number to complain about their bills, or reach billing to report fraud; they had to be transferred, and wait on hold at each step. A balance inquiry required an agent. Customers were angry, and the company's phone bill was rising.

At one point Capital One asked its customers to call less often, which only guaranteed more calls. One executive called it "a Homer Simpson moment."

In one of the most dramatic combinations of operations and technology business systems, the company's technicians suggested intelligent call routing, which at the time seemed impossible. Before a phone call was answered by someone at Capital One, computers would determine the purpose of the call and route it directly to the appropriate agent.

Fortunately, the pieces were in place to make it happen. First, 90 percent of all calls fell into one of ten categories, considerably narrowing the field. The data bank made it technically possible to establish the origin of an incoming call, thus identifying the customer. The computer's data banks could tell that this particular customer's interest rate had just been raised, or that a fraud stop had been put on his card, or just that he called every month to get his balance, so they could be programmed to determine the reason for this call with a high degree of probability. In effect, Capital One had identified attractive demand segments and strategies for meeting their needs. To progress to the technological system that would meet that demand—intelligent call routing—all Capital One needed was a sophisticated software program.

It would have to be dazzling. First came months of analyzing patterns of phone calls and grouping customers into clusters; that was followed by decision-tree programming, custom-built hardware, and of course, endless testing of the results. In 1998, the system finally was put in place, as were the organizational and operational structures to support it. Now, in the one-hundredth of a second between an incoming call's signal and the ring that the customer hears on her end, high-speed computers identify the caller and predict the reason for the call. Next, the computer reviews options based upon twelve different characteristics of the customer—account status, the products he or she already has, and her receptiveness to new campaigns. The call is then routed to the customer service associate who is considered the best match, determined by parameters including availability, skills, and training. The associate's computer displays critical information about the customer, as well as recommendations about suitable products to cross-sell.

Alternatively, the computers may draw their own conclusions and create a shortcut. A customer with a poor credit rating who threatens to leave will be shown how to cancel his or her card interactively, without bothering a representative. A customer who calls often for a balance is automatically answered by a machine: "The amount now due on your account is $587.43. If you have a billing question, press . . ." The question has been answered before it was asked, without tying up an employee's time; a call that might have lasted a minute took only ten seconds.

The company today says the computer predictions are right in 70 percent of all calls, up from 40 percent when the system was first installed. Indeed, the statistics suggest that the system is getting smarter: for example, if a customer calls from her office several times, the computer will associate that number with her as well as her home phone. As the systems grow more sophisticated, they come close to automating Demand Strategy, customer by customer. Soon the computers will be able to figure out language preferences and route calls to agents accordingly.

Marge Connelly, executive vice president of domestic card operations and information technology infrastructure, sums up Capital One's proprietary system this way: "The system gets information about customers and their accounts, and uses rules engines to create intelligence. . . . We have a lot of knowledge that we can apply to balancing the customer's desire for speed with the desire for a high-level experience."

Like many of its competitors, the company had been using bill stuffers and computer-dialed telemarketing to offer its cardholders goods and services ranging from calculators to cruises. But with intelligent call routing, Capital One, employing Demand Strategy, turned this system into the next big revolution of the business, and a major innovation in the field of marketing. "Credit cards aren't banking, they're information," Fairbank said. It was only logical to use the data bank to determine what cardholders wanted that they weren't getting, and to offer it to them. In other words, they are using the system to recognize demand, then developing the supply to meet it.

The spur to action was Capital One's poorly functioning outbound telemarketing system. Calls made at dinnertime were irritating too many customers. Perhaps worse for a company focused on long-term demand, Capital One's surveys showed that even when people bought something over the phone, they frequently never used the products.

The surveys also revealed that if the customer made the call, he or she was more likely to buy something than if the call came from a salesperson. In other words, Capital One realized that each of their millions of incoming calls was a sales opportunity. In hindsight, it seems both brilliant and obvious.

The first big inbound, cross-selling campaign targeted new customers who were required to call an automated line to activate their cards. When that was completed, a representative cut into the call with an offer to assume the unpaid balance from the customer's former card. That technique worked so well that it was expanded to include offers of insurance, long distance telephone service, and memberships in buying clubs—all services or opportunities that a sizable percentage of their customers were at least marginally interested in.

Though they didn't express it this way, Capital One's managers were responding to new sets of demand forces and industry factors that were reshaping competition in the industry. Interestingly, Capital One had created these changes themselves by expanding their database and initiating intelligent call routing. These steps made it possible to identify a new group of profitable customers, for whom new strategy options were created and put in place to meet the demand.

Capital One built a robust and competent strategy; the computers made it easy to make the adaptations that would allow incoming calls to be used for selling. In the one-hundredth of a second before the ring, the computer combed through the caller's records, identified his or her buying habits and demographics, and relayed suggestions for possible purchases to the agent handling the call. Then, when the customer's reason for calling was satisfied, the agent clicked on a blue icon that would reveal the products suggested by the computer. Someone reporting a lost card, for instance, would be a natural prospect for card insurance protection. A person calling to complain about a fee increase could be told how the added benefits of her new card actually saved money—then, because she recently bought a pair of skis, she could be offered a cut-rate weekend ski package.

Even with the successful completion of research and customer interface, technological and operational business systems, Capital One had only three of the four elements it needed in place. Not surprisingly, the fourth—organizational systems—became an issue. The primary organizational problem arose in setting up cross-selling: the agents, who saw their roles as service providers, were uncomfortable becoming salespeople. Capital One's solution was to show the agents how selling is a service. "If I've got this great product," says Marge Connelly, who runs all the Capital One call centers, "it might save a customer some money, or it might create convenience. If I'm committed to service, there's no way I'm not going to consider offering that product."

In operational terms, Capital One chose not to develop its own products to cross-sell. Instead, it partnered with other companies—for insurance, Liberty Mutual; for telephone services, MCI WorldCom; and for mortgages, Countrywide. Capital One now offers approximately three dozen products that are unrelated to their cards, and sells them at a pace of 1 million sales a year. Of its new credit card customers, 57 percent buy something else over the phone. And at this point, it is satisfying demand well beyond its core business of credit cards.

All told, says Rich Fairbank, Capital One is no longer a credit card company but rather "a marketing revolution that can be applied to many businesses." It surveys and tests new ideas relentlessly; in 2000, it ran forty-five thousand marketing tests, which is more than 120 campaigns every business day. Says Peter Schnall, senior vice president of marketing and analysis, "On a daily basis, we re-evaluate which programs are working best and which are working less well." Instead of developing quarterly campaigns, he adds, "we think about how to use our marketing budget day to day."

The test-and-control approach goes back to cofounder Nigel Morris's education in experimental psychology. As he puts it, "A lot of our information-based strategy . . . comes from the notion of empirically measuring consumer behavior and how it works." In the long term, his company's most important assets are the data it has collected about current and potential customers and the skills it has developed at turning that information into systems that deliver Demand Strategy.

Capital One intends to continue to build new systems to meet emerging demand. Perhaps it will do so to such an extent that credit cards will be incidental to its business. Marketing vice president Jory Berson says he wants the company to be the first place people look to find nearly everything: "When you get ready to buy a car, the first thing I want to go through your mind is, 'What kind of deal can Capital One get me on an auto loan or on auto insurance?' "

The speed of change can be a bit intimidating. "Fifty percent of what we're marketing now did not exist at this company six months ago," says Fairbank. "And 95 percent of what we're marketing today didn't exist two years ago. I'm proud of that fact—until I reflect on its implications. It means that 50 percent of what we'll be selling six months from now doesn't exist yet."

Whatever Capital One may morph into in midflight, it will almost certainly land on its feet. The company is not afraid to cut its losses. Once it realized that its cellular service was not going to live up to its sister operations, Capital One folded cellular and moved on to more fruitful endeavors.

As Capital One demonstrates, to successfully deliver on Demand Strategy, companies must have business systems with four key elements:

- Research and customer interface
- Operational systems and strategies
- Organizational systems and strategies
- Technological systems and strategies

Each area is critical, and must be coordinated with the others to ensure success. Each needs an individualized strategy and a system that works in conjunction with the others.

But these systems will work only if they reinforce your unique Demand Strategy. In other words, your systems must work together to deliver the Demand Value Proposition that you have developed for your targeted demand segments. The choices you make in these four areas will determine whether or not you succeed in implementing your Demand Strategy, a strategy that will create a positive experience for the customer and enable you to achieve your desired financial results.

RESEARCH AND CUSTOMER INTERFACE

The first set of systems used by a successful Demand Strategist drives new insights into demand and reveals how to serve high-profit customers better. These systems are a critical starting point because they set the objectives for all of your other business systems. As research and customer interaction identify changes in demand and new customer expectations, this information must shape the operational, organizational, and technological systems used to deliver on demand.

In Chapter 2 we described four companies—EMC, McDonald's, Medtronic, and Gatorade—and the formalized business systems for identifying emerging demand and improving the customer interface used by each. All of them have developed processes for assessing demand, including a detailed understanding of their customers' end customers. Each then works with its smartest and most valuable customers to determine how best to fulfill demand on an ongoing basis.

As we have seen, Capital One, too, has developed highly sophisticated systems for assessing demand and testing alternative means of fulfilling it. The data capture, data mining, modeling, and testing that are part of their information-based strategy give Capital One unique insights into demand and how to fulfill it profitably. As demand shifts at an ever-increasing rate, the near real-time information captured by Capital One's testing processes and database provide a distinct competitive advantage.

The customer interface includes both the ways customers are involved in developing offers—*who* and *how*—and the ways they are served. Capital One conducts over one hundred tests with customers each day to refine its offers. Determining exactly which types of customers to include in these tests is a critical part of conducting test research successfully. With accurate test results in hand, Capital One then leverages its other business systems to provide customers the offer and service they expect.

In a recent survey of corporate CEOs rating their satisfaction with the performance of functional areas, the research function was rated absolutely last. Although research is critically important to the ongoing health of any business, senior managers are least satisfied with its performance. In our experience, this is because research is frequently limited to reporting what happened in the past rather than identifying current and emerging demand. In addition, the customer-focused projections developed by research departments are often faulty. First, they typically fail to include the perspective of customers' own end customers. Second, they frequently include all customers in the research, rather than focusing on the company's most profitable demand segments. By not breaking out research results by segments, the researcher far too often leads her company astray, as almost happened at United Airlines when equal voice was given to both the once-a-year traveler and the twice-per-week traveler. Finally, they sometimes ask the wrong customers—unprofitable segments or infrequent users—and draw incorrect or misleading conclusions from their input.

OPERATIONAL SYSTEMS AND STRATEGIES

The second set of strategies and systems you need to implement a Demand Value Proposition are operational and process related; they involve the production and delivery of products and services to the target demand segment. These systems and strategies also track demand, govern the way decisions are made, develop innovations on an ongoing basis, and determine the flow of information (what gets measured, by what method, and who sees the results).

Supply-driven businesses have a myopic view of the process. Their operations and processes focus on supply-chain efficiency, rather than on fulfilling demand. Usually starting from production inputs, they move link by link along the supply chain until products and customers meet.

The new CEO at one such company described how his predecessor had focused almost exclusively on supply-chain costs for the past three years. While this generated significant new efficiencies for this integrated manufacturer-retailer, the supply it was creating was entirely out of step with consumer demand. As a result, the company's stores were filled with merchandise that, while low-cost to produce and ship, could not be sold without steep price discounts that erased profits.

In contrast, demand-driven companies develop strategies and systems that respond to customers' needs, then measure if they are meeting them adequately. Their first step is to understand demand, then to develop the operational processes, organization, and technology systems that can best meet that demand. Shifting to demand-driven strategies and systems requires a shift in perspective, in which demand is the determining consideration, and the goal is to add value to each step in the process.

How is this done?

To begin with, you must be guided by a view of the entire customer experience. Just delivering the product or service is not enough; value should be delivered at every step, as mastered by Commerce Bank.

As discussed earlier, the McDonald's Demand Value Proposition focuses on good food, speedy service, making kids feel comfortable, and a consistent experience everywhere in the world. Famous for its highly disciplined processes and training in support of its proposition, McDonald's has its employees attend Hamburger University to better understand the Demand Value Proposition and the business systems designed to deliver it. The restaurants are then run by the book, literally: thick process manuals and checklists govern all activities. To ensure consistency, McDonald's continually inspects and reviews franchise operations. Franchisees must comply with all McDonald's policies or risk losing the opportunity to own additional McDonald's restaurants.

Successful operational systems also use the best raw materials or supply required to fulfill the Demand Value Proposition—these may be produced within the company or may be outsourced. Rather than being vertically integrated to produce in-house all of the materials their finished products or services require, many successful companies are forging partnerships to outsource aspects of the business in order to provide better value to customers and cost savings to themselves. In this way they tap outside expertise and make it possible to enter new lines of business more rapidly and efficiently with less capital committed than if they were acting alone.

Capital One, for example, developed partnerships with other companies to offer additional services to their credit card customers, rather than trying to develop its own brand of insurance or telephone service.

Dell Computer conducts business this way as well. Instead of vertical integration, as Michael Dell explains, "We have more collaborative business systems. We have a kind of 'virtual integration' that is taking hold." Dell partners with IBM and Intel to produce PC components, and with Accenture and Gen3 Partners to build a new business in consulting services. It recently brokered a new agreement with

EMC to sell EMC's low-end storage equipment to smaller businesses, a demand segment Dell has targeted for growth. In forging such agreements, Dell can move into new fields quickly without having to retool its own complex operations.

Another crucial operational reform calls for eliminating the vertical-process "silos" that exist in many organizations and replacing them with integrated, horizontal processes. What do I mean by the silo approach? A silo organization has each functioning/operating group within its own imaginary silo. They work only on their own function. Products move from one silo to another so that the people responsible for making the product have little coordination; as a result, a single change within one silo requires changes in all silos.

The alternative is to assign each project to a functional team whose members represent every department involved in the project, from design and manufacturing to shipping and billing. When the teams are given the authority to run their projects (in what we refer to as *internal partnering*), traditional departmental boundaries are broken down as the teams cohere and gain experience.

General Electric's former CEO Jack Welch named this concept "boundaryless behavior." According to Welch, it is the soul of today's GE.

Medline Industries, Inc., a manufacturer and distributor of more than one hundred thousand medical products, provides a good example of this. With annual sales in excess of $1 billion, Medline is the largest privately held national manufacturer and distributor of medical supplies to hospitals, health care facilities, and nursing homes in the United States. To deliver on its mission of rendering "quality products and cost containment solutions to health care providers while enhancing the quality of patient care," Medline manufactures or outsources through partnerships 70 percent of the products it sells. In addition, Medline continually develops creative cost-saving solutions based on the changing demands of its customers.

In the early 1980s, the U.S. health care industry experienced a wrenching change as HMOs, Medicare, and Medicaid forced it to switch from cost-plus pricing to cost containment. As U.S. health care providers struggled under enormous pressure to reduce costs, Medline transformed itself from a distributor to a manufacturer, then to a business partner, in order to meet its customers' new demands. In addition to selling medical supplies, Medline now partners with health care customers to provide imaginative approaches to manage and lower the cost of supplies, sometimes by 10 percent or more.

Medline's response to the unique demand of some hospitals in the Rocky Mountains eventually became an innovation that changed the entire industry. In the winter, the snow in parts of Colorado, Wyoming, and Montana made the roads serving some of Medline's hospital customers impassable. The hospitals could neither pay in advance to stock supplies that would last until spring nor last all winter without new supplies. Medline's solution was a consignment program: the hospitals would receive a huge inventory of supplies before snow season, and pay for them as they were used. As a result, the hospitals were well stocked, and Medline earned itself loyal customers by finding an inventive way to respond to demand.

Medline's consignment program became an important customer benefit as the industry moved toward cost containment, and the company was able to expand the approach. As one of Medline's two CEOs, Jon Mills, notes, "Consignment is a real win-win. Many health care providers are short on cash, and consignment helps them finance the supplies they need. The care patients receive is improved because the supplies are available. It changed the industry to [become] consignment-based."

Today, Medline offers a number of innovative products and services designed to meet customer demand. Like its trailblazing consignment approach, each of Medline's programs has grown out of the company's partner-based operational excellence.

ORGANIZATIONAL SYSTEMS AND STRATEGIES

For a company to change its approach from a supply-driven perspective to a demand-driven one, everyone in the company must work together toward the central, organizing goal of implementing Demand Strategy. The changes may involve creating cooperative, cross-functional teams that can move across traditional departmental boundaries. As U.S. automakers painfully learned from the successes of their Japanese counterparts in the 1980s, a silo system can result in lower-quality and higher-priced products, and does so slowly. Many U.S. companies and industries outside of the auto industry continue to work via the silo system, even though integrated, cross-functional teams can produce superior goods more quickly, even when the product is complex.

Cross-functional teams are generally an improvement in any company—whether demand or supply driven. The many benefits include

- Keeping all functions closer to demand and an understanding of it
- Driving absolute clarity in communications rather than having messages altered or garbled with each handoff to another silo
- Resolving potential issues and gaining agreement to plans and priorities across functions before the fact, rather than trying to solve them midstream
- Aligning all of the functions to work toward a common goal rather than having each department focus on its own objectives

Cross-functional management teams are then focused on segments of demand or the channels serving those segments. Dell Computer, for example, now recognizes about a dozen business segments in the United States—including small business, health care, and consumer—according to founder and CEO Michael Dell. "We've found that if we segment our business, not only [can we] scale the business faster, but we start to understand the unique needs of specific customers. Instead of creating functional businesses that are really too big to manage and don't integrate very well, we divide and conquer the business." Dell's ability to know more about its most profitable customers than competitors almost surely would not have happened in a traditional silo structure. Each of Dell's cross-functional segment teams serve the specific demand of its target customers. This approach is nearly impossible in a siloed organization serving one mass market.

John Sculley, former CEO of Apple Computer and past president and CEO of PepsiCo, takes the concept of cross-functional teams one step further. According to Sculley, cross-functional project teams that come together to complete a specific project and then disband are replacing traditional functional organizations. In many cases these project teams include members from outside the organization. "Team members don't necessarily have to be just the members of your company . . . they may be vendors, customers and partners," says Sculley.

Solectron Corporation, a contract manufacturer of personal computers, was the first company to win the coveted Malcolm Baldrige National Quality Award twice. The Baldrige award, established in 1987, has become the most prestigious standard for performance excellence and quality among companies in the United States and around the world. Companies competing for the award are evaluated against seven stringent criteria, four of which reflect the business systems we've been discussing—customer and market focus, process management, human resource development and management, and information and analysis.

Solectron attributes its success to its customer-focused cross-functional teams. Solectron assigns each corporate customer to a team that includes salespeople, engineers, program managers, buyers, quality representatives, and line employees. One member of the team communicates daily with the customer to anticipate and solve problems. Solectron now has sixty-five active teams. Customers are asked to fill out a weekly report card on the company's performance. A grade of B minus or lower triggers a quality-improvement program for the team; a C rates an emergency review. From the chief executive to the billing clerks, Solectron people are expected to anticipate and respond to what their customers want, and play a role in delivering it.

As you shift from a supply-driven to a demand-driven model, it is critical that you make sure that the proposition you offer your own employees is structured to reward demand strategy.

Think of your employees as your first and most important customers. If employees don't understand your Demand Strategy and their role in delivering it, they cannot fully satisfy end-customer demand. To this end, we've helped build employee value propositions, motivation plans, and communications strategies for companies like Hilton Hotels, McDonald's, and Sears, among others.

For example, in our work with McDonald's we found that many of the teens working in their restaurants were highly motivated by personal recognition as well as the chance to contribute to their local community. McDonald's was able to use these insights to increase job satisfaction, job performance, and employee retention.

One program designed to capitalize on these insights, called Gifts of Joy, set a goal for each restaurant to sell 10 percent more McDonald's gift certificates than it had the prior year at Christmastime. The individuals who sold the most gift certificates received special recognition from the manager and the entire restaurant crew. Just as important, when the crew met its goal, McDonald's would contribute up to $250 on behalf of the entire crew to the community organization of the crew's choice.

We have found that demand-driven companies that develop and deliver on a carefully architected employee value proposition have much better performance per employee than their peers. Net income per McDonald's employee and market capitalization per employee, for example, are 2.8 times and 3.6 times higher, respectively, than those of its competitors. Medtronic has a net income per employee that is 2.1 times higher than competitors' and a market cap per employee that is 2.5 times higher than the competition's.

Clearly, having employees who are enthusiastic, well trained, and respected makes good business sense. It also makes strategic sense to have the most talented people possible throughout your organization. Dubbed "the War for Talent" by the consulting firm McKinsey & Company, the battle to attract and retain superior talent—the next Jack Welch or Lou Gerstner—continues despite changes in overall employment rates. Delivering on a compelling employee value proposition and a Demand Strategy that helps the company outperform competitors creates the exciting opportunities that attract the best managers.

TECHNOLOGICAL SYSTEMS AND STRATEGIES

Technological issues are inextricably interwoven with operational and organizational systems and strategies. But while it is relatively easy to understand how important operations and organization are to meeting demand, it can be more challenging to view technology from the same perspective. Many managers see technology as an end in itself.

In Demand Strategy, technology's value must be based on whether it adds value, real or perceived, that enables you to create supply or customer service that brings you closer to satisfying demand. Technology considerations refer first and foremost to information technology, but also include innovations in any areas—manufacturing, packaging, distribution—where it creates advantages in fulfilling demand. And specific strategies and systems are needed to exploit those innovations.

One example is Dell's famous build-to-order manufacturing and direct distribution model, which Michael Dell calls the "demand-supply" model. In Dell's model, the company sells directly to customers rather than through resellers; this allows for mass customization based on customer needs, thanks to Dell's build-to-order capability. Because customer orders provide continuous feedback about shifting demand for Dell and its component suppliers, Dell can anticipate and respond to shifts in demand. Dell also moved swiftly to take advantage of on-line opportunities. For fiscal 2001, it had average daily on-line sales of about $50 million per day, representing 50 percent of its total revenue.

As Capital One demonstrated, heavy investments in proprietary technology can rapidly propel a company to the top of its industry. In addition to its uncanny computerized handling of incoming calls, Capital One's unceasing, technology-driven, information-based probing of its broad customer base collects and mines data that tell it what products will be most profitable. Over the course of a year, Capital One uses this system to test some forty thousand offers and fine-tune them to accommodate a variety of customer segments. Its six thousand variations of Visa and MasterCard credit cards has brought the company as close to mass customization of products as any company has come.

Technology can rejuvenate and transform even the most successful companies. Medtronic, for example, identified the potential of integrating information technology with medical technology to create new and better ways of managing chronic diseases. Medtronic's Internet portal, Medtronic.com, provides patients and physicians with information about its products and treatments. It has also committed $100 million for an alliance with WebMD in order to allow consumers to access information on Medtronic. Remarks Syl Jones, a spokesperson for Medtronic, "We see people downloading more health-care information from the Internet. They're going into doctors' offices with reams of paper and saying, 'I want this pacemaker' or 'I want this defibrillator.' "

Medtronic is also integrating its product line with emerging technologies. It is currently conducting clinical tests with a new implanted heart-monitoring device named Chronicle, which transmits critical patient information to secure Internet sites. Physicians can then easily download the information and check for possible warning signs. The potential patient benefits are huge. The day may not be too far off, according to Medtronic engineers, when an implanted heart device detects a problem while a patient is sleeping, and automatically pages an ambulance to help deliver the required medical assistance.

Still, a word of caution regarding technology systems and strategies: if you have proprietary insights into demand and a compelling Demand Value Proposition, technology can enhance performance, as it did in the case of Capital One, but it remains a means to the end of meeting demand. Technology alone can neither solve a fundamental misalignment with demand nor fix a flawed business model. Technology should be improved when your Demand Value Proposition is in place. The goal of technology is to enhance each part of your proposition, which is the enduring formula by which you have chosen to compete.

To determine the best technological strategies and systems for your business, you must develop a fact base about the business you are in, the demand segment you have chosen, and the unique combination of demand forces and industry factors at work in your market. Only then can you see and assess the technological opportunities open to you and decide which options will provide the greatest advantages in driving your Demand Strategy. This assessment will also show you how the new technology will interact with your research and customer interface, organizational and operational systems and strategies.

To demonstrate how research and customer interface, operational, organizational, and technological business systems all come together to drive competitive advantage, consider the case of Computer Discount Warehouse (CDW) Computer Centers, Inc., a computer products retailer based in a Chicago suburb. CDW is an example of how to build a superior company with outstanding people driven by Demand Strategy even in a low-margin industry.

CDW's direct sales model focuses on telesales, catalogs, and the Internet to sell over sixty-five thousand computers and computer-related products manufactured by Compaq, Hewlett-Packard, IBM, Microsoft, and Toshiba. Conceived in 1984 at the kitchen table of thirty-year-old Michael Krasny, CDW today has blossomed into a Fortune 500 corporation with nearly $4 billion in annual revenues.

Krasny realized that CDW must remain focused on the value it adds every day in order to earn a profit and succeed as a retail middleman. One of his initial goals was to compete on more than just price. As Krasny points out: "Anybody who tries to build a business model strictly on a pricing model will lose. You have to build a business based on service and value to the customer." In many respects, CDW exemplifies the success of Demand Strategy's principles.

CDW continually refines its business approach to add greater value to the business proposition that it offers small and medium-sized businesses and government agencies, which account for 96 percent of its sales. One such addition is offering knowledgeable advice and troubleshooting expertise to small businesses struggling with information technology problems.

"In a small or mid-sized company," Gary Ross, CDW spokesperson, explains, "the IT director may have been volunteered for the job. In a tiny, 10-person company, for example, he was the only one who knew a little about computers, so he was 'elected' to purchase technology equipment, in addition to doing his regular job." Today, CDW operates as an extension of a firm's IT department.

CDW has also been a pioneer in developing and maintaining corporate extranets for its clients—secure sites, customized to individual businesses—that enable the businesses to track their existing orders, manage their technology assets, configure and order hardware and software, and give immediate access to dedicated account managers.

"We want to provide just about any information about our accounts that helps make our service better," notes chief information officer Jim Shanks. When a user sends e-mail, the extranet automatically flags it as a top priority for its intended recipient. Customers' dedicated account managers review all extranet orders to ensure that customers' new orders are compatible with their previously ordered equipment. They perform other quality checks as well. The extranets are also fully integrated with the rest of CDW's operations to increase operational efficiency.

To succeed with its target demand, CDW maintains a delicate balance. It has to provide exceptional service—expert advice, product availability, same-day shipping, and lifetime technical support—to value-conscious commercial customers who often have limited financial resources. Creating value for both customers and itself requires firm discipline across all aspects of CDW's business.

CDW's segment is fiercely fought for by companies such as Dell and Gateway, both of which manufacture their own products, and by Internet and catalog-based resellers like PC Connection. CDW also operates under the threat of crippling inventory write-offs, a constant danger in the fast-moving computer market, where hardware and software inventories rapidly become obsolete.

By necessity, CDW's business systems are finely tuned to provide high service at low cost. It manages to deliver convenient, direct delivery channels, knowledgeable and well-trained sales and technical personnel, and the right products, and does so in a tightly integrated package.

In fact, CDW's entire operating model is built around what it calls the "Circle of Service," which begins with customers and details every aspect of service that is provided to that customer. By consistently delivering the quality service its customers demand, CDW earns the loyalty and repeat business that closes the circle. Employees understand that if service fails at any point in the process, the circle is broken, and the company has very likely lost both a sale and a customer. As the framework for CDW's business model, the Circle of Service is so important that it is printed on the back of employees' business cards.

CDW's customers demand product availability, customization, and same-day shipping. To keep them satisfied, CDW analyzes demand in real time to make sure it has adequate inventory on hand. When an order comes in, if the product is in stock—as it is for 80 percent of all orders—it is immediately pulled from the warehouse. If the product is not available in the warehouse, the system automatically determines the fastest way to deliver the out-of-stock item to the customer.

Once the product is on hand, the order system determines whether it is to be shipped as is or needs customization. In a remarkable operational step, CDW warehouse conveyors automatically send products scheduled for customization to the CDW technicians who tailor the product to the exact specifications of the customer: they load software, add memory, or configure the product to fit into the customer's existing IT network. After the product is customized, it is shipped from the 450,000-square-foot distribution center. Their proprietary, state-of-the-art automated warehousing and order-fulfillment system enables the company to turn over its huge inventory twenty-six times a year.

Rather than organizing around products or geographic regions, CDW is focused solely on satisfying the demand of its customers. To improve service, it assigns personal account executives to every business and government client, regardless of order size. Technical experts and administrative personnel support CDW's account executives to ensure that customers get exactly the right equipment at the right time.

CDW's account executives are carefully screened before they are hired. Technical knowledge is not a key prerequisite. CDW has found that attitude and skills relating to customer service and sales are better indicators of future success.

One reason CDW can offer such a high level of service cost-effectively is its information systems. These detailed tracking systems allow each sales manager to monitor and coach as many as twenty-five account executives, instead of the ten they could effectively manage in the past.

The company backs up the service of its account executives with lifetime, toll-free technical support from highly qualified personnel. It ships 97 percent of credit-approved, in-stock orders on the same day. CDW's significant investments in quality service have paid off handsomely: customer satisfaction levels are so high that they generate repeat purchase rates representing 80 to 90 percent of sales.

Certainly one of CDW's keys to success is its extensive training process, conducted at CDW University, which is modeled on McDonald's Hamburger University. It provides full-time training for three to five months to newly hired employees at full pay. The account managers, who are so crucial to the company's success, are trained at the School of Sales within CDW University. CDW University's College of Technology provides initial and ongoing training for people hired into technical support positions.

This training is intensive and rigorous, with daily tests and mandatory attendance. CDW's professional training staff teaches the classes, and is aided by many of the vendors who sell products through CDW. The first phase of the training focuses on CDW itself and the Circle of Service, as well as the culture and the products the company sells. The second phase takes place in one of CDW's two retail showrooms and is designed to help trainees develop interpersonal skills by interacting with actual customers. The final phase is devoted to technology, and shows future account managers how to guide their clients through technical subjects and issues. The training process that begins with CDW University continues on a weekly basis even after graduation.

To help retain its well-trained and highly valuable employees, CDW provides an on-site gym, day care facilities, free dinners for night shift workers, and dry cleaning services. These efforts help to explain the company's presence on *Fortune*'s list of the one hundred best companies to work for over the last three years.

To enhance the service at the heart of its value proposition, CDW tightly integrates its technology into the rest of its operations. To improve customer service, the company made a deliberate decision to develop its system in-house rather than using a software package from outside. As Jim Shanks, the CIO, explains, "A packaged solution can dictate what you can and cannot do, how you handle a customer or a situation. We didn't want that. Our system is a competitive advantage."

CDW maintains an up-to-the-minute CRM data warehouse that captures customer information and stores it for access by any CDW employee. This facilitates in-depth understanding of customers' needs, ensures smooth service across CDW departments, and improves customer service in general. Massive information tracking systems continuously measure key performance benchmarks, such as calls per sales associate, average call times, order sizes, and the speed with which different products move off the shelves. CDW's system tracks demand very closely and can rapidly adjust pricing and marketing to maintain inventory balance. For example, items that are selling more slowly than originally predicted might be featured with price cuts. Of course, customer service measures are also closely watched: computer monitors outside Krasny's office show how long customers have to wait before they get to speak to a representative. On occasion, if the wait time gets too long, Krasny will take calls.

Like Capital One, CDW's business systems help it deliver on its targeted demand in ways that drive competitive advantage in its industry. In addition, CDW is continuously improving its integrated operations, organization, and technology in order to improve customer service and increase efficiency. Harry Harczak Jr., the chief financial officer, explains that "we're one of the lowest cost producers out there. Concentrating all our administrative, warehousing and sales activities under one roof brings us maximum efficiency with a minimum of capital. That's crucial when you're in an industry like we're in, where the prices are always on the decline." Indeed, between 1996 and 2000, CDW successfully leveraged its information systems to the extent that operating expenses as a percentage of revenues fell from 7.1 percent to 6.5 percent, even as the number of salespeople tripled.

SEVEN WAYS TO DELIVER ON DEMAND

Based on my experiences with many of the nation's top corporations, I have compiled a list of seven maxims, or best practices, for developing the business systems needed to successfully deliver a Demand Strategy. As you work to develop your research and customer interface systems, operational processes, organizational systems, and technological support, keep these seven best practices in mind.

1. As you build your business systems, don't lose sight of the broader forces and factors shaping demand. Your insights into demand, which include identifying the most profitable customers and formulating the value proposition that best meets their demand, provide your implementation blueprint.

2. Focus on the total customer experience—every interaction with customers is an opportunity to learn more about demand and refine your systems for delivering on it. It is essential to understand what matters most to customers and discover where there are real or potential gaps in your capacity to meet their expectations.

3. Communicate the Demand Strategy and the Demand Value Proposition across your whole company—and engage, empower, and motivate the organization to deliver on them. Delivering successful Demand Strategy begins with your employees, not your customers.

4. To meet the demands of your most profitable customers, you may need to develop partnerships and outsourcing arrangements instead of doing everything in-house.

5. Develop differentiated approaches and business systems that fit your Demand Value Proposition. Your investments should drive those benefits that are most meaningful to your targeted customer segments and make you stand out from your competitors.

6. Drive for efficiency throughout all your systems. Being demand-driven does not mean ignoring costs. Your company should strive for effective cost management, especially in outlays that do not add value for the customer or are not in line with industry averages.

7. Continuously improve the process. All of your strategies and systems—especially those for collecting data—need to be refined on an ongoing basis to remain competitive.

In the next chapter I will discuss the physical, financial, and intellectual resources you will need to keep Demand Strategy working full force—and how to allocate them.

THE FIFTH AND SIXTH PRINCIPLES

Allocate Your Resources and Execute Your Demand Strategy

long time ago, someone who turned out to be instrumental to my understanding of how business works asked me, "What is the most important job that a chief executive officer performs?"

I offered a litany of answers, including strategy, finance, personnel, and manufacturing. But he responded to each with a smile and a vigorous shake of his head, indicating that, no, that was not right either.

When I gave up, he acknowledged that everything I mentioned was important, but a CEO's single most important job is the allocation of resources. Doing it correctly gives the organization the best chance to carry forward its strategic and tactical plans. But if funds are allocated incorrectly, there is virtually no chance for the company to perform at its best.

Allocating resources correctly means using your dollars, the skills of your people, and intangible resources such as brand equity, intellectual capital, and customer relationships in order to get the highest financial return and have a greater impact on the market than your competitors. It also means gathering data at a level sufficient to enable managers to fully commit to growth and consistent performance while offering senior management confidence that the resources provided are the right amount to accomplish the agreed-upon objectives. It requires being effective at selecting the right investments and getting the highest return on each allocation. The key is in determining priorities.

I believe that in the demand economy, the margin for error in the area of resource allocation has diminished dramatically. Products have shorter life cycles, consumers can shop and compare prices more easily than ever, and the very oversupply of products reduces the margin for error.

In a supply economy, unpurchased products were discounted successively but were ultimately bought because the level of demand tracked closely with supply. This is not the case today. In the demand economy, a company must understand what its targeted demand segments want or suffer the penalty of having too few buyers for a significant percentage of its goods or service.

Throughout this book I have asserted that to succeed in the demand economy, you must understand demand before creating supply. Nowhere is this more evident or applicable than in resource allocation decisions. These critically important decisions should be based on a thorough understanding of demand and a sound fact base. In fact, by following the process and discipline of developing a Demand Strategy, resource allocation decisions should be much clearer and more successful.

The most important task for senior managers who have more than one product or service to budget for is approaching resource allocation as a means of defining priorities across a portfolio of businesses. Too often, promising high-growth and high-profit opportunities are starved in order to feed low-margin and low-growth businesses. This error makes the high-potential business weaker while destroying value through continued investment of funds and management talent in a poor business. More often than not, the real problem facing most businesses is not limited resources but limited insights into demand and how best to use resources.

In an influential book, *Value Imperative,* the consulting firm

Marakon Associates presented its fundamental discovery concerning the allocation of capital across business units: "In virtually every company we know, including companies that are very well managed in most respects, 100 percent of the value created is concentrated in less than 50 percent of the capital employed. That means that, year in and year out, resources are committed to activities that consume value." In one case the researchers found that for a large, "healthy" U.S. company with a projected return on equity of more than 20 percent, just 24 percent of the new capital and 21 percent of R&D was responsible for 100 percent of the company's value. At the other end of the spectrum, 56 percent of new capital and 47 percent of R&D actually lowered value by 42 percent!

In many countries, especially the United States, mergers and acquisitions (M&A) are a frequent use of resources intended to drive growth. While there are many examples of enormously successful M&As, they are the exception, not the rule. I believe that one of the major reasons so many M&As fail is that they are supply driven rather than demand driven. Frequently, M&As are based on driving operating synergies and cost savings across the supply chain. In many cases this results in substantially lower capabilities for fulfilling customer demand, as we have seen in retail banking. The real way to make M&As successful is to ensure that they enhance the ability to serve the most profitable demand.

In the last fifteen years, a number of academics and consulting firms have studied the outcomes of hundreds of mergers and acquisitions using criteria such as increased shareholder value and ability to earn back capital investments to measure M&A success. These studies consistently find that at best, only half of M&As are successful. In fact, many studies found that two-thirds or more actually failed to return the cost of capital.

I was very surprised when I first saw this data several years ago, but on reflection it makes sense. The difficulties of integrating different cultures, people, business processes, and philosophies make what looks good on paper highly problematic to execute. A recent study by Southern Methodist University found that postmerger management often focuses on driving costs down through operating synergies. In fact, the need to capture immediate cost savings, which is often the basis for the merger or acquisition, can prove such a distraction that revenue growth declines from pre-M&A levels.

Considering the issues related to M&A, I believe that in most cases the more certain way to succeed is by allowing your existing business to grow organically through superior strategy, execution, and additional resource allocation. If you have an appropriate opportunity, you can acquire promising small businesses, which will be far easier to integrate and which have their best growth still ahead of them. Alternatively, options other than M&A, such as strategic alliances and joint ventures, may help generate growth and unlock value without adding potential M&A-related issues.

Certainly I don't mean to communicate that mergers and acquisitions are never the right vehicle for growth. But the data suggest that poor due diligence, integration skills, and disappointing performance hinder growth and profit, despite numerous examples of M&A success. Putting your resources toward expansion efforts in the areas in which you excel may be the best way to grow organically, have more control over the outcome, and increase your shareholders' value. Wall Street disproportionately rewards profitable growth, rather than the cost cutting many mergers and acquisitions depend upon.

Demand Strategy enables a well-run business to reduce costs and increase revenue, margin, and profits. Once you make a commitment to managing your business as a Demand Strategist, you will find several efficient ways of allocating your resources, as a result of strategic choices regarding the specific demand segments you target, the Demand Value Proposition you have created, and the business systems that support it. The promise can be realized only if you have the discipline and executional excellence to fulfill the strategic and tactical steps suggested here.

Demand Strategy allows you to realize cost efficiencies by aligning your resources against demand. In other words, if you spend the right amount on what your target demand segment values, and very little on what it doesn't, you will get the highest return on your investment. One example I've already discussed is our international airline client that devoted itself to the 9 percent of customers who were frequent fliers. Among the vast majority of flyers, adding seat-based entertainment systems was a priority. However, for the 9 percent who were most valuable, these entertainment systems did not influence their choice of airlines at all. Using this new information, the airline halted the major entertainment system investment it was about to make. Instead it invested in the things that mattered most to its target and dramatically improved its business with them.

Our work with a national newsmagazine provides another example. This magazine was having trouble tapping into the demand from family readers that it believed existed. Like most organizations, the managers were vying for limited resources for their specific projects, and gaining family readers represented only one opportunity that needed funding. However, the president of the magazine believed families were critical and that the management needed more attention and resources to reach them. Our analysis of demand proved him right.

Like many general-interest magazines, the readership for our client skewed to older consumers. The average age of subscribers was almost fifty, and the majority were empty-nester households. This subscriber base raised three critical issues for the magazine's ongoing success: First, many advertisers in the magazine were looking to reach young families, rather than older consumers, because families are often the most valuable consumers of products and services, from cars and computers to cereals and investment advice. Second, the magazine's older consumers were the most likely to stop subscribing over time, and since the magazine was having little success among young families, there were few readers to replace subscribers when they left. Finally, we found that people who grew up with this magazine in their households were much more likely to become consumers of the category, and of this magazine specifically. Clearly, families were an important resource priority. Complicating matters was the fact that past efforts to gain family readers had largely failed.

In the course of our work, we found that the managers' demographic definition of families—any household with children—prevented them from a meaningful attempt at Step 2, identifying the most profitable customers and insights into their demand. Moreover, their very broad definition of "family" was causing subscriptions to drop because the needs of the families most valuable for this magazine could not be identified and therefore were not well served.

To overcome these formidable barriers, we identified different demand segments of families; we were able to understand their distinct motivations and what they wanted from the magazine. The most valuable target for the magazine was families who were "ardent news readers," that is, people who were interested in current developments and news, especially as they relate to the family.

These families found the magazine's infrequent articles on topics related to the family very interesting, but were frustrated that there was not more of them. In addition, we discovered that the segments with young children were particularly interested in having the award-winning kids' version of the magazine available at home; at that time, it was distributed only in schools.

With a new definition of "family" and new insights into their demands, we were able to address the needs of the most valuable families for our client and allocate appropriate resources to win them over. We added coverage of family-related topics, including a weekly page on families, and planned more cover stories with this group in mind. We then used our thorough understanding of the targets' needs to develop new offers and create strong direct-marketing approaches that have attracted record numbers of families.

In my experience, the foremost principle regarding allocation is that it should be based on a rigorous fact base encompassing past, current, and emerging demand. The fact base needed to optimize resource allocation decisions results from the type of analyses that are central to Demand Strategy. Based on this, my colleagues and I have developed several principles to guide more effective resource allocation decisions:

1. Both current and emerging demand must be assessed when making resource allocation decisions.

    In the demand economy, product life cycles are now shorter than ever, making it imperative that you understand how changes in demand might impact the profitability of your current business. In addition, demand and the desired supply must be thoroughly understood before making investments in products or services that could rapidly be made obsolete.

2. Resource allocation decisions should leverage not just dollars and people but all of the company's assets, including brands, talent, intellectual capital, and key relationships.

   Although most companies focus on the tangible assets of dollars and people, intangible assets can have an impact as big or bigger on driving success. For many businesses, their proprietary brand is the most valuable and enduring asset they own.

3. An understanding of the key activities that drive share of demand for your business is critical. Once the drivers of demand share are understood, the return on investment for each should be quantified.

   To succeed, you must have a clear understanding of the features and activities—service, convenience, product features, customization, and other benefits—that drive demand for your business and how investments in key areas can improve your performance.

With these principles as a framework, you can now determine how to divide your resources. Though there are no easy answers, there are several Demand Strategy criteria that will help you calculate the right percentages of your total resources so that each business will be nourished according to its contribution to your company's profits. The criteria are

- Impact of the various forces and factors on your business
- Current size and growth potential of your business
- Current and expected profitability
- Changes in the size of segment(s) targeted by business units
- Changes in your share of market, in demand share, or in the nature of your competition
- Size and growth of emerging demand versus current demand
- Ability to differentiate vis-à-vis competitors
- Level of insulation from competition
- Core competencies

- Competitive activities
- Distribution channels
- Profit margins
- Percent of portfolio you are willing to have at risk

Indeed, if you look closely at companies that are perpetually growing, you will see that they have a much broader understanding of their businesses and a firmer grasp of how they will evolve than their competitors. One of the distinguishing behaviors of demand-driven companies, as a result of performing force and factors analyses, is an understanding of demand at both the current and the emerging levels; that is, these companies think about their businesses in broader terms. Because they understand the key drivers of current and emerging demand, they can add specific product features, improve customer service, expand distribution, or leverage brand equity, among other options. They can determine the best use of resources to achieve their objectives. Then, on an ongoing basis they can measure the impact of their resource allocation decision and make any necessary adjustments.

Some companies plan so well and so far in advance, for example, that when they introduce a new product into the marketplace, they have already planned the next several generations of the product. At Medtronic, no product can be introduced unless the next four generations of product have been planned for and approved. This forces dynamic and forward-based thinking. Unfortunately, companies more frequently think only one or two years ahead, and their actions and resource allocations revolve around meeting those plans.

There are many IT-based tools to help model the complex trade-offs involved in resource allocation decisions. One such tool links traditional financial models with the strategic revenue and cost drivers of the business. It can provide profit-and-loss statements at the customer segment level and tie it back to the company level. Since you can change assumptions within the model, you can build scenarios that quantitatively assess the impact of investments in brand building, product development, customer targeting, portfolio alignment, channel alignment, and so on.

A company might, for instance, use such an approach to create a demand-driven allocation plan for raising shareholder value. Managers can model alternative resource allocations and determine the impact each scenario has on the key drivers of the business.

Jim Kilts, CEO of Gillette, has built a strong track record of turning around underperforming brands, businesses, and entire corporations throughout his career at General Foods, Kraft, and Nabisco. His approach reflects the core principles of Demand Strategy.

Kilts is perhaps best known for the hugely successful turnaround of Nabisco. At Nabisco, Kilts sold off peripheral businesses such as Fleischmann's table spreads and College Inn broths. As a result, Nabisco was able to focus on the core biscuit group (cookies and crackers, including Oreo and Ritz) and the U.S. foods group (including snacks such as Planters and Grey Poupon mustard). After Nabisco significantly improved U.S. sales and profits, Philip Morris acquired it for almost $19 billion, which includes $4 billion in debt assumption, in December 2000.

One of the first things Jim Kilts looks at with any business is how resources are being used. As he points out, "Most companies get into trouble not because they make a world-class blunder, although that happens sometimes. Most often, they get into trouble through a succession of well-intentioned but flawed decisions that build on each other until it becomes very difficult to unravel the problem."

One key insight into resource allocation that Kilts has made is what he describes as "the Circle of Doom." Unfortunately, many companies trap themselves in a downward spiral by setting unrealistic objectives at the outset of their resource allocation process. According to Kilts, "Saddled with objectives that are impossible to meet, companies tend to throw money at the problem. Overhead is built and extra capital is allocated. Then, in order to grow profits in the face of sales shortfalls, prices are raised. When higher prices cause an even sharper drop in sales, then the marketing budget is cut and funds are used to prop up the bottom line. Despite all these efforts, the company's earnings still fall short of Wall Street's estimates. So, the Circle of Doom continues and deepens." A fact-based understanding of demand—what is driving demand, how fast it is likely to grow, and what your specific opportunities are—is an important way to identify realistic opportunities for growth and profitability.

When a corporation spends money, that money is either an investment or an expense. If you properly categorize each allotment, the task of allocating resources will become much easier. However, these categorizations are not always straightforward. While, for accounting purposes, you may regard an expenditure in, say, training as an expense, it is in fact an investment in people, products, and your future. In general, expenses are costs that should be minimized; anytime the same benefit can be obtained at lower cost, the company is better off. Investments, on the other hand, should be optimized by providing funds to maximize benefits up until the point at which one begins to get smaller increments of return.

Demand Strategy can help guide the allocation of resources by reviewing the drivers of current and emerging demand and by allowing managers to model the impact of alternative resource allocations and track results on an ongoing basis. In contrast, many companies handle crucial resource allocation decisions based on past drivers of demand or by simply increasing the budget for the previous year in line with inflation.

A gap analysis is often a good way to identify critical resource allocation issues and priorities. There are several ways to perform a gap analysis. One is to identify the performance gaps between your own company and your competitors'. In Demand Strategy, a gap analysis looks at your performance on each individual DVP plank versus the performance of your competitors. Such gap analyses are likely to provide significant insight into your business performance, as well as that of your competitors. It may need to benchmark a particular category to other industries rather than direct competitors.

For example, when measuring customer service, a telecommunications client proudly noted that it provided the best in the industry. Unfortunately, consumers were dissatisfied with all of the service from all telecom companies, and our client's relative superiority did not make a significant difference. The standard for service customers sought came instead from great catalog retailers like L.L. Bean and stores like Nordstrom.

You begin a gap analysis by taking an inventory of existing initiatives and uses of resources. It is important to take a fresh look at your company's activities in light of the objective suggested by Demand Strategy and any new competition. A thorough gap analysis will produce four types of findings:

1. Systems and activities that are aligned with the Demand Strategy and that should be continued or even increased
2. Activities that need to be revised to some extent to align with the Demand Strategy
3. Initiatives that are inconsistent with the Demand Strategy and should be eliminated altogether
4. Systems and activities critical to delivering the Demand Strategy that are missing and need to be developed

The DVP is your guide. Writing the business plan, the manager can determine if an activity specifically fits any of the planks of his DVP. If it does not, it probably should be dropped from the plan. For senior management, the DVP is used to judge every expenditure on the basis of whether or not it will move a company further toward its goals of increasing sales and profitability.

A gap analysis helps you prioritize areas in relation to the Demand Value Proposition and identify where the business systems and strategies have to be changed, developed, or discarded.

The next step is to use the findings of the gap analysis to create a set of projects and activities that can potentially take you from where you currently stand to where you want to be. Such projects are designed to strengthen or differentiate one or more planks in the Demand Value Proposition—through training, through specific business systems, or through investments in physical or informational assets.

At this point you want to avoid the pitfall of choosing and allocating resources to projects out of habit. Too many companies simply fund the same activities each year without addressing their changing needs and priorities for success. Your decisions about where to allocate funds should be based on a fact base and an extensive economic analysis that will show you how each investment addresses the targeted demand. The analysis should point out the way for you to differentiate, as well as suggest how much value can potentially result.

Medtronic exemplifies a company that has successfully used Demand Strategy to guide its resource allocation decisions.

When Bill George (who recently stepped down after ten years as CEO) joined Medtronic in 1989, the business was a $1 billion market-capitalization company, deriving 80 percent of its revenues from pacemakers. By July 2001, its market cap had grown to almost $58 billion. During the fourteen-year period from 1985 to 1999, Medtronic's sales grew at a compounded rate of 18.8 percent per year, while earnings rose 25.4 percent annually over the same period. Today, pacemakers account for less than half of the company's total revenues, and this is likely to fall even further.

Much of the transformation that Bill George led can be explained by his implementation of the core principles of Demand Strategy to determine Medtronic's priorities and approaches regarding resource allocation.

I have already discussed Medtronic's forces and factors analysis, as well as its decision to focus on segments requiring chronic care.

From the outset, George understood that the medical device industry, which was in the forefront of the new demand economy, faced heightened competition from global companies, shortened product life cycles, rapid commoditization, and severe pricing pressure. Fierce competition in its core pacemaker market, for instance, drove Medtronic's market share down from 80 percent to only about 30 percent by the 1980s. Moreover, Medtronic's potential customers—physicians and surgeons—were among the most demanding and technologically astute customers in any industry. This was hardly surprising, given that technological innovation could prove to be the difference between life and death in their line of work.

The combination of forces and factors and its demand segment needs led Medtronic to make technology leadership the centerpiece of its Demand Value Proposition. In effect, Medtronic realized that technology leadership was a critical lever for capturing market share, and it was telling its target segment of physicians that its products were guaranteed to be the best technology available. Since delivering on this promise could be obtained—and maintained—only through R&D, that became the company's highest priority.

George's first step was to raise R&D spending from 8 percent per year to 10–11 percent. In effect, he performed a gap analysis to see whether or not Medtronic's current spending levels were adequate for delivering on this crucial driver of the Demand Value Proposition. George was guided by the principle that R&D was a long-term investment, which should be protected from short-term profitability requirements. In his opinion, a fast-growing company should, in fact, restrain profit growth. He described it this way: If "a company is growing profits at 40 percent and revenue at 18 percent, eventually, it won't get the revenue growth because it won't be investing enough in R&D and market development. You can get too greedy. What if you hit a flat spot in revenues? You can cut your R&D to keep earnings up. You can do that for a year or two, but you'll totally lose it. Clearly, our factory costs have to be cut. But we don't cut back on R&D."

However, George did much more than simply allocate additional money to R&D. The way he made specific allocations within R&D and the resources he allocated to other areas also contributed to Medtronic's success. Here's how he did it.

Customer Input

When he came into Medtronic, George discovered a crucial gap between his implicit promise to deliver the best technology and what the development engineers were actually designing. Essentially, they suffered from an inward-looking, "not-invented-here" syndrome. They certainly emphasized quality, but did not focus on demand. As a result, product development in 1991 took, on average, forty-eight months as researchers continually tweaked their products to make them more acceptable to doctors. To quicken this pace, George involved physicians in the product development process.

As George explained: "A lot of the quality gurus of the '80s took us in the wrong direction, toward internal measures and using quality as a motivating tool. That was wrong. The only measure of quality is in the eyes of the customers. We cut our product-development time from 48 to 14 months by setting up physician advisory boards. Every month, we go and sit with them to get their assessment, which forces our technologies to pass the market test. That shortens the development process."

The benefits are not found only in a faster product cycle but also in greater efficiency and improved market acceptance, as George pointed out: "We don't run down a lot of blind alleys. Our R&D is so focused with physicians that when we get going on a project we will wind up with a product on the market. By the time a product comes to market . . . the best doctors in the world in that field [have] look[ed at it]. And they know it's going to work, and they've treated several hundred or several thousand patients in . . . clinical trials."

George recognized the operating theater and surgical centers as fertile grounds for generating new ideas that would meet emerging demand. Perceiving a gap between the amount of time engineers were spending in their offices and the amount of time they were spending in the field, where ideas were developed, he devised a simple yet effective way to close the gap. "In medical technology, one engineer sitting with a doctor can come up with an invention," according to George. "Seven out of every 10 procedures that we do in the world have a Medtronic person in the operating room. And that's the way we stay creative."

Medtronic doesn't restrict its search for good ideas to the United States alone. Instead, it has built up relationships with leading academic and medical centers throughout Europe, as well as Australia and Japan.

Nearly fifteen years ago, French neurosurgeon Alim-Louis Benabid hypothesized that mild electric jolts delivered to certain portions of the brain might alleviate some of the symptoms of Parkinson's disease. Based on this hypothesis, Medtronic developed Activa, an implanted brain stimulator that is now in use worldwide. The company plans to develop similar devices for epilepsy, depression, and obsessive-compulsive disorder. Says Scott Ward, head of the company's neurological unit, "We are creating an entirely new field of medicine."

Medtronic has also developed internal systems and processes to ensure continued success in the demand economy. They include:

R&D Systems and Processes

To reduce the impact of commoditization and insulate the company from competitors, George implemented the concept of multigenerational product planning and development. For each new device that Medtronic brings into the marketplace, four additional generations have already been planned—a minor upgrade, a major one, and two longer-term technologies. Medtronic's goal is to derive 70 percent of its sales from products introduced within the previous two years. "That figure makes it hard for competitors to keep up," says George. "It's a barrier to entry because you are shooting at a moving target."

Moreover, successive products in the cycle, which grow smaller and more sophisticated with each change, must have lower manufacturing costs than their predecessors. The principle here is that it is better to cannibalize yourself than allow a competitor to do so.

The multicycle approach has additional advantages—it helps address emerging demand and also provides more stable cash flow because there is less risk that a competitor's product will suddenly take a big bite out of sales. The process through which the R&D budget is allocated is far from mechanical, however. According to a former Medtronic senior executive, "Most large corporate entities . . . fall into a rote allocation process. X percent of R&D goes in this direction, Y percent goes here, based on history. Medtronic allocates resources based on the future. Just because you got it last year does not necessarily mean you're going to get it again this year. You have to show what you're going to do."

The company has put in place a formal system by which developmental projects are funded, monitored, measured, and evaluated from beginning to end. Each plan has specific, clearly stated objectives, milestones, and decision points. Review processes at each decision point determine whether the project should be continued, abandoned, or redirected.

In some cases, when there is considerable uncertainty concerning the outcome, the company will simultaneously pursue two parallel approaches, and bring the winner to market.

Finally, while safeguards reduce risk, failure is assumed to be part of the R&D process. As a senior company executive stated, "At least

10 to 20 percent of R&D leads to nothing. That doesn't mean it was useless, because now you know what doesn't work."

Human Resources

The company uses small, cross-functional teams from different departments, including manufacturing, quality assurance, marketing, and R&D, to reduce internal bottlenecks and further accelerate the time to market. With no walls separating departments, people can easily shift in and out of projects as they are needed.

In order to ensure that the technologies that replace preexisting ones represent radical steps forward, the company uses research groups explicitly charged with cannibalizing the older technologies. As George explains, "We set up venture teams of people who aren't emotionally invested in the old product. Once the new has enough strength to stand on its own, we reintegrate the doubters. That's key. If you just [say] . . . 'here's the new product,' it demoralizes people. . . . You have to go from the venture team to integrating it into the mainstream business."

Creating and maintaining a culture that supports and encourages taking risks is essential to Medtronic's long-term success. As Mike James, vice president of marketing for its pacemaker business, says, "With all the pressure on short-term performance, it takes a real discipline to look at your asset mix to be sure you have a sufficient amount focused on the future. . . . But Bill [George] has established a culture that allows the dots [venture teams] to survive, because they are pretty fragile when they are little. Bill doesn't know about all of them but the culture . . . gives the middle managers the confidence to let those little dots live for a while to see if they are going to flourish or not. Bill encourages us to take those risks. There are many examples of risk-taking [being] rewarded and failures not ending with beheadings. I think that's the litmus test."

Part of the risk-taking culture is an initiative known as the Quest Program, which enables researchers to pursue ideas that are outside their primary responsibilities. Individuals are given seed money, up to

$50,000 per year, and Medtronic supports six to eight such projects annually. Inspiring creativity, Quest improves employee motivation, allows radical new ideas to take root, and lowers the risk of being blindsided by competitors.

Acquisitions

Although we at The Cambridge Group tend to prefer organic growth to mergers and acquisitions, some companies make excellent, profitable acquisition decisions, and Medtronic is one. The company devotes considerable managerial attention and resources to acquiring competencies and products needed to attain strategic objectives that are unavailable in-house. Meeting segment needs, filling product gaps, and moving into desired growth categories within chronic care are examples of these objectives. In 1999, Medtronic met a segment need by acquiring the Sofamor Danek Group, which made spinal technology products. Noting that the neurosurgeons using its neurostimulation products were progressively moving from the brain down to the spine, Medtronic followed them by providing the technology with which they could expand their capabilities.

Medtronic acquired Arterial Vascular Engineering in 1999 so that it could provide arterial stents as part of its cardiac line. Because in many hospitals purchasing committees, rather than surgeons and other physicians, were making crucial supplier decisions, Medtronic risked being left out if it didn't present a full line of surgical products.

The company also uses acquisitions to strengthen its position in important segments of chronic care, such as diabetes management. In 2001, for example, it paid $3.7 billion in cash to acquire MiniMed, a manufacturer of insulin pumps and wearable glucose monitors.

In choosing its acquisition targets, Medtronic does not use revenue gains or cost cutting as criteria; instead it looks for small targets that are rapidly growing and, at the same time, showing promise to design or make leading products. As Bill George points out, "There's a big risk if you make acquisitions just to add revenue. We could be a $30-

billion company . . . because we had the opportunity to acquire companies larger than we are. The market would have loved that in the short run. . . . We would much rather acquire industry leaders that are growing fast. I don't like mergers of equals. You get cost savings, but they really don't focus on growth."

Other Allocation Decisions

Historically, the need for FDA approval has created long lead times prior to product introductions. As a result, Medtronic concentrates its initial marketing efforts in Europe, where regulatory approval is often much faster. This directly benefits the company by improving profits and cash flow. Moreover, the experience gained in Europe and elsewhere provides valuable data for improving products and overcoming customer resistance in the U.S. market. At the same time, the company is not hurt by allocating resources to begin the regulatory approval process in Europe, because it will still be quicker to market than its U.S. competitors that deal only with the FDA.

Since regulation is a crucial industry force, Medtronic is often at the forefront of efforts undertaken to reform the regulatory process. With assistance from Steve Kelmar, a former high-ranking official from the U.S. Department of Health and Human Services, Bill George helped to get the FDA Modernization Act passed by Congress in 1997. As a direct consequence of that legislation, approvals that used to take an average of three years are now decided within six to nine months. While this is advantageous for Medtronic, it is, of course, of even more benefit to the patients for whom new drugs and medical devices can be the difference between life and death.

While the example of Medtronic is instructive in many ways, it is clear that there is no universal approach to resource allocation. The process needs to be tailored to the specifics of your company.

ALIGNING THE ORGANIZATION

The allocations behind a strategy will be successful only if that strategy is clearly understood and enthusiastically executed by everyone at every level of the organization. At The Cambridge Group, we have developed a process called Rashomon, which enables a company's management team to recognize the biases and misperceptions under which its members currently function. The name derives from a Japanese short story by Ryunosuke Akutagawa that was adapted into an Oscar-winning film in 1950 by Japanese director Akira Kurosawa. The fascinating story is organized in five parts. In the first part, an event involving four people occurs. In the remaining four parts, each participant reports the event from his or her perspective. Not surprisingly, the four stories differ vastly from one another.

The story parallels the way many large, multifunctional corporations operate. In my experience, senior officers in large corporations usually come together to discuss particular issues, rather than to share their views on the business enterprise in general. The observation in the film *Rashomon* that "where you stand depends on where you sit" has relevance for many corporations. Often, strategies fail because they are developed without the context of a cross-functional commitment.

The Rashomon process brings senior officers and functional leaders together to develop a view of the company and its strategic imperatives that they can share. Each functional leader conducts a discussion on the important issues in his or her area, for which they all prepare by using a common template. This approach raises and resolves issues—unlike separate, functional, silo discussions, in which concerns may be generated but are not addressed.

By the end of the Rashomon process, a shared point of view regarding the company's priorities has usually emerged. That is, the company has agreed upon what the most important issues are and how they will be solved.

As a result, differences and divisional resistance are more easily resolved, allowing the organization to pull together around the Demand Strategy. Managers are frequently surprised at the diversity of views within their teams.

Once senior managers are aligned, they can return to their departments and explain the resource allocation plan and the fact base that led to it so that everybody has the full understanding of how the decision was arrived at and can share in the enthusiasm and help execute the plan.

PERFORMANCE TRACKING

It is important to set up measurement and performance systems to evaluate the continuous progress of the Demand Strategy in relation to the agreed-upon priorities.

According to management guru Peter Drucker, "Today practically every business has a capital-appropriations process, but few use it correctly. . . . There is no better way to improve an organization's performance than to measure the results of capital spending against the promises and expectations that led to its authorization."

Continually tracking progress against the stated objectives of each specific resource allocation decision allows managers to determine whether or not progress is satisfactory, as well as to take appropriate action. If milestones are not being reached, driving to the root cause may indicate a significant change in the forces and factors impacting demand, new responses among competitors, or a flawed assumption that must be revisited. In addition, understanding the root causes may surface issues in the resource allocation process itself.

Three of the most critical measures to establish and track on an ongoing basis among your target demand segments are preference drivers, relevance, and differentiation. Preference drivers are those attributes that most influence the decision to use one product over another. In food products, for example, they might include taste, healthfulness, calories, convenience, and portability. As we have discussed, relevance to the target and positive differentiation vis-à-vis competitors are critical measures that are often indicative of the ongoing health of a business.

Implementation

In our experience, there are six critical elements that drive implementation:

1. *Why.* The objective and intended impact of the initiative as well as its connection to the Demand Strategy must be absolutely clear. Why is this initiative a priority, and what will it achieve?
2. *What.* The implementation plan needs to define the necessary action and the intended goal. What will be done and what will it achieve? The plan should also include an assessment of the total investment required and the intended payback on the investment. The investment must encompass all of the resources—capital, people, time—that are needed to succeed.
3. *How.* The approach for the initiative must be explicit, and if, over time, changes are made, they should be communicated to all stakeholders. Increasingly, some of the most successful companies are partnering with others to achieve objectives they could not have obtained on their own. By partnering, rather than trying to accomplish everything internally, they are getting to market faster with superior offers. Finally, establishing exactly how you will measure success is critical for tracking progress and taking corrective action.
4. *Who.* The leader and the team that are focused on the initiative must be accountable for delivering on it. To drive accountability, one person should be in charge of the effort. However, everyone on the team has to be motivated to achieve a common goal. In addition, the plan must unambiguously identify who will be affected, both externally and internally. Which customers will feel the changes? Which managers across the organization will feel the effects? Who will contribute to the effort? Finally, determining who will review and objectively assess the effort as it is progressing and once it is completed must be clearly established at the outset.
5. *When.* The effort's intended timeline and the key milestones that will measure its progress must be laid out in advance. This timeline must also incorporate the sequencing of events. What needs to be done now to facilitate follow-on initiatives?

6. *Where.* The project's geographic scope as well as where within your business system it will be located needs to be identified and understood.

In the discussion on the allocation of resources at the management level, I've mentioned an increasing array of modeling and predictive tools that take the guesswork and finger-crossing out of accompanied micro-level allocation.

For example, Spectra—a company that I co-founded fifteen years ago with my partner Steve Morris, former president and CEO of Maxwell House Coffee, and now the CEO of Arbitron—holds a dominant position in geodemography. This enables a manufacturer to understand the demand for every stock-keeping unit in every one of thirty-two thousand U.S. supermarkets. Steve and I had what seemed like a far-fetched idea in the late 1980s. We hypothesized that we could combine supermarket scanner data with a new software product called Prism, which determined the spending probabilities in every one of America's forty thousand zip codes.

It was possible, we thought, that if the *what* of scanner data was combined with the *who* of Prism, we would help manufacturers allocate their resources among thirty-two thousand supermarkets; the stores with the highest demand for certain products would receive increased supplies of those products, and the same would hold true of all products that indexed highly in all supermarkets in America.

As it turned out, our idea was workable, and under several years of John Larkin's inspired leadership, Spectra has prospered and now has the capacity to predict individual store demand in grocery, mass-merchandiser, convenience, and department stores. With that information, you can allocate additional resources and inventory to those retail stores where the demand for your products is heaviest. This is a large step toward granular resource allocation, and at the same time it reduces costs and increases revenues, margins, and profits.

When senior management has multiple products or categories to contend with, it is best to organize them as a portfolio to ensure that businesses with high potential get the attention and resources they deserve. A rigorous analysis is essential to identifying the potential of each business and to allocate resources to it accordingly.

Keep in mind:

- A gap analysis is often a good way to begin the resource allocation process. In Demand Strategy, the analysis reflects where you stand on your Demand Value Proposition in relation to where you have determined you wish to be. The result of the analysis will clearly prioritize areas where you need to invest people, time, and money.
- For resource allocation to succeed, it is essential that each level of the company understand and behave according to the priorities established by the Demand Strategy. A well-planned group exercise such as Rashomon is a useful way of getting key management on board.
- Implementation of the allocation plan needs to be mapped out in detail, including the *why*s, the *what*s, the *how*s, the *who*s, and the *when and where*s.
- Last but not least, when you deploy resources within an organization, it is vital that you regularly track performance on the measures that have been agreed upon earlier, such as differentiation relative to the competition, segment level profitability, and margins.

CHAPTER 9

GATORADE WINS ON DEMAND

n 1983, Phil Marineau, now president and CEO of Levi Strauss & Co., was a thirty-seven-year-old marketing executive at the Quaker Oats Company. Early one Monday morning, his president, Bill Smithburg, shared his long-term dreams for Gatorade with Marineau. Smithburg then assigned him a huge new job that could be viewed as either a dream come true or a nightmare. As it turned out, the dream prevailed, because Phil Marineau and the team he assembled had a natural gift for understanding demand.

In the first of a series of shifts in the food industry, Quaker Oats paid $250 million to buy Stokely–Van Camp, Inc. Many analysts complained that Quaker Oats bought a lesser company with only one asset—the offbeat sports drink Gatorade, which was then selling nationwide at the pace of $85 million a year. If that figure sounds impressive, it represents only 0.1 percent of the U.S. beverage business.

Marineau, a seasoned pet food marketer who knew little about Stokely–Van Camp and less about Gatorade, was put in charge of the new acquisition. "You're there to figure out what to do," his president told him. "More precisely, you're there to grow Gatorade and make sure we pay off this acquisition."

Over the next twelve years, Marineau's response became a classic example of Demand Strategy.

Gatorade was born at the University of Florida, in Gainesville, where oppressively hot weather often flattened the football team, known as the Gators. In the late 1960s, the team doctor enlisted various university colleagues to help develop a rehydrating drink for Gator players. He wanted something that would quickly replenish not just the water they lost but also the glucose and minerals that streamed from their pores in Florida's steam-bath humidity.

The scientists decided that the drink should be isotonic—that is, able to enter the bloodstream as quickly as water. So they laced it with electrolytes to speed its passage through intestinal tissues.

No sooner did the Gators start drinking the new beverage during games than their football fortunes soared. In 1966, they astonished even themselves by winning nine games and losing two in the regular season. Soon called the Comeback Kids, they became famous for trailing until the third quarter, then rebounding to victory as their opponents wilted in the heat. They credited their physician's elixir, by then dubbed Gatorade.

After the Gators soundly beat Georgia Tech in the 1967 Orange Bowl, the losing coach told reporters, "We didn't have Gatorade. That made the difference." That comment appeared in *Sports Illustrated,* and coaches and trainers everywhere began to understand the importance of replenishing body fluids during a game.

The doctor and his colleagues formed a company to market the drink, and got a break in 1970 when the Kansas City Chiefs took Gatorade to the Super Bowl and won. The Chiefs' coach, Hank Stram, snagged further publicity for Gatorade by praising it in the media. Again, *Sports Illustrated* picked up the story. But Gatorade was still a small player in a niche market for athletes when its developers sold it to Stokely–Van Camp.

With a modest television advertising campaign, Gatorade rode the sports boom to nationwide distribution over the next thirteen years. But it remained concentrated in the Southeast United States and sold mainly to athletes and former athletes. Though millions of Americans had apparently heard Gatorade's singular name, Marineau told me, "they had no idea what it was," let alone what it could do for them.

Marineau brought two clear questions to his new job: How big an opportunity did Gatorade offer? And what strategy should he use to make the most of it? He quickly organized a core team of about ten executives, mostly from Quaker Oats but including a few marketers from

Stokely–Van Camp. They launched a study of Gatorade, from its unique qualities to its potential market.

A version of Demand Strategy evolved. Though the term had not yet been conceived, Marineau's people were guided by the same principles and disciplines that now comprise Demand Strategy. After all, Demand Strategy is, at its essence, a way of thinking.

Marineau began assembling the fact base for his new business. Apart from Gatorade's basic history—which, of course, made a beguiling story—one of the most important facts was the nature of the drink itself. "It was not, at that point, going to be a social beverage," Marineau remembers. "The sugar content is only about half of what you get in a soft drink, and any more would ruin the rehydration process. Then there are the electrolytes and the sodium—not much sodium, but enough. It's an acquired taste. But nothing tastes better after a five-mile run."

The next key issue involved Gatorade's distribution. Unlike major soft drinks, which rely on regional bottling companies to buy concentrate from the manufacturer and distribute it to retailers and vending machines, Gatorade sold its product either to wholesalers or directly to major retail chains. That gave the company a bigger profit on each bottle sold but made it more difficult to expand distribution—and virtually ruled out fountain service and vending machines.

What's more, the team discovered that Gatorade's established location in supermarkets was not with the soft drinks but with the fruit juices and fruit drinks. That had advantages and disadvantages: while it shut Gatorade out of the big-stakes competition, the location boosted its markup since juices and fruit drinks sell at a higher price per ounce than soft drinks.

The next question was whether or not Gatorade had any competition. After looking at all the scientific papers they could find on rehydration, they determined that plain water was their only competition—and, of course, it didn't have the benefits of Gatorade's added glucose and sodium.

Marineau's team's next step was to identify the forces and factors that affect the beverage industry as a whole. Their key findings:

- The business was huge and growing. Per capita consumption of nonalcoholic beverages in the United States had already hit record levels—an average of $350 a year for every man, woman, and child—and the country appeared thirstier than ever.
- There was an obvious seasonal factor—more beverages were sold in hot months than in cold—and given the fact that Gatorade was used for rehydration, the seasonal factor would be inescapable.
- The nationwide trend toward exercise and physical fitness had taken hold. As Marineau puts it, "Baby-boomers were saying, 'I don't want to get old and fat like my parents and grandparents.'"
- Compounding all this, the United States was on the verge of a new infatuation with sports, triggered by the explosive growth of television. With cable television spreading, available channels proliferating, and coverage mushrooming in the media, the prospects for any good sports-related product were likely to grow exponentially.

Putting it all together, Marineau told me, "There was going to be this physical need for Gatorade driven by people's greater participation in exercise and sports, and there was also going to be the imagery associated with what they saw being consumed by real people, real athletes. So we determined that the emerging potential of Gatorade was nothing short of phenomenal."

That analysis brought the team to another key part of Demand Strategy: determining the most profitable demand segment to go after.

Given the nature of the product, Marineau recalls, this was straightforward: "The core bull's-eye target was men—men in hot and sweaty moments, whether at work or in athletics." And after further study of how many potential hot and sweaty moments might be waiting for rehydration, the team concluded that this demand segment could indeed be profitable. From golfers and joggers to construction workers, even people watching sports in the stands or on television, the odds in favor of Gatorade moments seemed almost limitless. If Gatorade slaked the thirst of only a small percentage of the hottest and thirstiest, it could become one of the best-selling thirst quenchers on earth.

For the targeted men, Marineau explains, sports provides some of life's best moments: "These are times you get together with your buddies, let your hair down, really enjoy. Times you know you've played a terrific game. Whether you've won or lost, you've had a great time—a Gatorade time. Gatorade is part of that whole sense of personal self-satisfaction and affiliation."

Given the fact base, the forces and factors, and their chosen demand segment, the team next had to review its options. Should they try to reposition Gatorade to compete with soft drinks? How could they change the distribution system to expand their reach? How could they maximize their core competencies? What level of risk would they tolerate to reach the growth rate and financial returns they wanted? How and where should Gatorade compete? Was there a way to get into vending machines without going through regional bottlers?

Now they had to make the choices between the many attractive options at hand. Marineau and his team's first decision here was tough: not to alter the product. Gatorade was unique in the field. Though it was tempting to add sugar, improve Gatorade's flavor, and tackle the giants, they decided it would remain a thirst quencher, with an emphasis on sports.

The distribution system had its faults, Marineau says, and, "We saw the virtues of a direct-store delivery system, but we didn't have one. We couldn't afford to build one if we wanted to, and the people we could try to hire as store deliverers weren't as good as the Coke and Pepsi deliverers, who weren't available to us. So we decided we could live with the system we had."

The price of that decision was doing without some sales outlets and limiting the potential for fountain service or vending machines—potentially huge opportunities. But the wholesale system also provided the advantage of higher margins, which could be reinvested in the business.

In fact, Gatorade's position in the juice aisle of supermarkets gave the team a chance to increase its margins. Ounce for ounce, it was less expensive than its neighbors on the shelves. If the price were raised, it would still be competitive, and the added revenues could be used for a marketing campaign. The decision was to do it.

Perhaps the most critical choice was where and how Gatorade should compete. Here the key decision was to think of demand in terms of hot and sweaty occasions, not to aim for some vague share of the beverage market. In other words, Marineau was thinking about how to meet demand. The team's conclusion was that Gatorade had to be available as near as possible to the "points of sweat," the places where men get hottest and sweatiest, notably athletic fields and hard-work job sites, including factories, farms, and mills.

As they studied the demand, Marineau's team found that one of their biggest opportunities was in convenience stores. Driving home hot and tired from work or play, Marineau says, men stop at a convenience store, "buy a bottle of something from beer to Gatorade, and usually drink three-quarters of it before they leave the parking lot."

The Demand Strategy upshot: Gatorade would build national distribution through supermarkets, grocery stores, and anywhere else close to points of sweat, where demand for a thirst-quenching product is the highest. In particular, Marineau remembers, "We were going to be the preeminent supplier of beverages in convenience stores—even beyond Coke and Pepsi. And that turned out to be a huge idea. We became very important to convenience stores."

Now the team started to pin down the specific strategies and business systems needed to win. Gatorade's proposition to its chosen customers had taken shape.

To deliver that proposition, the team committed itself to a five-part strategy:

1. Gatorade had to establish its ownership of the value it was offering—in other words, anyone thinking "sports beverage" or "thirst quencher" should automatically associate it with Gatorade. But to do that, Marineau explains, "We would have to advertise at a level much higher than the size of our business would normally justify." In fact, they would have to advertise—at least in Gatorade season—at a level approaching the promotion of the soft drink giants, just to keep Gatorade's proposition from being drowned out.

   Thanks to the price increase permitted by Gatorade's location in the fruit juice aisle, the company could afford the marketing expenditure. Its current customers accepted the higher price because they thought the product was worth it; to new customers, that was just the price of Gatorade. In other words, Gatorade's price was inelastic because there was no substitute for it.

The advertising linked Gatorade with male bonding and sports, implying a value that carried over from play to work, including lawn mowing and other do-it-yourself projects. And Gatorade's scientific credentials were reinforced in every television commercial by "demo man," an outline of a human body filling up with replenishing moisture.

2. The advertising would also establish Gatorade's ownership of the hot and sweaty occasions that prompted people to want rehydration. Any such moment should make people think of Gatorade.

3. To turn thinking into drinking, Gatorade distribution was focused on convenience stores and supermarkets. Where Coke's strategy was that it was always "within arm's length of desire," Marineau explains, "We wanted to drive brand availability to the point of sweat."

To attract new Gatorade customers, Marineau and his team developed new flavors and packages. When Marineau first showed up at the Stokely–Van Camp offices, he found a plan for a fruit punch flavor to be added to the existing lemon-lime and gave the go-ahead to roll out the flavor. In addition to offering greater variety, he reasoned, the added punch flavor would give Gatorade more shelf space and presence in stores.

Equally important was the packaging. In 1983, Gatorade came in just two sizes, thirty-two ounces and forty-six ounces, both in glass bottles. There were no cans, no trial sizes, no easily carried reclosable plastic bottles.

One oddity about the beverage market, the team discovered, was that many people have more container loyalty than brand loyalty. If they're used to buying their favorite drink in a certain can or plastic bottle, they will switch brands only if the new drink comes in the same kind of container. Clearly, it behooved Gatorade to offer more shapes and sizes resembling its competitors' containers.

The team's first packaging innovation was a sixteen-ounce trial-size bottle. Cannily, they flouted beverage convention by making it with Gatorade's usual wide mouth—a chugalug convenience that underscored the product's thirst-quenching properties.

Plastic bottles presented a bigger challenge. Unlike conventional soft drinks, Gatorade is bottled at a high temperature—so hot that it would warp the usual plastic bottle. It took two years of research, but Gatorade finally became the first nationally distributed beverage to be bottled hot in plastic bottles. Today the line comes in ten different containers, none of which is glass.

4. To establish its sports identity, Gatorade set out to "own the sidelines, from kid to pro." This involved a hugely ambitious five-year plan (it stretched to eight) to establish a presence at nearly every organized sports contest in the country.

The team identified six sports that together attract more than 90 percent of both participants and observers—football, basketball, baseball, hockey, golf, and track and field. For all players at all levels in these sports, from grade schools to pro teams, Gatorade made all its products available free during games. To viewers, the planners figured, the sight of an athlete scoring a touchdown and swigging Gatorade would be an implied endorsement of the drink's thirst-quenching power. For an athlete, seeing a coach dispense the stuff gave it instant credibility. According to Marineau, this sideline tactic became the fulcrum of the whole Gatorade strategy, cementing the ownership of rehydration, the ownership of the hot and sweaty occasion, and the availability of the brand.

Starting in 1983, the sideline tactic was progressing rapidly in all six professional sports and making inroads at the lower levels. In 1986, the New York Giants were on their way to the Super Bowl. With millions of viewers watching, linebacker Harry Carson undertook the customary ritual of drenching the winning coach, Bill Parcells, with water. But this time, instead of water, Carson saturated the coach with a very visible cooler of Gatorade. Suddenly, the green drench acquired symbolic value, a bit like baptism.

That was a happy accident, Marineau recalls—"We didn't pay anybody to do it"—but in addition to providing great publicity for

Gatorade, it woke up the competition. As other beverage makers tried to muscle their way onto the sports sidelines, the cost of completing Gatorade's coup kept escalating.

Nonetheless, it was worth whatever it cost. Given the sight of star athletes officially swigging Gatorade, the drink's very ubiquity tended to keep competitors at bay. "All you see on the sidelines is Gatorade," says Marineau. "I mean, is there really any other sports thirst quencher?"

5. The final plank in Gatorade's Demand Strategy was Marineau's protection of its franchise by making sure his team became experts on the science of fluid replenishment. The planners wanted to make sure no one else could steal a march by coming up with new science or technology that would turn Gatorade into yesterday's faded fad.

Gatorade built a sports physiology laboratory and established relationships with sports physiologists around the world, enlisting them in some of its research projects to enhance and reinforce Gatorade's knowledge and credibility. The move was sheer genius. Even though it had no competition, Gatorade protected itself by making sure that it would always know more about the physiology of thirst quenching than any upstart competitor. In its first major project, the lab provided just what Marineau hoped for—actual evidence that Gatorade was even faster than water in getting from the stomach into the bloodstream.

Marineau's planners had now reached the point of allocating resources. Having defined the demand for Gatorade and shaped strategies for meeting and boosting that demand, the team had to decide what it needed to make all this happen and ensure Gatorade's enduring success as well.

Once a company has identified demand, allocating the appropriate resources may appear straightforward. Specific items cost specific amounts. But the decisions aren't always easy. Gatorade's sports-physiology lab is a case in point. At some companies, cost-conscious managers might question an investment as seemingly tangential to bottom-line concerns. At Quaker Oats, the pressure to justify a controversial acquisition gave Marineau and his planners a license for action. Any resource that could possibly help create demand for Gatorade was approved for their use.

Carrying out demand strategies involves making specific choices, being disciplined, and having varied input. So it went for Gatorade. In the early years, Marineau's team tried to keep Gatorade's success as quiet as possible—hoping to stay below the radar beams of the big beverage players, who might sense an opportunity in a sports thirst quencher. "We were trying to create a safe harbor from competition," Marineau remembers.

For a while, it worked: the only competitors who attempted to enter the market were small and easily beaten back. No one put a serious dent in Gatorade's 90-plus percentage of the demand. But by the time Carson dumped Gatorade on Parcells, the secret was out. "Sooner or later, people start noticing," Marineau says. "They couldn't miss it. And so, back in the late eighties and early nineties, we saw Coke and Pepsi coming with POWERade and AllSport."

By then, Gatorade had its game on. "No one has been able to build a better product," explains Marineau. "They've all tried 'Tastes Better.' They've all tried 'Works Better.' For them, nothing works." Experts warned that Coke and Pepsi would threaten Gatorade with distribution, but Gatorade's demand-based system proved up to the battle.

In the one area where Marineau's team sensed that Gatorade might be vulnerable, it made a preemptive, bold strike.

As part of its own-the-sidelines tactic, Gatorade had deliberately steered clear of getting endorsements from star athletes. It was more powerful and believable, the team felt, to have the drink associated with all sports, everywhere, than with a few major players. But now they feared that Coke or Pepsi might blitz them with star power.

How to respond? "We said, 'Well, ideally, we could get the world's best-known athlete to endorse our product,'" Marineau recalls. "He'd be the only one we'd use, but everyone else would pale by comparison." In the late eighties, that meant, inevitably, only Michael Jordan. Gatorade wooed him for two years, waiting for his contract with Coca-Cola to run out. Then the company got him.

The slogan was brilliantly simple: "Be like Mike." "We're not really trying to have Michael shill the benefits of Gatorade," says Marineau. "Everyone knows about that. Let's just make sure that when they say Michael Jordan, what does he believe in? Nike. Gatorade. 'Be like Mike.' And it worked phenomenally. Who are you going to put up against Michael Jordan to say, 'Well, I drink POWERade, so you ought to, too'? It really was the final nail in the competitive defense."

At last reading, Gatorade's worldwide sales totaled $1.8 billion, and its share of demand was in the high eighties. Moreover, in 2000 both Coke and Pepsi bid to acquire the Quaker Oats Company—primarily to obtain Gatorade. Pepsi won and acquired Quaker Oats for over $13 billion.

CHAPTER 10

COUNTRYWIDE CREDIT INDUSTRIES

n 1969, two enterprising New Yorkers, Angelo Mozilo and David Loeb, set out to change fundamentally the way mortgage banking is practiced in America. They were determined to create opportunities for more Americans to own their own homes by cutting costs, increasing efficiencies in lending, and speeding and easing the mortgage process. So they started a company in California in an office with only two desks but an extremely confident name on the door: Countrywide Funding Corp.

Little more than three decades later, Countrywide Credit Industries is one of the giants of the mortgage industry, and co-founder Angelo Mozilo remains at the helm as chairman and CEO. (David Loeb, his co-founder, retired from Countrywide in 1999.) In fiscal 2001, Countrywide created $69 billion worth of new home loans—a mortgage every forty seconds—and serviced a $300 billion portfolio of existing loans for 2.4 million customers. In an industry with severe pricing pressure and gyrating interest rate cycles, it has achieved compounded earnings growth at a staggering annual average of 33 percent in the decade ending in 2001, when it chalked up post-tax profits of $374 million. Even more remarkable, Countrywide's growth has been primarily organic, not the result of acquisitions or mergers.

In Demand Strategy terms, Countrywide's story would probably come closest to the history of Southwest Airlines, which began operations in the same era, or Dell Computer, founded more than a decade later. Like Southwest and Dell, Countrywide targeted the demand of value-conscious buyers and invented a completely new and different business system to serve it profitably. Having discovered this profitable segment, Countrywide spent the next three decades perfecting its Demand Strategy, broadening and deepening its reach, refining its Demand Value Proposition, and evolving its business systems to maintain profitability and growth despite numerous challenges along the way. Since 1997, it has been one of the five hundred companies that make up the Standard & Poor's stock market index.

Countrywide's first few years were far from easy: the young firm, still trying to find its footing in the industry, either lost money or made only meager profits. Much of the problem could be traced to the structure of the industry at the time. Mortgage banks employed loan officers, whose job it was to build contacts with the local real estate brokers and home buyers. These relationships generated loans for the mortgage bank but also produced hefty commissions for the loan officers, sometimes approaching 1 percent of the total loan. Not surprisingly, the mortgage banks in each region of the country competed vigorously for the best salespeople by dangling higher commissions as a carrot. When the loan officers took the highest bid and left for a new bank, they took their broker relationships, loan volumes, and profits with them.

This bidding war not only sapped profits for Mozilo and Loeb but frustrated their long-term goal: their vision of nationwide innovation was being held hostage by the spiraling commissions they had to pay to keep their sales staff. But after several years of frustration, the pair had an epiphany: studying the forces and factors in their market, they found a demand segment of customers not currently addressed that they could target. Mozilo estimated that roughly a quarter of home buyers were highly price sensitive and would sign up with the bank that had the lowest mortgage rate. The challenge was to find a way to meet this demand profitably.

By 1974, they had their new plan in hand. It was a classic of Demand Strategy: a decision to differentiate themselves not by pushing the same commodity the competition was offering, but by betting on a product that aligned with the demand of their targeted demand segment. First, Mozilo and Loeb fired Countrywide's entire commissioned sales staff and replaced them with salaried employees who had no special contacts but could efficiently provide loans to home buyers who applied. Next, they used most of the money they saved on commissions to lower their interest rates and thus meet the targeted demand. The rest of the savings went for bold advertising to promote their lower rates. At first, working with a shoestring budget, they advertised on postcards; as the business grew, they began using radio and television as well. At one stroke, they had cut operating costs enormously and passed the savings on to their customers. And as Mozilo puts it, "Advertising gave us full control over our message."

The steps Mozilo and Loeb took to get off the commodity treadmill are a classic of Demand Strategy.

First they established a forces and factors context. Then they identified the customer segments who would be most profitable for them. Next they differentiated themselves by creating a product that was targeted at the 25 percent of home buyers whose need for a lower-cost mortgage wasn't being met. To deliver on this demand, they built a proprietary business system composed of branch offices, salaried rather than commissioned salespeople, and customized information systems. Finally, they reallocated precious resources by passing savings on to customers in addition to using advertising to let people know that Countrywide was the best place to get a low-cost mortgage.

The new strategy paid off handsomely. Countrywide's rate-cutting ads roused ire among its competitors but found a ready response among home buyers. By 1980, Countrywide was able to expand to forty branches in eight states.

As Countrywide expanded, it gained a deeper understanding of its targeted demand segment. In fact, the segment turned out to include not just home buyers but also the brokers who were selling them houses and who often helped them with their mortgage applications by steering the buyers to a preferred lender. The company saw that some of these brokers fit the Countrywide business model better than others. In an interview conducted in the mid-1990s, Mozilo defined his target: "We're looking for the real-estate agent who's looking for the most efficient execution. We are not looking for an agent who needs his hands to be held."

To serve this segment of brokers and their customers, Countrywide gave its branch lenders considerable authority to make fast decisions. Each branch could approve its own loans, process them, and write its own checks to borrowers. With no decisions from headquarters to wait for, a real estate agent acting for a customer could deal with the source and close a deal before the buyer changed his mind.

As Countrywide expanded, Mozilo and Loeb also realized that they could profitably serve a market segment considerably larger than the price-sensitive home buyers they had initially targeted. Their customers included many inexperienced home buyers who valued Countrywide for its ability to explain and simplify the steps involved in obtaining a mortgage. Countrywide's salaried staffers were well equipped to handle this; they could demystify the process by patiently outlining all the details, without any high-pressure sales tactics. Here again, the branch-level control helped free the staff to provide a convenient and straightforward experience that was valued by this group of customers.

This is an excellent example of why a Demand Value Proposition well done is inclusionary rather than exclusionary. While building products and services for their target, Countrywide found that tens of thousands of people in different demand segments wanted the simplification and care offered by Countrywide.

The network of Countrywide branches was also carefully structured to serve target demand profitably. Mozilo explained that the branches would remain small, with about one thousand square feet of space and only three or four staffers in each one, so that they could be close to their customers and close to the core of the real estate community they serve. Each branch, he said, would need to make only a few loans to be profitable, but there could be many branches in a given community. Countrywide's aim, even then, was to grab at least a 5 percent share of any market it competed in, and a national penetration of 5 percent. (At last count, it had more than 550 branches across the country.)

Countrywide's constant pursuit of a proprietary understanding of demand enabled it to differentiate itself to its target segments in an otherwise commodity-driven marketplace. But to serve its segments profitably with its DVP, Countrywide had to have the business systems and strategies to support its Demand Strategy.

One key business system was, as discussed above, the decentralized branch system staffed by salaried employees. But there were other forces and factors that Countrywide had to address as part of its strategy.

In the mortgage industry, a bank's fortunes rise and fall with interest rates. When rates are high, demand for new mortgages dries up, but when rates start falling, mortgage origination ramps up quickly. Falling interest rates also trigger a boom in refinancing mortgages at lower rates, as happened between 2000 and 2001. But the industry must live with the fact that it has no real control over its own pricing: interest rate movements in the United States are largely controlled by the Federal Reserve.

In the early 1980s, interest rates of nearly 18 percent withered demand and ravaged the mortgage industry. As a result of this, Mozilo realized Countrywide had to diversify in order to reduce its dependence on the interest rate cycle. At the same time, it had to retain its focus on the mortgage industry, where its competencies and brand could be leveraged. The company addressed these objectives by developing a business-to-business unit named Countrywide Securities Corporation. Countrywide Securities Corporation is a broker-dealer that bundles loans into pools and sells them to investors as securities, backed by the underlying mortgages. The venture has since grown into an important subsidiary, now known as Countrywide Capital Markets. In fiscal 2001, it traded $742 billion worth of securities and generated $44.5 million in profit, accounting for nearly 8 percent of Countrywide's total pretax earnings. Countrywide learned a larger, more important lesson from the high interest cycles of the 1980s: that the company had to be flexible and search continually for new ways to keep costs low. Only then could it be sure that there would be revenues, profits, and growth in lean years and good ones alike. As Mozilo decreed, "I never want to be behind the competition. I never want to try to catch them. We need to leapfrog them."

One key to flexibility was a business system that Mozilo called a "dynamic production operation." This involved staffing up with temporary employees when interest rates were low, and letting them go when rates rose again and originations dried up. The small branch offices in Countrywide's network were similarly geared for flexibility; they could be easily closed and reopened as economic conditions fluctuated.

Countrywide also realized, better than any rivals at the time, that technology could help the company provide loans faster, more accurately, and more cheaply—goods that were essential to its DVP. As early as 1980, it began to develop proprietary technology to automate many back-office functions, the first step in a long line of technological innovations.

In 1990, Countrywide introduced a proprietary processing software named EDGE that allowed a single entry of data for all the processes involved in a loan, such as document production and underwriting.

In 1992, the company launched CLUES (Countrywide Loan Underwriting Expert System), an automated underwriting program that used artificial intelligence technology to approve or deny routine loans. Years ahead of Countrywide's competitors, CLUES made sure that all the necessary information about a potential loan was taken into account, without compromising on credit quality or fairness to the applicant. A decision on a loan, which formerly took weeks as employees gathered all the necessary paperwork, now took thirty seconds.

Richard Jones, chief technology officer of Countrywide, says CLUES originated in the refinancing boom of 1991, when a shortage of underwriters clogged the company's systems and created a backlog of loan applications. "We were doing a huge volume and we needed to automate," he says. "This is consistent with Countrywide's philosophy. All along, [our idea] was to use technology to gain a competitive advantage, and that was our thinking in 1991."

Automated underwriting turned out to be a vital system for Countrywide in the boom of the 1990s, making it possible for the company to launch new products rapidly and frequently. As Jones explains, CLUES can be easily adjusted to make decisions based on a new set of criteria. Thus, he says, "If a new product is invented by marketing, we're able to support that with [an] automated underwriting decision within a one-month release cycle."

Smart Call, similar to the intelligent call-routing system pioneered by Capital One, allows Countrywide to speed up routine customer service, while simultaneously lowering costs and freeing up employees to work on more complex tasks. Introduced in 1997, the system handles more than 40 percent of the twenty thousand calls that come in from customers every day on tax questions and payment issues. Smart Call automatically identifies the home owner who is calling, accesses the account to predict the reason for the call, and provides the answers to five questions it has predicted will be asked by the caller. As a result, the cost per service call has fallen from $4 to sixty cents, saving the company $6 million a year.

Perhaps the most important system that Countrywide invented to smooth out the interest rate cycle was what its managers call the "macro hedge." Since mortgages have a lifespan of as long as thirty years, the business splits naturally into two parts—originating loans and servicing them—which may actually be done by separate companies. In mortgage origination, the loan is actually approved and funded; servicing involves the collection of payments from the borrower and the routine paperwork of accounting and tax reporting for the duration of the loan. The servicing company guarantees the payments and collects a fee, which can be as low as a quarter of a percentage point or as much as 3 percent, depending on the riskiness of the loan. In its early years Countrywide focused on originating loans, but in the late 1980s, as the industry came off another interest rate cycle, the company made an interesting observation about the forces and factors at work: when interest rates are low, high originations generate revenues and profits, while servicing revenues fall as people prepay their mortgages through refinancing. But when interest rates rise and originations dry up, fewer people refinance, and older mortgages continue to generate servicing fees.

Thus Countrywide developed its justly famous macro hedge: in addition to its own originations, Countrywide began to build up its servicing portfolio by buying loans from other companies. That way, at both turns of the interest rate cycle, Countrywide was guaranteed steady revenues and profits.

The hedge came in handy when rates shot up dramatically in 1994 after a long-term low in 1993. The refinancing boom of 1993 dried up, and while the company chalked up a $95 million decrease in origination revenues, it more than made it up with a $230 million gain in mortgage servicing fees. Countrywide ended the year with an overall profit, no mean achievement in a rising-interest-rate environment.

While Countrywide pioneered the macro hedge, it is also one of the few mortgage companies that can actually make it work. Most companies use origination as a loss leader and make their profits on servicing fees. Countrywide's flexible, low-cost structure lets it profit from both operations.

Countrywide's Demand Strategy truly came of age in the 1990s. As part of their continuing analysis of the forces and factors in their market, including long-term demographic trends, its managers were ahead of the competition in recognizing that the mainstream home ownership market had become increasingly saturated. At the same time, ownership rates remained low for such nontraditional borrowers as African Americans, Hispanics, immigrants, and lower-income groups in general. Toward the end of the 1990s, 74 percent of Caucasian Americans owned their own homes. The rate for all other groups was only 45 percent. As Mozilo put it, "There was a whole segment of the population that was left out, because the system built by the government was unintentionally creating barriers that kept nonwhite, non-English-speaking people out of home ownership."

The gap, troubling as it was on social and political grounds, was easily explained: nontraditional home owners were perceived as presenting higher risk because of their lower incomes and assets. Often they did not have the documentation required for loans and could not come up with the down payment of 20 percent typically required for traditional mortgages.

But this perception of risk, Mozilo decided, was exaggerated. "Early on," he recalls, "I went to people's homes to interview them for loans. I'd try to get these round pegs to fit in a square hole. With tears in their eyes, people would promise me they'd take on second and third jobs to make the loans, because home ownership would make such a difference. I saw by interviewing thousands of these people that they were right—they'd make the payments, the system was wrong."

For Countrywide, the home ownership gap was a demand force. Potentially, it could be a fast-growing, profitable business opportunity, and it was also a chance for the company to help level the playing field for minorities and first-time home buyers.

So Countrywide has gone after this market aggressively. In 1998, the company pledged to provide $50 billion (later increased to $80 billion) in affordable mortgage financing for low-income and minority borrowers over a five-year period. It has also come up with a host of new products and services that help nontraditional borrowers overcome the hurdles associated with obtaining a loan.

A borrower with few assets who has maintained an excellent credit record, for example, may borrow 100 percent of a property's value, and in most states, an additional 3 percent for closing costs. Another such program offers a first mortgage of 95 percent of a home's cost, with the remaining 5 percent financed through a home equity loan.

Measured under the terms of the Home Mortgage Disclosure Act, Countrywide's efforts make it the nation's top lender to Hispanics, the third largest lender to African Americans, and the top lender to lower-income communities and borrowers. Moreover, despite the fact that it is not regulated under the Community Reinvestment Act (which was designed to protect underserved borrowers), it has a better fair lending record than most banks that do fall under the CRA.

It's a record that deserves—and gets—praise. "Hats off to Countrywide," says Matthew Lee, director of an activist group that has been sharply critical of many lenders. "They're not subject to CRA, and they have still invested the time to penetrate these markets. In that sense they're a leader among nonbank mortgage companies."

One would expect that lending to first-time home buyers and lower-income groups involves an increased risk of delinquencies: for all their good intentions to make timely payments, these buyers lack resources to weather financial emergencies. Such defaults can be very costly. First, there are direct foreclosure costs of around $2,500 for each failed mortgage. Moreover, once the foreclosure has occurred, Countrywide loses the lucrative fees from servicing the loan. Third, higher delinquency rates adversely affect Countrywide's standing with the investors who fund its loans, making future financing more difficult or expensive. The most damaging effect of foreclosures, however, may be the bad word of mouth in the communities where the company operates. Even though most foreclosures are driven by unforeseen events among borrowers such as job loss, divorce, or health issues, a lender with many foreclosures develops a reputation: "Don't go to Countrywide—they'll foreclose on you."

For all these reasons, Countrywide takes extraordinary steps to minimize the default rate on its loans to lower-income borrowers and first-time home buyers. In Demand Strategy, we'd say that they've built an extraordinary business system to support a profitable product and a demand segment that requires a bit of extra service. The process actually starts the day the loan application is received, and ends only when the loan has been paid off in full. The company uses a model to assess how large a loan a borrower can afford, given the family's background and income. It also has a home ownership education program, to prepare first-time owners for the responsibilities and potential costs of owning a home. To make sure money earmarked for mortgage payments does not get diverted to pay for unanticipated repairs, the program includes home inspection services and also a home warranty for electrical products.

If loans from disadvantaged borrowers do fall delinquent, Countrywide keeps them in a separate portfolio, recognizing that such people do not have the financial cushion or easy access to credit that conventional borrowers possess.

And the company has a toolbox of workout programs for such defaulters, including payment plans, loan modifications, and assistance with mortgage insurance. Richard De Leo, managing director of loan administration, says these measures "can help borrowers avoid foreclosure and get back on track with their mortgage payments." For instance, he says, payments may be suspended for three months if a borrower loses his or her job.

Countrywide has teams of "loss mitigation specialists" whose job is to offer counseling to lower-income defaulters, using the toolbox to create a workout program tailored to their special circumstances. The teams recognize that embarrassment, fear, or denial keeps defaulters from initiating contact with the company, so when payments are skipped, they reach out with telephone calls, pamphlets, letters, even a mailed videotape. All these messages are couched in friendly, non-threatening terms, with offers to provide counseling and relief.

Says one defaulter who received a hand-addressed letter from Countrywide: "I saw the pamphlet and said, 'Yeah, sure.' But I called and they seemed real supportive, real helpful. When I got off the phone, I thought, 'This was too easy; there has to be something else.' " But his fears proved unfounded: Countrywide's team reworked his loan to make it repayable over a new thirty-year period, reducing his interest rate by nearly half a percentage point in the process.

None of these measures is unique to Countrywide. Its real differentiation is the way it combines the toolbox with its teams of loss-mitigation specialists and its insights into the attitudes and behavior of its targeted customers. As De Leo says, "There is nothing special that we have that other companies don't have, but what sets Countrywide apart is how we successfully utilize the tools that we are given to avoid foreclosure."

And on the whole, the foreclosure reducing system has been highly successful. As many as 80 percent of early-stage delinquent loans to low- and moderate-income borrowers are worked out quickly. Even the remaining 20 percent, delinquent for 120 days or more, are not abandoned. Fully 40 percent of these defaults are eventually worked out as well. The end result: a mere 12 percent of Countrywide's delinquent mortgages end in foreclosure.

In the 1990s, a new force on the market—the Internet—seemed to pose a threat to Countrywide. As with all financial transactions, the information involved in processing and granting loans could, in principle, be transferred entirely to the Web, effectively bypassing real estate brokers and, with them, the entire branch system that was the core of Countrywide's retail business. Even while the Internet was in its "early adopter" phase, companies such as E-LOAN were gearing up to handle the entire mortgage origination process on-line.

Mozilo recognized this danger and was prepared to meet it. However, with an insight into emerging demand that looks truly astonishing in hindsight, he also recognized that what we now call a "clicks and bricks" strategy would be essential to serve all the various segments of the mortgage market.

Countrywide.com was launched in 1996, and related Web sites were quickly added as consumers and business partners saw the benefits of the new Internet channel. Prospective Countrywide borrowers can apply on-line, and can be preapproved on-line in more than twenty-five states. Applicants and borrowers are constantly kept informed about the status of their loans. As recently as 2000, Countrywide's major competitors, including Wells Fargo and Chase, still had not caught up with the company in the range of services offered over the Internet.

But even as Countrywide built up its Internet presence, it stayed true to the clicks and bricks vision articulated by Mozilo in 1995. "The Web site remains a cornerstone of Countrywide's growth plans," Stan Kurland, the company's executive managing director and chief operating officer, wrote in a recent article. "The clicks-and-bricks strategy recognizes that different customers have different comfort levels when it comes to shopping for a mortgage on the Internet."

In practice, this means that every loan application received on the Internet is sent automatically to the branch office closest to the applicant, where it is processed just like loans from walk-in customers, using all the company's technology and automated systems. But if the on-line applicants have doubts or questions at any point in the process, they can call the company directly for further help. Says Mozilo, "Do as much as you want on the 'net, but when you get stuck, we're there."

Countrywide's e-commerce strategy has been a success: its collection of Web properties (including separate channels for wholesale mortgages) currently generates 40 percent of its loan originations. However, says David Espenschied, head of Countrywide's e-business unit, "It's just beginning to pay off. The best is yet to come."

E-commerce was only one of the powerful forces and factors at work on the mortgage industry in the 1990s, and some of the others had more immediate impact. Tremors of the demand economy—

increased competition, pricing pressure, and the loss of differentiation—were beginning to be felt by the whole industry, and Countrywide was no exception.

In a detailed essay on the evolution of the industry, Michael Jacobides, a professor at the Wharton Business School, describes how standardized underwriting eroded the differences between lenders and increased price competition. Meanwhile, real estate professionals and potential home buyers took advantage of the information explosion to shop around for the best deal, and the industry played right into their hands. As Jacobides puts it, "Given the availability of information and commoditization of the product/service offered, most of the savings was passed on to consumers through competition. . . . Transparency and reduced search and transaction costs led to increased rivalry and the erosion of profits."

In sum, the traditional basis for competitive advantage in the mortgage industry was vanishing. "Being local and embedded did not cut it any more," wrote Jacobides. "Like the Red Queen's soldiers in *Alice in Wonderland,* mortgage firms had to run to keep their place and run even faster to stay alive." The increased competition created severe pricing pressures: fees and charges for origination fell almost 40 percent within a few years. Several big players, such as First Union, actually left the industry. There was also a spate of mergers and acquisitions as many concluded that being bigger would help them survive.

In 1990, the top twenty-five originators had about 30 percent of the new loan market, while the top twenty-five servicers had slightly more than one-fifth of their market. These share figures had been steadily rising over the decade, and by 2000 had mushroomed to around 60 percent of each market.

Countrywide itself was feeling the pricing pressure: its net margin fell from 28 percent to 20 percent between 1995 and 2000. As a true Demand Strategist, however, the company has anticipated and responded to these pressures. As it did in dealing with nontraditional home owners, Countrywide stepped up its efforts to identify new demand opportunities and create profitable products to serve them. Today the company has no fewer than eighty-four distinct products to serve various subsegments of consumers with specific needs.

One example is the eEasy Rate Reduction Plan, which allows borrowers to reduce their mortgage rate automatically as interest rates fall, without going through the cumbersome process of refinancing the loan. By exercising this option, a borrower with, say, a $100,000 fixed-rate mortgage could save nearly $1,300 over a five-year period. This product has created a large new market for Countrywide: Lehman Brothers estimated that more than 30 percent of borrowers would prefer to use Countrywide's offering rather than refinance in the traditional manner. As an added benefit, as the first company to launch this kind of product, Countrywide was able to obtain a price premium: it charged 2.5 percent of the outstanding balance as its fee for the service. It could have made a profit with a fee as low as 1.5 percent. Even so, most borrowers found the fee lower than the cost of a traditional refinancing.

More recently, Countrywide has promised a new type of product that combines the features of a mortgage with those of a credit card and has tax advantages as well. This instrument will automatically provide a credit line based on the difference between the current value of the home and the outstanding mortgage balance.

Countrywide, however, is all too aware of the shortened product cycles of the demand economy. The eEasy Rate Reduction Plan, for instance, was matched soon after its introduction by a similar offering from Greenpoint Financial, and the 2.5 percent fee seems likely to dwindle. Even before its launch, Countrywide's combined mortgage and credit product faces competition from Wells Fargo, which has plans for a similar bundle. Such competitive pressures ensure that Countrywide will continue the search for new opportunities in the years ahead.

Reduced margins and commoditization in the core mortgage business have also led Countrywide to diversify its activities. However, its leaders have stayed largely within the boundaries of the mortgage industry. They have also focused on offerings that reinforce the Demand Value Proposition they have developed over the years. For instance, they aim to create a one-stop shop for all the services associated with loan origination: title insurance, appraisal, escrow, credit reports, processing, and closing. As it is, these processes require a borrower to deal with as many as eight different organizations. But as Mozilo sees it, "It should be one seamless process, with all services in one location from one source."

Countrywide already has a springboard for this operation. Its subsidiary LandSafe provides appraisal, credit, flood risk determination, and title and escrow services, while another subsidiary, Countrywide Insurance, offers home protection and other policies.

Countrywide has also dipped a toe in the European market. In a joint venture with Britain's Woolwich plc, the company is adapting its lending technology to the regulations and customs of the British mortgage market, where it sees major opportunities to cut costs and increase homeownership rates.

And in the end, Countrywide's Demand Strategy requires branding that will seal its differentiation in the customer's mind. As early as 1995, Mozilo told an interviewer: "When people think of hamburgers, they think of McDonald's. When people think mortgages, we want them to think of Countrywide. It's a thirty-year odyssey we are on."

Less than halfway through that time frame, Mozilo and the company he co-founded have traveled a good chunk of the distance.

EMC'S DEMAND PROPOSITION

Almost certainly there's never been an entrepreneur who hasn't endlessly played the "What if" game. This is a simple game where you imagine your new business being successful, and the "What if" represents sales growth, profits, or any other objective measurement of your own choosing. Sometimes I think that it must be an extra chromosome that only entrepreneurs are born with. In business we're taught to do the "What if" game as a pro forma business plan. That makes the exercise much more disciplined and much closer to reality, while at the same time taking all the fun out of it.

Dick Egan and Roger Marino, the two founders of EMC, played the "What if" game, but even in their wildest dreams they couldn't have asked themselves, "What if our company is so successful that its stock grows faster over a ten-year period than any stock in the history of the NYSE?" It would have been impossible for them to imagine ten years ago that their fledgling company, then based in a small second-story walk-up office over a restaurant, would appreciate 80,575 percent in the 1990s.

Named after Egan, Marino, and a third founder (who dropped out early on), EMC was able to accomplish this amazing feat because of the company's understanding of the coming demand for computer data storage. EMC then used its insights into demand to dominate the rapidly growing storage market. EMC's achievement is even more remarkable considering the fact that it came from nowhere to take on established giants like IBM, Hewlett-Packard, and Sun Microsystems, among others.

Back in 1979, Egan and Marino had no business plan, no product, no market, no capital equipment. All they had was electrical engineering degrees and a sure instinct for understanding and meeting demand.

In those days, information technology customers were frustrated by proprietary technology products designed to accept only expensive add-ons made by the original manufacturers. Users wanted freedom to customize information systems at a reasonable cost. Providing that freedom became EMC's raison d'être.

First, however, the two entrepreneurs had to reap seed money. Working for a California furniture company, Egan and Marino sold computer desks to New England businesses at a hefty commission of 55 percent. Manhandling desks into customers' offices, the two soon built up the funds they needed to begin a new venture. They started out representing and selling Intel's add-on memory packages, a growth business at a time when companies were computerizing as fast as possible.

EMC's real future began in 1981 when the partners were turned down by one prospect, a research scientist at the University of Rhode Island. He had no interest in Intel memory chips. He used a computer aimed at scientific users—the Prime thirty-two-bit minicomputer—and told them, "I wish EMC sold Prime-compatible memory."

As Egan says, "In that moment, an idea was born. For the next five months, Roger and I spent every weekend in a university computer lab designing . . . testing . . . perfecting our own Prime-compatible product. The professor who led the Boston Prime Users' Group ran that lab; he got very excited when he saw our first unit working. He wanted us to publicize our success. Everyone he knew needed more Prime memory but couldn't pay $36,000 per megabyte for it—Prime's price was that high."

When the partners made a stab at publicity, Prime Computer quickly sued EMC for allegedly stealing proprietary information. When Egan and Marino threatened to countersue Prime for monopolistic behavior, the computer company backed off. EMC was in the clear, and began to take off.

"When our payroll grew to 12," Egan recalls, "we stopped worrying about how much we spent in restaurants. And every day, we heard users expressing a need for more memory for Prime . . . and for Wang, for DEC VAXs, for nearly every minicomputer. Roger started building a direct sales force by recruiting college graduates. Those enthusiastic, high-energy kids sold a lot of memory. And they gave us the confidence to look for another product line to develop and sell.

"Everybody had been segmenting the computer market into a pyramid shape according to memory size: high-speed memory for minicomputers formed the point of the pyramid; low-cost tape formed the base. We started seeing a new variable that actually changed the shape of the market. We realized that if EMC 'walked down the pyramid,' it could reach a big but under-publicized market: disk storage. Storage turned the pyramid into a diamond with a plump center reflecting a potentially huge demand.

"We set our sights on creating peripherals for IBM computers. After all, the real money wasn't in college labs; it was in corporate data centers."

But what IBM mainframe user would buy a storage device from a dozen guys with an office above a restaurant? Moreover, EMC had no chance of landing mainframe business (that is, competing with IBM) until it could make an IBM-compatible disk drive system that worked better than IBM's.

In an ironic twist that Adam Smith would have appreciated, EMC's efforts to do so triggered a response so ferocious (price slashing, breakneck improvements) that the digital David was forced to fight Goliath by creating truly breakthrough products. EMC created an even better and cheaper alternative to IBM by using eight-inch commodity disks and combining them with RAID (redundant array of independent disks) technology to deliver higher performance and fault tolerance.

With the company growing rapidly in 1988, Egan and Marino hired Michael Ruettgers to improve the company's manufacturing quality and efficiency. A former Raytheon executive who had played an important role in the Patriot missile program, Ruettgers launched a continuous improvement program that became the first step to EMC's impressive customer response system. (Ruettgers's outstanding management abilities were clear from the very beginning, and he was made chief executive officer in 1992. At the start of 2001 Ruettgers was succeeded as CEO by Joseph Tucci, when Ruettgers was promoted to EMC's executive chairman.)

By the early 1990s, EMC had mastered the hardware side of data storage with its evolving Symmetrix family of intelligent information storage systems for mainframe users, and had taken an enormous share of mainframe storage from IBM. It then surveyed the next logical step—software for information protection, management, and sharing.

Before getting into software, Egan and Marino had to be sure there was sufficient demand to justify plunging into that side of the business. Their first step was to analyze the forces and factors at work in the software side of the industry.

One of the most important forces and factors to emerge at EMC occurred during a working session of a group of senior officers. At one point the group was looking at the letters *IT* on the board in one of their workrooms. Suddenly, one of the senior officers leapt to his feet and said, "That's it, that's it, everyone's been focused on the technology and no one has paid nearly enough attention to the information, which is really what it's all about." It has led EMC to focus their attention on how to store and move information wherever and whenever it's needed. While the technology and all of its benefits are critical, the real end result is what can be done with the information. Fortunately, businesses were awakening to the real essence of their ability to compete: their ability to capture and harness all of the critical information in their enterprise. The volume of information was mushrooming and they needed access to this information many more hours each day.

EMC realized that the most important thing about computing was not the power of the processor but the speed and reliability of access to the data. The problem was that data was on multiple "islands" scattered throughout the corporation—on a heterogeneous collection of mainframes and servers. There was no centralized access to it, and its safety and integrity in the event of a fire or some other disaster were far from assured. EMC saw that software could help solve their problems and decided to pursue this avenue.

The decision to pursue software was a major one for EMC. Their storage business was booming. Why would they want to risk their resources and their growth by entering a new business?

The forces and factors analysis made the answer clear. Customers wanted to extend the functionality of storage. They wanted it to move from being a static, isolated container to being a dynamic, networked container. There was, of course, a desire to protect the information within storage while making the availability of storage more rapid even in the face of much higher demand on the storage system. In other words, what customers were asking for was software that would give them simpler, more cost-effective ways to safeguard, preserve, move, copy, view, analyze, and especially manage their information. EMC answered the call.

EMC soon realized that the key to the future of data storage was *functional* storage. Customers wanted to store and retrieve data from remote locations. EMC's Symmetrix 3000, unveiled in 1995, combined hardware with advanced software to solve this problem. It was the world's first platform independent storage system for open systems, and could seamlessly interoperate to gather data from all the different "islands" within the enterprise.

EMC also created software that eliminated the chances of losing data following a disaster. "We involved our lead customers to participate with our engineers both in our facilities as well as in their own. The customers invented more ways to use a key EMC software product called Symmetrix Remote Data Facility (SRDF), including data center consolidations and migrations.

"It was clear that the combination of hardware and software—an integrated offering—increasingly served as the basis of differentiation in a market growing more competitive daily."

Software has been a key source of EMC's growth. By 1997, more than 70 percent of EMC's engineers were dedicated to software development, and software sales rose from $20 million in 1995 to $445 million in 1998 and to $1.4 billion in 2000, making EMC the fastest-growing major software company in the industry.

In past chapters you've seen the power of industry forces and demand factors and their ability to provide insights about changes in demand that are forming or are about to change in a meaningful way. Most often, forces and factors are applied during annual planning or as part of an acquisition study. Not so at EMC, because of the speed of change in the information technology industry. Virtually everybody at EMC is devoted to uncovering the next emerging demand. The main reason is Mike Ruettgers's and EMC's constant sense of urgency. When Ruettgers goes by some of the formerly prominent names in IT on Interstate 495 and Route 128 in Massachusetts, whose buildings are now empty, they are a constant reminder to him that one should be skeptical of success.

According to Ruettgers, "I think the defining characteristic of our culture is a sense of urgency. This primes us to seize opportunities that are only just emerging as well as to execute our existing plans. For example, when we launched our open storage product in 1995, I set a goal of $200 million in sales for the year. At the end of the first quarter, we were way behind our sales target, even though we had built enough products to meet them. So to make sure everybody understood how important this was, we took the extra inventory and put it in people's offices. They had to climb around crates to get to their desks. Miraculously, by the end of the next quarter we had met all our sales targets. And all of the offices were empty.

"We help fuel this sense of urgency by setting quarterly goals for the 800 or so executives in the organization. We measure and pay against those quarterly goals. I continue to be amazed at companies that still have annual goals for executives. I understand a profit target for the year but just can't imagine turning them loose and saying 'As long as you get this done by the end of the year, it's okay.' "

This sense of urgency and skepticism help to achieve EMC's objective to have more accurate and up-to-date information about its customers than any of its competitors. Ruettgers remains relentless in EMC's understanding of what its customers want and value. This constancy of purpose, he says, is vital.

EMC believes that the key to its ability to fully satisfy its customers is that most companies lack a lens through which to view and interpret their customers' world. EMC's lens keeps it focused on the sine qua non for customers: fast, reliable access to all of their corporate information no matter where in the enterprise it resides. Note that EMC views and interprets its customers' world, not its own, which enables it to fully and accurately understand demand before creating supply.

Recently, Mike Ruettgers told me a story about the value of meeting with customers. In the mid-1990s when the Internet was just beginning to show its commercial application, there was a great deal of conjecture on what uses the Internet would offer to customers in a B-to-B setting. Ruettgers, visiting a French insurance company, was having a meeting with the head of their IT department. "Since we hadn't arrived at a firm answer, I wanted to know what our customers thought about the Internet, so I asked the question of everyone I met in Europe. How were they using the Internet today, how might they use it tomorrow, and what were the benefits they were looking for? The French insurance IT leader told me that they were using the Internet to file claims. Instantly, the opportunity that the Internet represented became clear. I did approximately five hundred additional interviews that year, and not one person provided an answer as clear and as meaningful as our customer in France."

Here are some of the ways EMC stays on top of the forces and factors in its industry:

- Both the executive chairman Mike Ruettgers and CEO Joe Tucci meet with several hundred customers each year, individually or in small groups.
- A written questionnaire is sent to nearly 850 customers each year.
- EMC's service organization is trained to spot problems and opportunities.
- Customer councils are formed where customers directly participate in creating the next generation of products.
- The sales force is specially trained to identify emerging demand.

- EMC uses a six-quarter rolling planning process to link strategy with execution and discern changes in demand pattern.

When information from these sources is brought together, it forms a multifaceted view of demand forces and industry factors, allowing senior management to continuously challenge EMC's assumptions and anticipate customers' evolving requirements as well as the next big thing in storage technology. This revalidates EMC's current plans and activities and provides insight and direction regarding emerging demand and the next generation of products from EMC.

The second step of demand strategy is selecting the customers you intend to target and figuring out how to work with them.

I doubt there is a company anywhere in the world that earns a closer and more interdependent relationship with its customers than EMC.

When you visit EMC and hear its managers talk about customers, or observe their interactions with customers, it becomes immediately apparent that their definition of a customer is very different from most other companies'. Usually a customer is someone to whom you sell a product or a service, and that transaction results in a profit for you. At EMC, customers have a remarkably collaborative relationship, in which more of a partnership is formed. EMC opens virtually every part of its company to its customer advisory council, and its customers are open and candid with EMC.

When Mike Ruettgers and Joe Tucci each see several hundred customers per year and dedicate time to listening, not to selling, that's a devotion to customers that is very rare. You'll remember that several pages ago we talked about EMC's lens, which keeps it focused on storage: fast, reliable access to all of corporate information, no matter where in an enterprise it resides.

EMC believes that its abiding focus on storage, and only storage, gives it a significant competitive advantage. Every dollar it spends is spent on storage. Every engineer and every employee spends his or her days thinking about how enterprise storage can help EMC's customers.

Not surprisingly, one of EMC's principles is called "Creating the Customer Trust Loop."

When EMC talks about a trust loop, it doesn't merely talk about frequency of appointments or entertaining the client. "Creating the customer trust loop involves a process of listening, responding, validating, refining, revalidating, delivering, fine-tuning, and repeating the process." As Mike Ruettgers says, "every company with a pulse asks itself the question, 'what is of value to our customers?' The real challenge lies in knowing whether what we think matters to customers is in fact what matters to them." As you can see from the list above, it's not just talking to your customers that matters, it's asking the tough questions as well: validating, refining, and then revalidating what the demand is, and gauging whether you can, in fact, deliver what matters to them.

One of the most candid and valuable customer interaction programs I know of is EMC's customer councils. These are held twice a year in North America and Europe and once a year in other markets. Unlike many customer get-togethers, these are neither sales meetings nor golf outings. The sessions bring together fifty to sixty of EMC's most respected customers and involve two and a half days of intense discussion about storage and IT. Rather than golf clubs or tennis rackets, customers are asked to bring completed homework assignments that are sent out to them a week before the meeting.

The working sessions are about methodically exploring product requirements from customers, validating product concepts and long-term business direction, and above all, creating a climate for collaborative innovation.

A great deal of care goes into selecting the fifty to sixty customers who are invited. Only those individuals who are their companies' acknowledged experts, strategists, and key decision makers participate. Each individual must agree to a minimum eighteen-month commitment, and sign nondisclosure agreements.

First EMC presents what it believes to be the most troublesome short- and longer-term problems facing the industry and its customers' businesses. Next, it attempts to confirm that EMC's understanding of customers' concerns dovetails with EMC's experience and that the problems EMC is focusing on are, in fact, the problems that its customers are challenged with. If it appears that EMC is on the same page with its customers, the company presents a detailed look at EMC's work-in-process solutions to these problems.

At this point, EMC's senior management probes to find out if their proposed solutions will solve their customers' specific problems, and if, once these problems are solved, the solutions will have a meaningful business impact. Across hours of discussion, they try to discover new requirements and fine-tune their offering. There is talk about how to best implement the solution, including which strategic partner customers would like EMC to work with. All of this acquired knowledge is integrated by EMC into a coherent product design.

At the next session, EMC management shows customers how their product has changed based on their customers' directions. Between sessions, council members can log on to a special Web site to share information with peers at their company. These councils are a powerful learning tool for everyone. EMC helps customers plan their IT future, and they help EMC plan its future as well. The customer councils are truly partnerships, with genuine give-and-take between the participants. The reason they are so effective is that they are linked to a common objective, to create storage and related IT products that solve problems and create opportunities. EMC does it by selecting its best customers, getting the best input and direction it can get, and in all likelihood converting these people into early adopters of the products that they helped to create and bring to market.

EMC has experienced firsthand the power of disruptive technologies; it started as a tiny company with zero share in mainframe computer data and just four years later overturned IBM's lead in mainframe storage. By 1999 it had a 60 percent share of the market and had transformed computer storage from a passive container without strategic value to a solution for making information immediately and continuously available across the corporation.

EMC has adopted the philosophy "Disrupt or be disrupted"—otherwise defined as "Get them before they get you."

As I mentioned earlier, one of the ways EMC builds highly sophisticated technologies and then keeps extending what these technologies can do is that the company operates with well-designed, time-tested processes that provide both comfort and direction. EMC has identified four preconditions for creating a disruptive technology:

- First, be intimately in tune with your marketplace and take the widest possible view of that marketplace—not just your existing customers but potential and even unlikely customers.
- Second, have a special lens through which to view and interpret customers' current and future needs.
- Third, offer a new solution that meets those needs precisely while, ideally, redefining your industry.
- Fourth, scour the landscape for a corresponding change in market dynamics or customer attitudes to ensure that your new solution can quickly gain a large, receptive audience.

EMC put these conditions to work in the early 1990s. There was a strong movement back to centralized computing from distributed computing. In ever-increasing numbers customers were consolidating information into the strategic hub of their technology operations. The volume of information was exploding, and access to the information was needed many more hours each day, without risk of downtime.

It was here that EMC realized the potential for a disruptive technology—i.e., intelligent storage systems. This technology had a self-diagnostic capability that would monitor and proactively alert customers about potential problems with their storage.

The intelligent storage system, with advanced self-monitoring diagnostics and even self-healing capabilities, has been central to EMC's reputation for outstanding customer service.

But how does a company like EMC go about *creating* a disruptive technology?

First, by staying in tune and in step with its marketplace. This seems easy enough. Yet as we've seen throughout this book, if you don't research deeply enough you can quickly find yourself in trouble. Asking your customers is not enough. Most customers think only of their immediate needs and tend to ask for very basic changes that will make products or services faster, cheaper, or better than those they already have. EMC uses five different approaches to identify promising technologies and transform them into products:

1. A market requirements group looks out eighteen months or so, focusing on the special requirements of customers from key industry segments like financial services, telecommunications, and airlines. In other words, they are focused on current demand.
2. EMC's emerging technologies group zeroes in on technologies that will become important to EMC and its customers nineteen to sixty months out. They focus on emerging demand.
3. EMC's engineers interact intensively and regularly with customers, concentrating on applying the emerging technologies to solve customers' emerging requirements.
4. Every one of the more than one hundred thousand intelligent storage systems EMC has placed with customers has a self-diagnostic technology that is in contact twenty-four hours a day with one of EMC's customer centers. This service often detects errors before they become serious and threaten data availability.
5. EMC works closely with a very broad array of strategic partners whose complementary skills can accelerate the company's time to market.

To sum up EMC's Demand Value Proposition simply requires a review of their most valued business strategies and practices:

- Providing customers with fast, reliable access to all corporate information, no matter where in the organization it resides
- Always having more information about customers than its competitors
- Creating trust loops with customers to maintain the collaborative innovation, which is at the heart of its customer councils
- Using its defining idea of information centrality, which provides assurance that the company stays true to its focus on storage and doesn't try to be all things to all people at some point in the future
- Maintaining an "environment of urgency and skepticism"

EMC is one of the very best examples of the power of Demand Strategy. In the past two years EMC has continued to widen the gap between itself and its competition in the major areas of data storage. A third-party evaluation of customer satisfaction showed EMC received an all-time high rating of 97.7 percent. This not only ranked higher than any other storage provider, it was higher than any other IT provider.

While the results are impressive, they are made possible because of the remarkable discipline, leadership, and proven business principles used by Mike Ruettgers. EMC's success has not been a series of on-off decisions but a process that takes place on a daily basis, in which it builds a proprietary understanding of current and emerging demand.

At the deepest level, EMC understands that it has a responsibility not only to their direct customers, but to their customers' customers, whose own competitive advantage is enhanced when EMC's customers make the best possible use of data and information. Several years ago the company set what seemed to be an almost impossible hurdle by committing itself to reinventing its category every two years. EMC has met this challenge by relying on its one-of-a-kind business system and its worldwide knowledge web, which identifies emerging and changing demand and works hand in hand with EMC engineers to develop proprietary products to capture an ever-increasing share of this demand.

Early in Chapter 1, I introduced you to a very simple value equation: value = benefits/price. Despite competing with the world's leading technology companies, EMC is able to consistently add proprietary benefits that provide its customers with great value and enable EMC to enjoy reasonable price premiums.

No matter how great its past success, EMC has the humility and business wisdom to know that it has to continue growing and differentiating its products in order to sustain its leadership. Early in 2001, it introduced AutoIS, which reduces the growing complexity of technology and enables its customers to enjoy both increased efficiency and effectiveness. The AutoIS system provides very high levels of automated support that greatly simplifies the herculean task of managing information throughout a worldwide business enterprise across thousands of users in real time.

As it has done so many other times in the past, EMC has used its understanding of demand to create AutoIS, which addresses the rapidly growing problem of IT complexity. It's not surprising that EMC is the first and only company to offer such a solution, having built the system in collaboration with those customers who had the best understanding of the demand which had to be satisfied.

EMC's ability to make commitments and keep them came sharply into focus during the unfortunate events of September 11, 2001: it was vital to maintain across-the-board information continuity in the face of this disaster and the confusion and problems caused by its aftermath. The performance level of EMC's symmetric system and SRDF software led *Information Week* to name it "the gold standard" in information and business continuity.

As EMC looks to the future, it will continue to bring its most visionary customers inside its development process so that it continues the collaborative efforts that honor its commitment to reinvent storage every two years. EMC's constant focus on storage and its expert understanding and usage of the new law of demand and supply ensure its leadership for a very long time to come.

EPILOGUE

On January 28, 2002, long after this book was completed, Thomas E. Weber wrote an article in the *Wall Street Journal* in which he argued that many companies and senior managers who thrived when success was defined by *supply* are now finding it difficult to adapt to the fact that it is now being measured by demand.

In his article "Broadband Advocates Should Fight to Increase Demand, Not Supply," Mr. Weber pointed out that most consumers "don't see a compelling reason to shell out an extra $20 or $30 a month for a zippier Net link." Yet, in its haste to make broadband a national priority, the industry has overlooked that fact. While we are hearing a lot about tax credits and building out networks, very little is being said about why customers would clamor for these services.

Weber wrote:

> "Build and they will come" is, in essence, the rallying cry of the broadband cheerleaders. But this time it has been built, and the masses aren't coming. Until efforts to promote broadband begin to address demand instead of supply, the big broadband push isn't going anywhere.
>
> A few key numbers sum up the story. Anywhere from 70 to 80 percent of U.S. households can already sign up for high-speed cable modem Internet access if they want it . . . but fewer than 10 percent of those homes have subscribed.

Weber goes on to describe FCC statistics:

> Numbers for phone-company DSL lines tell a similar tale; with an estimated 51.5 million U.S. homes able to get the service at the end of 2001 . . . less than 10 percent signed up.

If the high-technology industry learned anything during 2000 and 2001, it should have been that creating more supply, regardless of the numerous functions it may enable, is not an answer to lagging sales. In fact, those who created supply without understanding demand are saddled with write-offs amounting to hundreds of millions, even billions, of dollars.

This book shows that the telecom industry, more than any other, should understand how imperative the shift to a Demand Strategy is. Nonetheless, it's no surprise that people who attribute their success to their having worked the supply side of the street will be slower to adapt to the rules of the demand economy. And the essential rule is this: If you want customers to purchase your products, you must understand demand first; only then will you be prepared to create the supply that aligns with and satisfies that demand. Without that knowledge, creating supply is simply guesswork.

Because many established businesspeople are resistant to learning new tricks, enormous opportunities await today's leaders who thoroughly understand and are comfortable with the realities of the demand economy.

The growth of EMC stock by 80,575 percent, the increase in Sears Credit's profits and margins despite losing its monopoly, and Nokia's victory over Motorola in its sales of mobile telephones aren't isolated examples. Demand-side economics underlie the success of a product such as bottled water and a company such as Commerce Bank. My hope is that this book will help you recognize and grapple with the opportunities of the new demand economy.

I selected the cases for this book from the multitude of companies that ascribe their prosperity to Demand Strategy. I studied a broad cross-section of business-to-business and business-to-consumer organizations; from financial services to food, high tech to retail and tiny start-ups like EMC, which started 1990 with zero share of mainframe storage compared with IBM's 60 share, and closed the decade with a 60 share compared to IBM's 20.

Furthermore, because Demand Strategy requires neither enormous sums of capital nor a huge workforce, everyone can make use of it. Only a few years before it entered the storage business, EMC was an office furniture sales company located on the second floor of a building above a restaurant. You don't have to be large or wealthy to achieve success using Demand Strategy. You need only understand that our entrance into a global economy marks a new era shaped by demand.

Because they will be identifying their most profitable demand targets instead of chasing an ill-defined mass market, I believe that companies committed to Demand Strategy can look forward to lower costs while they increase revenue, margins, and profit. By understanding the demand of their most profitable customers, companies can achieve inelastic pricing and, in so doing, safeguard their competitive advantage. And most important, those leaders will have taken control of their organizations' future.

CHAPTER 1: Why Demand Strategy? Why Now?

2   *"I doubt if there is a single company"*: Larry A. Bossidy, "Reality-Based Leadership," *Executive Speeches,* August 1, 1998.

4   *now have an estimated twenty times more*: "Too Much Fibre for the World to Digest," *Financial Times,* June 29, 2001; "Overbuilt Web: How the Fiber Barons Plunged the Nation into a Telecom Glut Staff," *Wall Street Journal,* June 18, 2001.

7   What *commodities will be produced*: Paul A. Samuelson, *Economics,* 1st ed. (New York: McGraw-Hill, 1948).

7   *"Every society must have a way"*: Paul A. Samuelson and William D. Nordhaus, *Economics,* 17th ed. (New York: McGraw-Hill, 2001).

8   *"conspicuous consumption"*: Thorstein Veblen, *The Theory of the Leisure Class* (Amherst, N.Y.: Prometheus Books, 1998).

10   *"always start from the satisfaction"*: Joseph Schumpeter, *The Theory of Economic Development* (Piscataway, N.J.: Transaction Publishers, 1982).

10   *"It is still the case"*: Fred Smith, "The Commanding Heights of Global Commerce," speech at the Economic Club of Chicago, October 13, 1998.

12   *from 8 percent to 18 percent*: www.solectron.com, accessed September 27, 2001.

12   *nearly 30 percentage points*: "No Fear," *Electronic Business,* February 1, 2001.

12   *virtually from scratch*: Juniper Networks Annual Report, 2000.

12   *"It is the maxim"*: Adam Smith, *Wealth of Nations* (Amherst, N.Y.: Prometheus Books, 1991), bk. IV, ch. II.

13   *"globalization is forcing prices down"*: Lester C. Thurow, "Building Wealth," *Atlantic Monthly,* June 1999.

13   *a hundred new microprocessors*: Intel Microprocessor Quick Reference Guide, www.intel.com, accessed July 6, 2001.

14   *When the Procter & Gamble Co.*: "Clorox Was Once Part of the Family," *Cincinnati Post,* February 29, 2000.

17   *Population growth in the United States*: statistical analysis with data from the U.S. Census Bureau; Bureau of Economic Analysis—National Income Accounts; Federal Reserve Statistics on Industrial Utilization, Capacity and Production.

18   *In the steel industry*: "Reaching for Maximum Flexibility," *Iron Age New Steel,* January 1, 2000.

18   *In 1999, the auto industry*: "Too Much Capacity for Automakers," *Detroit News,* April 4, 2000.

18   *By 2002, analysts predict*: "DaimlerChrysler Takes a Stake in Mitsubishi to Join Automobile Alliance Trend," *St. Louis Post Despatch,* March 28, 2000.

18   *"As large multinational companies"*: W. Lazer and E. H. Shaw, "Global Marketing Management: At the Dawn of the New Millennium," *Journal of International Marketing,* January 1, 2000.

18   *The Federal Reserve Board's study on productivity*: Stephen Oliner and Daniel Sichel, "The Resurgence of Growth in the Late 1990s: Is Information Technology the Story?" (Washington, D.C.: Federal Reserve Board, May 2000).

18   *sellers increased their advertising*: statistical analysis with data from *Universal McCann's Insider Report,* December 2000.

18   *the space in which retail goods*: statistical analysis with data from the National Research Bureau Shopping Center Census 1999 and the U.S. Census Bureau.

18   *imports exceeded exports*: statistical analysis based upon data from the Bureau of Economic Analysis—National Income Accounts.

19   *producers maintained only 70 percent*: analysis based upon data from the Bureau of Economic Analysis—National Income Accounts; Bureau of Labor Statistics—Producer and Consumer Price Indices.

19   *"The conclusion is straightforward"*: Stephen Roach, "On Pricing Leverage," Global Economic Forum, www.morganstanley.com, June 6, 2001.

20   *A recent study of one thousand*: Dwight Gertz, "Beating the Odds," *Journal of Business Strategy,* July 1, 1995.

21   *"In this supply-focused economy"*: Fred Smith, "The Commanding Heights of Global Commerce."

21   *"The strategic logic"*: Michael E. Porter, *Competitive Advantage* (New York: Simon & Schuster, 1998).

21   *Many companies have tried reengineering*: Michael Hammer, and James Champy, *Reengineering the Corporation: A Manifesto for Business Revolution* (New York: Harper Business, 1993).

24   *"by adding new features"*: Scott Thurm, "The Outlook: Germ of Tech Rebirth Seen in Price Cutting," *Wall Street Journal,* August 6, 2001.

25   *"Listening, for Motorola"*: "Softer Sell: Once-Mighty Motorola Stumbled When It Began Acting That Way," *Wall Street Journal,* May 18, 2001.

25   *Nokia jumped into digital*: "Nokia Bets on Tarzan Yells and Whistles," *Wall Street Journal,* July 2, 1997.

25   *In 1996, Motorola had a lock*: Estimated from *Global Wireless Equipment Investor,* Dataquest/Salomon Smith Barney, June 7, 2001; "Outlook: Nokia H1." *AFX News,* August 4, 1997; *Wall Street Journal,* May 18, 2001.

26   *according to an Interbrand survey*: "World's Most Valuable Brands," Interbrand, 2001.

CHAPTER 2: Demand Strategy

30   *"You can't just look"*: " 'Lousy' Sales Forecasts Helped Fuel the Telecom Mess," *Wall Street Journal,* July 9, 2001.

30   *"All the conversations I was having"*: ibid.

36   *annual research and development budget*: "Medtronic: Pacing the Field," *Forbes,* January 8, 2001.

36   *one or more Medtronic:* "Say Goodbye to Managed Care," *Chief Executive,* December 1, 1999.

36   *Medtronic controls more:* "Medtronic: Pacing the Field."

38   Ford Motor Company's *market share:* "The Power of Smart Pricing," *Business Week,* April 10, 2000.

39   *only 2.2 percent:* Erik Brynjolfsson and Michael Smith, "Frictionless Commerce? A Comparison of Internet and Conventional Retailers," *Management Science,* April 2000.

39   *sold the name to barnesandnoble.com:* "Don't Write Off Barnes and Noble," *Upside,* June 2000.

40   *Luxury hotels in Malaysia:* Akshay Rao, Mark Bergen, and Scott Davis, "How to Fight a Price War," *Harvard Business Review,* March 2000.

40   *"If we can be totally connected":* "How MTV Stays Tuned to Teenagers," *Wall Street Journal,* March 21, 2000.

40   *"We actually in some cases":* ibid.

41   *"Just as you get accustomed":* ibid.

48   *"The scarcest resources":* Peter F. Drucker, *Management Challenges for the 21st Century* (New York: Harper Business, 1999).

CHAPTER 3: Sears Credit Wins on Demand

54   *the mean rate on other cards:* "The Card Industry Rides a Wave of Prosperity," *Credit Card News,* April 1, 1994.

CHAPTER 4: The First Principle

65   *coffee consumption was falling:* Horticultural and Tropical Products Division FAS/USDA, June 2001; Coffeeresearch.org.

65   *he approached 242:* Howard Schultz and Dori Yang, *Pour Your Heart into It* (New York: Hyperion, 1996).

74   *"in crisis—and spending":* John Barry and Evan Thomas, "The Pentagon's Guru," *Newsweek,* May 21, 2001.

74   *Fred Smith:* "Federal Express Wasn't an Overnight Success," *Wall Street Journal,* June 6, 1989.

74   *Early in 2000, Medtronic's:* William W. George, "Medtronic Vision 2010," Medtronic Global Strategic Direction Employee Meeting, January 11, 2000.

78   *In 1999, electronics:* US-China Business Council, 2000.

78   *when the World Trade Organization:* www.wto.org, accessed October 20, 2001.

80   *In 1999, when Mexico unexpectedly teamed:* "Crude Cuts: Will Oil Nations Stick or Stray?" *Wall Street Journal,* March 26, 1999.

81   *Xerox Corporation provides a striking:* "Downfall: The Inside Story of the Management Fiasco at Xerox," *Business Week,* March 5, 2001; "Xerox's New Strategy Will Not Copy the Past," *New York Times,* December 18, 1994; "Inventor of a New World," *Los Angeles Times,* March 14, 1999.

83 *3M (which invented videotape)*: Akshay Rao, Mark Bergen, and Scott Davis, "How to Fight a Price War," *Harvard Business Review*, March 2000.

83 *In 1965 Gordon Moore*: Gordon E. Moore, "Cramming More Components onto Integrated Circuits," *Electronics*, April 19, 1965.

84 *"It's not an innovation"*: personal conversation with Alvaro de Souza.

84 *While Windows 95, 98, and 2000*: www.microsoft.com/persspass/corpprofile.asp.

84 *the $7 billion game*: "Video-Game Sales Surge More Than 30%," *Wall Street Journal*, July 26, 2001.

85 *When Lunchables were introduced*: "Introducing a Neat Package Deal for a Lunchtime Crowd," *San Francisco Chronicle*, March 28, 1990.

86 *Today, the concept has been extended*: "It's Lunchable!" *Brandmarketing*, May 2000.

86 *now worth almost $1 billion*: "Kraft Launches Lunchables for Snack Attacks," *Advertising Age*, March 12, 2001.

86 *commands 85 percent*: "It's Lunchable!"

87 *Today, businesses are trying*: Neil Howe and William Strauss, *Millennials Rising: The Next Great Generation* (New York: Vintage Books, 2000).

87 *"the single most important"*: Peter F. Drucker, *Management Challenges for the 21st Century* (New York: Harper Business, 1999).

CHAPTER 5: The Second Principle

108 *3M launched a flanking*: Akshay Rao, Mark Bergen, and Scott Davis, "How to Fight a Price War," *Harvard Business Review*, March 2000.

109 *the same voice recognition*: ibid.

111 *Though members of this group*: "No, Really, We're a .Com," *Worth*, November 1999.

111 *In 2000, UPS had*: UPS 2000 Annual Report.

111 *compared with FedEx's 2000*: FedEx 2000 Annual Report.

112 *"the Internet is the neural system"*: "No, Really, We're a .Com."

112 *Cisco, which transacts 90 percent*: "Cisco Determined to Turn Tide of '100-Year Flood,'" *Internet Week*, June 11, 2001.

112 *In 2001, AOL charged $23.90*: "Battle of the ISPs: Rivals AOL, MSN Slug It Out for Your Dollars," *Gannett News Service*, October 8, 2001.

113 *AOL's 31 million*: "Top US ISPs by Subscriber Q2 2001," *ISP Planet*, August 17, 2001.

113 *"easy ways to do online"*: "AOL–Time Warner Merger Portends Perils and Benefits for the Nation," *Tampa Tribune*, January 16, 2000.

113 *"something magical"*: "The Internet Is Mr. Case's Neighborhood," *Fortune*, March 30, 1998.

114 *as subscribers swelled*: "A Case of Timing, Knowledge," *Washington Post*, January 11, 2000.

114 *"You can already check e-mail"*: www.corp.aol.com/careers/aolinside/changing.html, accessed December 13, 2001.

115   *20 percent of U.S. cable subscribers:* "Harry Potter and Canadian Cultural Woes," *Toronto Star,* November 21, 2001.

CHAPTER 6: The Third Principle

126   *The importance of relevance and differentiation:* Young & Rubicam, Brand Asset Valuator, 2000.

136   *"diametrically opposed to the 80/20":* "A Bank Where the Customer Is Always Right," *ABA Banking Journal,* March 2001.

138   *"A Home Depot is":* "Local McBanker: A Small Chain Grows by Borrowing Ideas from Burger Joints," *Wall Street Journal,* May 17, 2000.

139   *"Our competition can't copy":* interview with Vernon Hill, September 2001.

140   *"Our growth rates":* ibid.

141   *"They're all advertising":* "You Want Fries with That Withdrawal?" *Business News New Jersey,* July 27, 1998.

141   Statistical data and remaining quotes from Vernon Hill: compiled from interview
142   with Vernon Hill, September 2001, and "The Commerce Story," Commerce Bank, Cherry Hill, N.J., July 2001.

CHAPTER 7: The Fourth Principle

144   *approximately one out of:* "This Is a Marketing Revolution," *Fast Company,* May 1999.

144   *"information-based strategy":* www.capitalone.com/about/corpinfo, accessed November 28, 2001.

145   *"When we started this company":* "This Is a Marketing Revolution."

146   *Capital One offered:* ibid.

146   *company offers six thousand:* ibid.

146   *Its 33 million cardholders:* "Growth Formula," *ComputerWorld,* July 2, 2001.

146   *Capital One had thirty-five hundred:* "Scratching the Surface: Capital One Revolutionizes Credit-Card Marketing," *Washington Post,* October 30, 2000.

146   *lost-card:* "This Is a Marketing Revolution."

146   *"Homer Simpson moment":* ibid.

146   *90 percent of all calls:* ibid.

147   *in the one-hundredth:* "Growth Formula."

147   *Alternatively, the computers:* "This Is a Marketing Revolution."

148   *The company today says the computer:* "Scratching the Surface."

148   *"The system gets information":* "Capital One: Fanaticism That Works," *US Banker,* August 1, 2001.

148   *"Credit cards aren't banking":* "This Is a Marketing Revolution."

149   *the agent clicked:* "Scratching the Surface."

149 *"I've got this great product"*: "This Is a Marketing Revolution."

150 *for insurance, Liberty Mutual*: "Aboard the Money Trail—Capital One Financial," *Kiplinger's Magazine*, September 2000.

150 *offers approximately three dozen*: "This Is a Marketing Revolution."

150 *57 percent buy something*: "Capital One—Expert of Cross-Selling," *US Banker*, May 2000.

150 *"a marketing revolution"*: "This Is a Marketing Revolution."

150 *in 2000, it ran forty-five thousand*: "Growth Formula."

150 *"On a daily basis"*: "Solid Growth, Smart Marketing Help Capital One Score with Customers," *Card Marketing*, March 2000.

150 *"A lot of our information-based"*: "To Be or Not to Be on Web? Debate at Capital One Enters Final Round," *American Banker*, May 19, 2000.

150 *"When you get ready to buy"*: "This Is a Marketing Revolution."

150 *"Fifty percent of what"*: ibid.

154 *"We have more collaborative"*: Michael Dell, "Leadership in the Internet Economy," keynote address, Canadian Club of Toronto, April 7, 2000.

154 *Dell partners with IBM*: "Dell, Intel Announce Initiatives to Enhance Future Enterprise Computing and Internet Technologies," Dell press release, April 28, 1998; "IBM, Dell Announce $16 Billion Technology Agreement," Dell press release, March 4, 1999.

154 *with Accenture and Gen3*: "Dell Enters E-Consulting Alliances with Gen3 Partners, Arthur Andersen," Dell press release, April 5, 2000.

154 *brokered a new agreement*: "Dell, EMC Sign Multi-Billion-Dollar Enterprise Storage Agreement," Dell press release, October 22, 2001.

155 *Medline manufactures or outsources*: Medline news release, May 3, 2001.

156 *Medline's two CEOs, Jon Mills*: conversation with Jon Mills, July 2, 2001.

157 *"We've found that if we segment"*: "The Dynamics of the Connected Economy," Michael Dell keynote address, Atlanta, June 25, 1999.

158 *"Team members don't necessarily"*: "Former Apple Computer CEO Discusses Effects of Internet at Chicago Convention," *Chicago Tribune*, October 14, 2001.

158 *The Baldrige award, established*: 2001 Criteria for Performance Excellence, Baldrige National Quality Program, www.quality.nist.gov, accessed November 5, 2001.

158 *Solectron now has sixty-five active teams*: Solectron Corp., *Industry Week*, October 19, 1998.

159 *Net income per McDonald's employee*: analysis over 1996–2000 using data from Compustat; competitor list taken from Quicken.com.

159 *Dubbed "the War for Talent"*: "The War for Talent," *Fast Company*, August 1998.

161 *It has also committed $100 million*: "Innovate Your Heart Out: Fittest 50 Winner Profile," *Darwin*, October 2001.

161 *"We see people downloading more"*: "Conference Previews 'Revolutionary' Net-Enabled Monitors, Pacemakers, Defibrillators," *Electronic Engineering Times*, May 7, 2001.

161 *The day may not be too far off*: ibid.

162   *nearly $4 billion in annual:* www.cdw.com, accessed July 5, 2001.

162   *"Anybody who tries to build":* "Computer Retailer Michael Krasny—He Keeps the Human Touch While Selling High Tech," *Investor's Business Daily,* April 20, 2000.

162   *"In a small or mid-sized company":* "High Touch in a High-Tech Era," *Target Marketing,* April 1, 2001.

162   *"We want to provide just about":* interview with Jim Shanks, July 27, 2001.

163   *When a user sends e-mail:* "CDW @Work Works Hard for IT Buyers," *PC Week,* May 24, 1999.

163   *The extranets are also fully:* "High Touch in a High-Tech Era."

163   *CDW's segment is fiercely fought:* "CDW Clicks by Keeping People in Sales Picture," *Chicago Tribune,* August 16, 2000.

164   *If the product is not available:* "CDW Keys Up Profits," *Chain Store Age Executive,* November 1, 1999.

164   *company to turn over:* www.cdw.com.

164   *regardless of order size:* ibid.

164   *CDW has found that attitude:* "High Touch in a High-Tech Era."

164   *twenty-five account executives:* interview with Paul Kozak, executive vice president of operations, CDW, August 2, 2001.

165   *representing 80 to 90 percent:* "Baby Dell," *Forbes,* November 27, 2000.

165   *School of Sales:* "High Touch in a High-Tech Era."

165   *College of Technology provides:* www.cdw.com.

165   *The training process that begins:* "High Touch in a High-Tech Era."

165   *one hundred best companies:* "Baby Dell," *Forbes,* November 27, 2000.

165   *"A packaged solution can dictate":* "High Touch in a High-Tech Era."

166   *"we're one of the lowest":* "CDW Keys Up Profits."

166   *from 7.1 percent:* "Baby Dell," *Forbes,* November 27, 2000.

CHAPTER 8: The Fifth and Sixth Principles

170   *lowered value by 42 percent:* James McTaggart, Peter Kontes, and Michael Mankins, *The Value Imperative: Managing for Superior Shareholder Returns* (New York: Free Press, 1994).

170   *actually failed to return the cost of capital:* Alexandra Lajoux, *The Art of M&A Integration* (New York: McGraw-Hill, 1998).

170   *often focuses on driving costs down through operating synergies:* "Why Mergers Fail," *McKinsey Quarterly,* 2001, no. 4.

176   *Fleischmann's table spreads and College Inn broths:* "Nibbling at Nabisco: Cookie King Fighting to Keep Its Dominance," *The Record,* January 10, 1999.

176   *Philip Morris acquired it for almost $19 billion:* Nabisco 10K for fiscal year 2000.

176   *"Most companies get into trouble":* conversation with Jim Kilts, August 10, 2001.

176 *"Saddled with objectives that are impossible"*: ibid.

179 *the business was a $1 billion market-capitalization company*: "Bill George Revolutionized Medtronic, One of the World's Leading Medical-Device Companies," *Economist,* September 2, 2000.

179 *deriving 80 percent of its revenues from pacemakers*: "Heart and Soul," *Industry Week,* May 4, 1998.

179 *earnings rose 25.4 percent annually over the same period*: "Say Goodbye to Managed Care," *Chief Executive,* December 1, 1999.

179 *pacemakers account for less than half of the company's total revenues*: "Heart and Soul."

179 *down from 80 percent to only about 30 percent by the 1980s*: ibid.

180 *from 8 percent per year to 10–11 percent*: ibid.

180 *"But we don't cut back on R&D"*: "Product Development That Can Fill Prescription for Success: How to Handle the Demands of a Company That's Growing Quickly," *USA Today,* May 30, 2000.

181 *"That shortens the development process"*: ibid.

181 *"they've treated several hundred or several thousand patients in . . . clinical trials"*: "Say Goodbye to Managed Care."

181 *"And that's the way we stay creative"*: ibid.

181 *"We are creating an entirely new field of medicine"*: "Medtronic: Pacing the Field," *Forbes,* January 8, 2001.

182 *"you are shooting at a moving target"*: ibid.

182 *"show what you're going to do"*: "New Product Machine: Medtronic Picks Up Pace of Medical Device Development to Stay Ahead of Competition and Ensure Success," *Star-Tribune* (Minneapolis and St. Paul), June 5, 1995.

183 *"now you know what doesn't work"*: ibid.

183 *projects as they are needed*: ibid.

183 *"integrating it into the mainstream business"*: "Product Development. . . ."

183 *"I think that's the litmus test"*: "Heart and Soul."

184 *Medtronic supports six to eight such projects annually*: ibid.

184 *providing the technology with which they could expand their capabilities*: "Say Goodbye to Managed Care."

184 *a full line of surgical products*: "How Smart Is Medtronic Really?" *Fortune,* October 25, 1999.

184 *it paid $3.7 billion in cash to acquire MiniMed*: "Medtronic to Buy MiniMed and Medical Research," *Wall Street Journal,* May 31, 2001.

185 *"You get cost savings, but they really don't focus on growth"*: "Product Development. . . ."

185 *where regulatory approval is often much faster*: "New Product Machine."

185 *decided within six to nine months*: "Say Goodbye to Managed Care."

186 *Japanese director Akira Kurosawa*: Ryunosuke Akutagawa, *Rashomon and Other Stories* (New Haven, Conn.: Liveright, 1952).

187 *"the promises and expectations that led to its authorization"*: Peter F. Drucker, *Management Challenges for the 21st Century* (New York: Harper Business, 1999).

CHAPTER 9: Gatorade Wins on Demand

201 *Pepsi won and acquired Quaker:* "PepsiCo to Acquire Quaker for $14 Billion; Stock Deal Gives Firm Control of Gatorade," *Washington Post,* December 5, 2000.

CHAPTER 10: Countrywide Credit Industries

202 *David Loeb, his cofounder:* Countrywide Factsheet, www.countrywide.com, accessed November 5, 2001.

202 *In fiscal 2001:* Stanford L. Kurland, "Countrywide Credit Industries, Inc.," presentation at Sanford Bernstein Strategic Decisions Conference, June 6, 2001.

204 *The rest of the savings:* "Last Man Standing," *Forbes,* November 27, 2000.

204 *"Advertising gave us full control":* "Leaders & Success: Countrywide's Angelo Mozilo," *Investor's Business Daily,* November 22, 1996.

204 *By 1980, Countrywide was able:* About Countrywide, www.countrywide.com, accessed August 15, 2001.

204 *"We're looking for the real-estate":* "Mortgage Machine," *ABA Banking Journal,* October 1, 1995.

205 *To serve this segment of brokers:* ibid.

205 *Mozilo explained that the branches:* interview with Angelo Mozilo, *Dow Jones Investor Network,* November 29, 1995.

206 *it traded $742 billion:* Kurland, "Countrywide."

206 *"I never want to be behind":* conversation with Angelo Mozilo, September 2001.

207 *"dynamic production operation":* "Mortgage Machine."

207 *As early as 1980:* "Countrywide Enters Its Fourth Decade on the Cutting Edge," *Community Banker,* January 1, 2000.

207 *In 1992, the company launched:* "Tech-Driven Efficiency Spurs Economic Boom," *Los Angeles Times,* February 22, 2000.

207 *"We were doing a huge volume":* "Countrywide's CTO," *Mortgage Banking,* April 2001.

207 *"If a new product":* ibid.

208 *provides the answers:* "Mozilo Says the Big Players Will Dominate," *Real Estate Finance Today,* November 13, 2000.

208 *the cost per service:* "Tech-Driven Efficiency. . . ."

209 *The hedge came in handy:* "Desensitizing: Countrywide Credit Industries Inc. of Pasadena, CA, Uses a Successful Strategy to Keep Earning," *Forbes,* February 12, 1996.

209 *Most companies use origination:* "Caveats on Countrywide—Mortgage Banker's Fortunes Are Booming Now, But . . . ," *Barron's,* November 25, 1991.

209 *Countrywide's flexible:* "Mortgage Machine."

209 *Toward the end of the 1990s:* "Countrywide Credit Industries, Inc., CEO Interview," *CNBC/Dow Jones Business Video,* November 3, 1999.

209 *"There was a whole segment":* conversation with Angelo Mozilo.

209 *"Early on," he recalls:* ibid.

210 *the company pledged:* "Countrywide Enters. . . ."

210 *A borrower with few:* ibid.

210 *the nation's top lender:* CNBC/Dow Jones Business Video.

210 *top lender to lower-income:* "Countrywide Downsizes, Seeks New Markets Amid Hard Times," *Capital Markets Report,* October 18, 1999.

210 *"Hats off to Countrywide":* "Full Steam Ahead for Countrywide Execs," *American Banker,* October 20, 1998.

210 *there are direct foreclosure:* "In the Nick of Time: Loan Companies Help Families Save Homes from Repossession," *San Diego Union Tribune,* December 17, 2000.

211 *The process actually starts:* "Affordable Housing 'Tool Box' Helps Countrywide Minimize Delinquencies," *National Mortgage News,* December 6, 1999.

212 *"I saw the pamphlet and said":* "In the Nick of Time."

212 *"There is nothing special":* "Affordable Housing. . . ." ibid.

212 *As many as 80 percent:* ibid.

212 *"early adopter":* "Mortgage Mania," *Chief Executive,* January 2000.

213 *Countrywide.com was launched:* www.countrywide.com.

213 *As recently as 2000:* "Mozilo Says Selling Countrywide Is No Longer Out of the Question," *American Banker,* May 16, 2000.

213 *"The Web site remains":* "Countrywide Enters. . . ."

213 *"Do as much as you":* "Countrywide Downsizes. . . ."

213 *Countrywide's e-commerce:* www.countrywide.com.

213 *"It's just beginning":* "Tech-Driven Efficiency. . . ."

214 *"In a detailed essay":* "Mortgage Banking Unbundling: Structure, Automation and Profit," *Mortgage Banking,* January 1, 2001.

214 *The increased competition:* ibid.

214 *Several big players:* "Last Man Standing."

214 *In 1990, the top twenty-five:* Kurland, "Countrywide."

214 *Countrywide itself:* "Last Man Standing."

215 *One example is the eEasy:* "Rate Reduction Products to Revolutionize Mortgage Mart," *Capital Markets Report,* November 19, 1999.

215 *More recently, Countrywide has promised:* "Two New Mortgages to Offer Line of Credit," *Baltimore Sun,* February 11, 2001.

215 *Greenpoint Financial:* "Rate Reduction Products. . . ."

215 *Even before its launch:* "Two New Mortgages. . . ."

216 *"It should be one seamless"*: "Full Steam Ahead. . . ." ibid.

216 *Its subsidiary LandSafe provides:* www.countrywide.com.

216 *"When people think of hamburgers"*: "Countrywide Aims to Be a Household Name," *American Banker,* December 15, 1995.

CHAPTER 11: EMC's Demand Proposition

217 *walk-up office over a restaurant:* www.emc.com/about/emc story/early days.jsp, accessed December 4, 2001.

217 *would appreciate 80,575 percent in the 1990s:* www.emc.com/news/in depth archive/millennium011200.jsp, accessed December 3, 2001.

217 *Named after Egan, Marino, and a third founder:* www.emc . . . early days.jsp.

218 *a hefty commission of 55 percent:* ibid.

218 *"I wish EMC sold Prime-compatible"*: ibid.

218 *"In that moment, an idea was born"*: ibid.

219 *"When our payroll grew to 12"*: ibid.

219 *Egan and Marino hired Michael Ruettgers:* ibid.

220 *A former Raytheon executive:* "Managing for the Next Big Thing: An Interview with EMC's Michael Ruettgers," *Harvard Business Review,* January 2001.

220 *made chief executive officer in 1992:* ibid.

220 *At the start of 2001:* emc.com/about/management/tucci.jsp?openfolder=all, accessed December 4, 2001.

220 *when Ruettgers was promoted:* www.emc.com/about/management/ruettgers.jsp? openfolder=all, accessed December 4, 2001.

220 *By the early 1990s:* A Brief History of EMC Through 1998, www.emc.com/ about/emc story/brief history.jsp, accessed December 11, 2001.

220 *Suddenly, one of the senior officers:* personal conversation with Michael Ruettgers.

221 *"We involved our lead customers"*: ibid.

222 *the fastest-growing major software company:* www.emc.com/about/milestones/ index.jsp?openfolder=all, accessed December 4, 2001.

222 *"I think the defining characteristic of our culture"*: "Managing for the Next Best Thing."

223 *Recently, Mike Ruettgers told me a story:* personal conversation with Mike Ruettgers.

223 *Both the executive chairman:* Michael Ruettgers, "I Pledge Allegiance to This Company: From Customer Satisfaction to Allegiance," *Chief Executive,* September 1999.

223 *A written questionnaire:* Michael Ruettgers, "Thriving in the Information Economy," speech, New York, May 13, 1999.

223 *Customer councils are formed:* Ruettgers, "I Pledge Allegiance. . . ."

225 *When EMC talks about a trust loop:* ibid.

225 *"The real challenge lies"*: ibid.

225 *One of the most candid and valuable:* ibid.

226 *and just four years later:* Michael Ruettgers, "Disrupt or Be Disrupted: Overturning Conventional Thinking in the Information Storage Industry," www.emc.com/about/management/speeches/overturning.jsp, accessed December 11, 2001.

226 *By 1999 it had a 60 percent share: ibid.*

227 *EMC has identified four preconditions:* ibid.

227 *It was here that EMC:* ibid.

228 *EMC uses five different approaches:* ibid.

INDEX

Page numbers in *italics* refer to figures and tables.

C U R R E N C Y ▽ D O U B L E D A Y

If you like the ideas in this book and are interested in learning more, become a member of **The Currency Connection**—an informal network of business leaders, thinkers, and readers interested in learning about the newest and boldest practices, strategies, and ideas about work.

Visit **www.currencybooks.com** and sign up for our free newsletter today.

CURRENCY MEANS BUSINESS™